Should You Choose to Live Forever?

In this book, Stephen Cave and John Martin Fischer debate whether or not we should choose to live forever. This ancient question is as topical as ever: while billions of people believe they will live forever in an otherworldly realm, billions of dollars are currently being poured into anti-ageing research in the hope that we will be able to radically extend our lives on earth. But are we wise to wish for immortality? What would it mean for each of us as individuals, for society, and for the planet?

In this lively and accessible debate, the authors introduce the main arguments for and against living forever, along with some new ones. They draw on examples from myth and literature as well as new thought experiments in order to bring the arguments to life. Cave contends that the aspiring immortalist is stuck on the horns of a series of dilemmas, such as boredom and meaninglessness, or overpopulation and social injustice. Fischer argues that there is a vision of radically longer lives that is both recognizably human and desirable. This book offers both students and experienced philosophers a provocative new guide to a topic of perennial importance.

Key Features:

- Gives a comprehensive overview of the main arguments for and against living forever.
- Uses lively examples from myth, literature, and novel thought experiments.
- Highly accessible—avoiding jargon and assuming no prior knowledge—without sacrificing intellectual rigour.

- Includes helpful pedagogical features, including chapter summaries, an annotated reading list, a glossary, and clear examples.

Stephen Cave is the Director of the Institute for Technology and Humanity at the University of Cambridge, UK. His other books include *Immortality* (Crown, 2012), *AI Narratives* (with Sarah Dillon and Kanta Dihal, Oxford UP, 2020), and *Imagining AI* (with Kanta Dihal, Oxford UP, 2023). He also advises governments around the world on the ethics of technology and has served as a British diplomat.

John Martin Fischer is a Distinguished Professor in Philosophy at the University of California, Riverside, and in 2017 he was appointed a University Professor in the University of California, one of twenty-two in the ten-campus system, and the only philosopher. He has published widely on the topics of this debate, including: *The Metaphysics of Death* (Stanford UP, 1993), *Our Stories: Essays on Life, Death, and Free Will* (Oxford UP, 2009), and *Death, Immortality, and Meaning in Life* (Oxford UP, 2020). From 2012 to 2015, he was the Project Leader of The Immortality Project, funded by the John Templeton Foundation.

Lord Martin Rees is a British cosmologist and astrophysicist. He is the fifteenth Astronomer Royal, appointed in 1995, and was Master of Trinity College at Cambridge University, from 2004 to 2012, and President of the Royal Society between 2005 and 2010.

Little Debates About Big Questions

About the series:

Philosophy asks questions about the fundamental nature of reality, our place in the world, and what we should do. Some of these questions are perennial: for example, *Do we have free will? What is morality?* Some are much newer: for example, *How far should free speech on campus extend? Are race, sex, and gender social constructs?* But all of these are among the big questions in philosophy and they remain controversial.

Each book in the *Little Debates About Big Questions* series features two professors on opposite sides of a big question. Each author presents their own side, and the authors then exchange objections and replies. Short, lively, and accessible, these debates showcase diverse and deep answers. Pedagogical features include standard form arguments, section summaries, bolded key terms and principles, glossaries, and annotated reading lists.

The debate format is an ideal way to learn about controversial topics. Whereas the usual essay or book risks overlooking objections against its own proposition or misrepresenting the opposite side, in a debate each side can make their case at equal length, and then present objections the other side must consider. Debates have a more conversational and fun style too, and we selected particularly talented philosophers—in substance and style—for these kinds of encounters.

Debates can be combative—sometimes even descending into anger and animosity. But debates can also be cooperative. While our authors disagree strongly, they work together to help each other and the reader get clearer on the ideas, arguments, and objections. This is intellectual progress, and a much-needed model for civil and constructive disagreement.

The substance and style of the debates will captivate interested readers new to the questions. But there's enough to interest experts too. The debates will be especially useful for courses in philosophy and related subjects—whether as primary or secondary readings—and a few debates can be combined to make up the reading for an entire course.

We thank the authors for their help in constructing this series. We are honoured to showcase their work. They are all preeminent scholars or rising stars in their fields, and through these debates they share what's been discovered with a wider audience. This is a paradigm for public philosophy, and will impress upon students, scholars, and other interested readers the enduring importance of debating the big questions.

Tyron Goldschmidt, Fellow of the Rutgers Center for Philosophy of Religion, USA
Dustin Crummett, University of Washington, Tacoma, USA

Published Titles:

Should You Choose to Live Forever?: A Debate
by Stephen Cave and John Martin Fischer

What Do We Owe Other Animals?: A Debate
by Anja Jauernig and Bob Fischer

What Makes Life Meaningful?: A Debate
by Thaddeus Metz and Joshua W. Seachris

Do Numbers Exist?: A Debate
by William Lane Craig and Peter van Inwagen

Is Morality Real?: A Debate
By Matt Lutz and Spencer Case

What Is Consciousness?: A Debate
By Amy Kind and Daniel Stoljar

Do We Have a Soul?: A Debate
By Eric T. Olson and Aaron Segal

Can War Be Justified?: A Debate
By Andrew Fiala and Jennifer Kling

Does Tomorrow Exist?: A Debate
By Nikk Effingham and Kristie Miller

Should Wealth Be Redistributed?: A Debate
By Steven McMullen and James R. Otteson

Do We Have Free Will?: A Debate
By Robert Kane and Carolina Sartorio

Is There a God?: A Debate
by Kenneth L. Pearce and Graham Oppy

Is Political Authority an Illusion?: A Debate
By Michael Huemer and Daniel Layman

Selected Forthcoming Titles:

Consequentialism or Virtue Ethics?: A Debate
By Jorge L.A. Garcia and Alastair Norcross

For more information about this series, please visit: https://www.routledge.com/Little-Debates-about-Big-Questions/book-series/LDABQ

Should You Choose to Live Forever?

A Debate

Stephen Cave and
John Martin Fischer

FOREWORD BY LORD MARTIN REES

NEW YORK AND LONDON

Cover image: © Jonatan Linderman / UnSplash

First published 2024
by Routledge
605 Third Avenue, New York, NY 10158

and by Routledge
4 Park Square, Milton Park, Abingdon, Oxon, OX14 4RN

Routledge is an imprint of the Taylor & Francis Group, an informa business

© 2024 Stephen Cave and John Martin Fischer

The right of Stephen Cave and John Martin Fischer to be identified as authors of this work has been asserted in accordance with sections 77 and 78 of the Copyright, Designs and Patents Act 1988.

All rights reserved. No part of this book may be reprinted or reproduced or utilised in any form or by any electronic, mechanical, or other means, now known or hereafter invented, including photocopying and recording, or in any information storage or retrieval system, without permission in writing from the publishers.

Trademark notice: Product or corporate names may be trademarks or registered trademarks, and are used only for identification and explanation without intent to infringe.

ISBN: 978-0-367-61539-0 (hbk)
ISBN: 978-0-367-61540-6 (pbk)
ISBN: 978-1-003-10544-2 (ebk)

DOI: 10.4324/9781003105442

Typeset in Sabon
by MPS Limited, Dehradun

Contents

Foreword	xi
LORD MARTIN REES	

PART I
Opening Statements   1

1. Why You Should Not Choose to Live Forever   3
   STEPHEN CAVE

2. Why You Should Choose to Live Forever   54
   JOHN MARTIN FISCHER

PART 2
First Round of Replies   107

3. Reply to John Martin Fischer   109
   STEPHEN CAVE

4. Reply to Stephen Cave   134
   JOHN MARTIN FISCHER

PART 3
Second Round of Replies   159

5. Reply to John Martin Fischer's Reply   161
   STEPHEN CAVE

x   Contents

6. Reply to Stephen Cave's Reply   177
   JOHN MARTIN FISCHER

   Further Readings   191
   Glossary   195
   References   200
   Index   206

Foreword

Lord Martin Rees

Humans have long sought the elixir of youth, so it is not surprising that even non-scientists closely follow the latest research into ageing. But is the ageing process—what most people consider simply a fact of life—actually a 'disease' that can be conquered? Or is there some insurmountable limit to the lifespan of human bodies?

Of course, almost everyone, as they get older, yearns for at least a moderate extension of their lifespan—provided that they retain their health and faculties. But if we could survive only with the help of extreme measures, many of us would opt instead for non-resuscitation and solely palliative treatment. We might also find comfort in having the option of 'assisted dying' as soon as our quality of life and our prognosis dipped below a certain threshold. We would dread the fate of the Struldbrugs depicted in Swift's 'Gulliver's Travels'—remaining alive, but in a decrepit state repulsive to those with 'normal' lifespan.

But suppose that the ravages of ageing could be held at bay, would you then opt to live for centuries? Doubts are raised by the famous fictional example of Čapek's 'Makropulos' who succumbs to ennui after a few centuries as an opera singer. But that response doesn't necessarily ring true. You would surely not have been bored—at least if your station in life were fortunate—if you'd participated in several centuries of European history.

Makropulos is envisaged as unique, living on in a world where all around her die. But what if the 'elixir' had been taken by others too? There would obviously be a fundamental inequality between those who had taken the elixir and those who had not. And if everyone's life was extended, how could an overcrowded and unsustainable world be avoided?

xii Foreword

In this book, the two authors deploy and debate wide-ranging arguments pro and con life extension. They elucidate the various 'grades' of lifetime enhancement, from a mere doubling of lifespan to permanent indestructibility. They address the philosophical issues of whether 'personal identity' can be preserved indefinitely—so that after thousands of years you would still be 'you' in a meaningful sense.

But what makes the book timely is that these issues are no longer fantasy—some could soon be part of 'practical ethics', just as euthanasia is today. Biologists are exploring seriously whether ageing can be 'cured', so that our physical bodies remain in good repair for centuries. And futuristic technologists argue that AI and robotics are advancing so fast that one day human brains may be 'downloadable' into a near-immortal electronic simulacrum, which would perpetuate their consciousness and memories with a precision that would preserve the personality of their flesh-and-blood precursors. So the book's themes range from those that seem conceivable within a few decades, to flakier speculations that must await a remote post-human era.

In the former category is serious research that focuses on telomeres—stretches of DNA at the end of chromosomes—that shorten as people age. By adjusting the telomeres of nematode worms, for example, experimenters have managed to increase the lifespan of these creatures tenfold, although the same approach has less effect on more complex animals. The only effective way to extend the life of rats is to give them a near-starvation diet. (But the naked mole rat may have some special biological lessons for us; some of them live more than 30 years—several times longer than the lifespan of other small mammals.)

The powerful desire for a longer lifespan creates a ready market for exotic therapies of untested efficacy. For example, Ambrosia, a US start-up founded in 2016, offered Silicon Valley executives a transfusion of 'young blood', although the company halted the treatment following a warning from US regulators. Another recent life-extending craze was metformin, a drug intended to treat diabetes, but which some claim can stave off dementia and cancer in otherwise healthy people.

More credibly, human-genome analysis has yielded insights into our vulnerability to some diseases. And there is a realisation that the thousands of species of bacteria in our gut constitute an internal ecosystem whose 'balance' may be crucial to our health.

Three 'Altos' laboratories have now been set up—two in California and one in Cambridge (UK)—to focus on extending the healthy lifespan. They are well funded by billionaires and have 'poached' researchers of high repute from other institutions. Even though few experts are optimistic about achieving drastic enhancement, there is at least a hope of beneficial spin-offs—just as President Nixon's 'war on cancer' in the 1970s boosted our understanding of cell biology. But this kind of piecemeal progress probably won't satisfy the founders of these labs: when they were young, they wanted to be rich. Now they're rich they want to be young again. That's not so easy!

But what if a breakthrough were indeed achieved? Some would view a huge increase in life expectancy with foreboding: it could have undesirable and far-reaching consequences for society as a whole. If it were affordable only by the rich, we'd confront a fundamental new form of inequality: a privileged long-lived 'caste' (though its members would be less unacceptable if they actually became wiser with age!). But if life extension were available to everyone, its implementation would drastically alter population projections and create a massive 'demographic shock'. The social effects, while obviously huge, would depend on whether the years of senility were prolonged too; whether women's age at menopause would increase; and how families would be structured if many generations were alive at the same time. (And unless childhood development were to be slowed, children would be a smaller and more precious segment of the population; any accidental death would deprive the victim of centuries of life, not just decades.)

Hardcore longevity enthusiasts hope to achieve a metaphorical 'escape velocity', when medicine advances so fast that life expectancy increases by more than a year each year, offering the prospect of immortality. But some worry that this 'take-off' won't be achieved before they face natural death—they therefore want their bodies frozen until technology advances sufficiently. I know some academics in the United Kingdom who have signed up for such 'cryonics'. The contract is with an Arizona based company called Alcor, which replaces the blood of dead bodies with liquid nitrogen. They accept that the chance of resurrection is small, but point out that it would be zero otherwise.

I find it hard to take this aspiration seriously, and I would rather end my days in an English churchyard than an American freezer. And I don't think it would be good if cryonics ever did succeed.

xiv Foreword

Let's suppose Alcor stays in business and dutifully cares for its cryogenically frozen bodies for the requisite number of centuries. The corpses would then be revived in a world where they would be strangers – refugees from the past. Perhaps they would be treated indulgently, as most people believe distressed asylum seekers or displaced Amazonian tribespeople should be treated today. The difference, however, is that the thawed-out corpses would be burdening future generations by choice, so it is not clear how much consideration they would deserve.

But I don't want to end on a sceptical note. As an astronomer I'm aware of the immense future lying ahead. The marvellous biosphere of which we're a part is the outcome of about 4 billion years of Darwinian evolution. But our Sun is less than half way through its life; and the wider cosmos has a still longer—perhaps infinite—future. So we're nearer the beginning than the end of the emergence of ever more intricate complexity, which may well encompass near-immortal intelligences.

The prospect of human immortality has long been the stuff of science fiction. The world will face new risks and challenges if it is enabled by technological advances. But there are scenarios that are benign and exciting—for humans and for posthumans. That is why this book—presented as a lively debate between two astute thinkers—is such an enlightening and engaging read.

Part I

Opening Statements

Chapter 1

Why You Should Not Choose to Live Forever

Stephen Cave

Contents

1 Introduction	3
2 Living Long, Living Longer, Living Forever	4
2.1 How Long Is Forever? Four Categories	4
2.2 What Do We Mean by Living On? The Identity Criterion	7
2.3 What Do We Mean by 'Should'? The Prudential and Ethical Criteria	11
2.4 Why the Question Matters	14
3 Prudence: Would Living Forever be Right for Me?	18
3.1 Boredom	19
3.2 Ennui	25
3.3 Meaninglessness	26
3.4 Procrastination	32
3.5 Weighing the Prudential Arguments	35
4 Ethics: Would It be Right for Society for People to Live Forever?	39
4.1 Overpopulation	39
4.2 Social Justice	48
5 Preliminary Conclusions	51

1 Introduction

We are all on the way to the grave—like all humans, all animals, all living things. But unlike other living things—or at least, the great majority of them—we humans are painfully aware that our days

DOI: 10.4324/9781003105442-2

are numbered. As far as we can tell, tulips, beetles and even long-lived tortoises do not have the mental capacities required to grasp the future. But our astonishing, massively complex brains have given us a kind of superpower: to predict the future and plan for it. This has brought us great prosperity, but also a curse: to know that we are mortal.

While we might acknowledge this mortality in the abstract, few of us like to confront the reality of our own deaths. Indeed, all across the world, and as far back into history as we can see, we humans have been telling ourselves stories about how we can escape death and live forever, whether through potions or prayer, sacrament, or science.

It is understandable, if we are enjoying life, that we should not want to die. But does that mean that if we could choose to live forever, we should? I will argue that the answer is no. Life is good, and more might be better, but unending life would be too much. I will argue—in Part 3 of this opening statement—that living forever would be the wrong choice for each of us with regard to our own welfare. And I will argue in Part 4 that it would be the wrong choice with regard to society and the planet as a whole.

But first, in Part 2, I will do what philosophers always do before trying to answer a question: clarify what it means.

2 Living Long, Living Longer, Living Forever

2.1 How Long Is Forever? Four Categories

Some people are clear about what they want from living forever: to not die, at all, at any point—to just keep going without end. This matches the primary meaning of forever: 'for all future time' (OED 2021). They want not merely to live for a hundred years, or a thousand, or a million, or a thousand million. All of that would just be a start, a mere fraction of infinite time—indeed, an infinitely small fraction.

However, sometimes people use the term 'forever' more loosely. A small ad that says 'cute puppies seeking their forever home' would not expect the lucky owner to still be looking after the dog when the Sun expands to swallow the Earth seven and a half billion years from now. They mean something more modest—in this case, something like for the puppy's full natural lifetime. Similarly, when some people say they want to live forever, they do not mean until the heat death of the universe and beyond. Instead, they mean that they want to live much longer than the usual human lifespan, perhaps a thousand years instead of a mere eighty.

These different forevers have some very different implications, so we should distinguish between them. For our purposes, it will be helpful to distinguish between four different categories:

2.1.1 Moderate Life Extension ·

I will use the term 'moderate life extension' to mean extending life expectancy to somewhere between 120 years (about the longest any human has ever lived until now) to 160 years (about double the current life expectancy in developed countries). This would be an incredible achievement, which would require many breakthroughs in our understanding of ageing as well as of diseases such as cancer. But it might be reasonable to expect such life extension if medical science and technology continue to advance as rapidly as they have in the past century. I do *not* think we should consider living to 160 to be 'forever'—that would be a gross misuse of the word. But arguments for or against living forever are often wrongly conflated with arguments for or against moderate life extension. So it will be helpful for our discussion to clearly distinguish this category.

2.1.2 Radical Life Extension

By radical life extension, I mean defeating ageing and disease, so that people could live indefinitely, unless and until some outside shock such as a meteor strike puts an end to them.[1] This would require us totally mastering our own biology, but not everything else in the universe. Although we can imagine radical life extension brought about by swigging an elixir, in reality if it were ever to come about, it would likely involve a great deal of regular and intrusive medical treatment: to radically extend our lives would require some radical changes to our bodies.

---

1. In my distinction between moderate and radical life extension, I am largely following John K. Davis (Davis 2018). In earlier works, both John and I have sometimes referred to this category as 'medical immortality'. However, it is at least highly unlikely, if not impossible, that immunity to ageing and disease would lead to living forever—or even more than a few millennia. In this opening statement, I reserve the term 'immortality' for categories that do allow the possibility of endless lives.

6 Stephen Cave

In theory, people might live centuries or millennia or more if immune to ageing and disease. But in practice, the chance of accident—not to mention the prerequisites of continued prosperity, political stability, and uninterrupted advanced medical treatment—would ensure that radical life extension did not literally mean forever. In fact, my life expectancy would become directly proportional to the risk of dying by causes other than disease in a given society. So my life expectancy would for example be lower in the US, which has relatively high rates of fatal shootings and car accidents, than in safety-conscious Japan. Actual lifespans would also likely be wildly varied, with some people dying while mountain climbing in their teens, and others making it to a ripe old age of five thousand. We can assume in scenarios in this category that people can at any time choose to stop receiving their elixir, and so bring about their demise.

2.1.3 Contingent Immortality

Immortality literally means not dying—not being mortal. An immortal being is therefore one that at least *could* live forever. Contingent (in the sense I am using it here) means dependent on other factors. We can define contingent immortality as being able to live forever—immune to ageing and disease, *and* accident or violent death, etc.—but also being able to die if one so chooses by discontinuing whatever processes are keeping one alive.

I find it hard to imagine anyone achieving this state in the known universe, given the possibility of radical shocks (a meteor strike that completely destroys the Earth, for example). But people do try to imagine it, and so we can explore whether the visions they conjure are genuinely ones we should want. For example, some people imagine this in science fiction terms: imagine in the future we will all regularly make 'backups' of ourselves—full brain and body scans perhaps. If then a meteor struck me, the backup factory would just produce a new me based on the scan, and I would be able to pick up where I left off pre-meteor. There are lots of problems with this idea, philosophical as well as practical, but it has its advocates. Other people might imagine contingent immortality in more mystical terms: for example, some people might believe we have a soul or self that cycles through different bodies, as some theories of reincarnation suggest, but also that we could choose to end this cycle if we wished.

2.1.4 True Immortality

As mentioned, being *im*mortal means not being mortal. Some people interpret this as being an entity that *cannot* die, no matter what happens or whether one wants to live on or not. This is the kind of immortality often associated with gods and other supernatural beings. But it is also a very common view of humans. Many people believe that my true self is my soul, and that my soul *just is* immune to ageing, disease, and drive-by shootings. No elixirs or medical breakthroughs required. Billions of people believe that they have a soul in this way, and that this soul survives the death of the body—around 65% of people in Europe, for example, and 70% of Australians (Pew Research Center 2018, 125; Moore 2021).

The details of these beliefs vary. Some people believe that their souls are reincarnated in new bodies, whereas some people believe they will go to other realms, such as heaven or hell. In many cases, they believe that their souls are not the kinds of things that could ever die: that they are essentially immortal, and will necessarily live forever. This is what I will refer to as *true immortality*: the view that someone cannot cease to exist. In scenarios of true immortality, unending life is much more like a sentence imposed upon us, rather than a choice.

These four categories do not capture all the possible variations of lifespan and who can choose to extend or end it, and under what conditions. For example, in my accounts of radical life extension and contingent immortality, I am assuming that people can still choose to die. But we can imagine situations where this is not the case. For example, in the episode 'White Christmas' of the TV show *Black Mirror*, a sentient digital clone of a person is created and then tortured (through isolation and boredom) until they agree to work as a personal assistant. These digital people have no way of ending their own miserable lives—but they are not true immortals, as someone else could end them (Tibbetts 2014). Nonetheless, the four categories give us a clear starting place for our discussion, which we can always vary if we need to explore other possibilities. The categories are summarised in Table 1.1.

2.2 What Do We Mean by Living On? The Identity Criterion

Imagine that a great scientist, Professor Vitalonga, offers you eternal life. Given her reputation, you are curious, even cautiously optimistic. Vitalonga explains to you that all she needs to do is scan

8 Stephen Cave

Table 1.1 Categories of very long life

Category	Life expectancy	Immune to ageing and disease	Immune to accident, etc.	Able to die
Moderate life extension	120–160	No	No	Yes
Radical life extension	Centuries or more	Yes	No	Yes
Contingent immortality	Millennia or more	Yes	Yes	Yes
True immortality	Forever	Yes	Yes	No

your brain. Her scanner is wonderfully sophisticated and will record every detail of every neural connection. This, she argues, will capture your mind—the real you. Unfortunately, she can only capture this level of detail by removing your brain from your skull and cutting it into wafer-thin slices. These she will scan one-by-one, then vitrify and keep for her archives. Then she will take the complete scan of all your neurons and save it on an ineradicable disk, which she will keep in her indestructible safebox for evermore. Voila, immortality!

Now imagine a different scenario. Guru Whitbeard tells you that he can ensure this life is not your last: if you follow his daily regime of breathing exercises, you will be reincarnated in a new body, born the moment this one dies. Indeed, if you give him just ten thousand dollars, he will invest it wisely and transfer it tenfold to you in your next incarnation! You ask if your next incarnation will remember this one, your current life. Oh no, the Guru answers: just as that wee baby will be a freshly born body, so it will have a clean slate of memories, preferences, foibles, and so on. What then, you ask, will survive of you and migrate on to this new body? Your ineffable aura, he replies, which he can unerringly detect.

Would you accept Vitalonga's or Whitbeard's offers? I suspect not. You might have many reasons for your hesitance, including scepticism about whether they could deliver on their promises. But even if they could, I suggest we should still be hesitant—because what they are promising does not really sound like living on at all. In the case of the professor, it might really be a scan of *your* mind in her safebox, but a disk in a safebox does not sound like the kind of thing that could have a *life*. It would be inert, more akin to a book containing your biography on a library shelf. In the case of the guru, on the other hand, the baby that he claims is you will one day certainly be alive. But what would connect this new creature,

Why You Should Not Choose to Live Forever 9

with its new body and new mind, to you now? Whatever an ineffable aura is, it does not sound like the kind of thing that can guarantee your survival.

As we saw in the previous section, there are many different scenarios that have been put forward as ways of living forever. But not all of these will seem genuinely like living on at all. Some sound like living on in a metaphorical sense only. Socrates argued that women and some men gain immortality by having children, while men who are 'pregnant in the soul', pursue instead 'an immortality of fame' (Plato 2015). But we do not literally live on through our children: my three daughters are all clearly separate beings with their own experiences, and when I die nothing will happen to transfer my life to theirs.[2] Similarly, the great Greek hero Achilles is not still with us to experience the world, even though the stories of his exploits at Troy are still told. As Woody Allen once said: 'I don't want to live on in the hearts of my countrymen; I want to live on in my apartment'.

When we consider various scenarios in order to help us answer the question of whether we should choose to live forever, we should first check that what is happening in that scenario really is an instance of the same person living on. This is usually referred to as the *identity criterion*.

Philosophers distinguish between two quite different meanings of 'identity', and we need to be clear which one we are talking about. **Qualitative identity** refers to two objects having exactly the same qualities. For example, two bottles of beer from the same factory could be identical in this sense, or even two human twins. That is not the kind of identity we need here. When I ask whether some person in the future is *really* me—say, a person who has just rolled out of the backup factory based on my latest scan—then I am asking about **numerical identity**. If x and y are numerically identical, then they are one and the same thing. For example, the baby born to my mother in January 1973 in Cornwall is numerically identical with the person typing these words—we are one and the same human being, even though we look very different.

This is a very important distinction, though it is sometimes blurred in discussions of immortality. Someone—let's call them

---

2. While this is clear for humans, it is much less clear for some creatures: for example, bacteria, which are single-celled organisms, reproduce by dividing—so literally becoming both their offspring.

Aleph—might say that if they lived for a million years then the resulting person would 'not really be them'. What Aleph might mean is that over the course of such an expanse of time, they would have changed to become utterly unrecognisable to their original self. Their appearance, beliefs, preferences, values, and even name might have changed. Let us call that future person Beth. It seems quite likely that Aleph would have little in common with Beth. However, this is a way of saying that they are not *qualitatively* identical—that they do not share all the same qualities. But this is also true of my current self and the baby born to my mother in January 1973. It does not tell us whether Aleph and Beth are *numerically* identical—whether they are one and the same person, just at different phases of their life.

Day-to-day, we rarely have trouble working out whether a certain person at one time is one and the same as a person at another time. We assume that people *are* their bodies (or at the very least that they continually inhabit their bodies), and bodies can be recognised, whether by the naked eye or more sophisticated means such as fingerprints or DNA. Consequently, if ten people leave to climb Mount Everest and only three return, we do not usually have trouble working out which of them are the survivors.

But millions of people around the world have beliefs about what they can survive that are much harder to verify. Many Jews, Christians, and Muslims, for example, believe that after they have died and rotted away there will be a Day of Judgement when they will be physically put back together (resurrected) to live again. Others, as we have discussed, believe they will live on as a soul in another realm. It is easy to tell a story that makes it sound like someone survived some extraordinary process (like 'she closed her eyes and breathed her last ... then awoke bathed in light in the presence of angels'). But it is much harder to come up with a rigorous account of what a person *is* that would make such a story actually plausible. The questions of what a person *is*, and therefore what a person can survive, form a lively area of philosophical debate known as **personal identity theory**.

If we wanted to definitively answer the question of whether we *could* live forever, we would need to decide which theory of personal identity we think is right. For example, if you think a person's identity over time consists in the survival of a particular human organism, you would likely think we could not live forever. But if you think a person's identity over time consists in the

Why You Should Not Choose to Live Forever 11

continuation of their indestructible, immaterial soul, you would reach a different answer.

However, our question is not whether it is possible to live forever, but the hypothetical one of whether we should choose to, if it were possible. For this question we can keep a more open mind about which theory of personal identity might be right. Nonetheless, we should also keep in mind that when talking about someone 'living forever', we are assuming that the identity criterion is being met. In some cases this will be a more plausible claim than in others.

2.3 What Do We Mean by 'Should'? The Prudential and Ethical Criteria

Our concern in this book is with whether we should choose to live forever. We have discussed the various meanings of 'forever', and what it means to live on. Now we need to explore what we mean by asking whether we should choose it.

Sometimes, whether we should choose a thing or not is simply a matter of taste. Say we are choosing T-shirts. You choose a blue one, and I choose a red one. I don't think you are wrong to choose a blue one—I accept that it is simply your preference. You can't explain *why* you prefer blue—you just do, just as I don't have a reason for why I prefer red. Let us also assume that nothing further depends on our choice of colour: you choose blue, and I choose red, and that's the end of it.

Is the question of choosing to live forever like that? Might you simply prefer to live forever, while my preference is to live to be 1,384? Most people who consider the question think not. It is too important and complex to be merely a matter of preference. The way we answer the question is related to what we value in life, our ideas of the future and of our place in the cosmos. If someone told us that they wanted to die at the age of 80 or of 1,384 or never, we would expect them to give reasons for this attitude, reasons that relate to their life goals, their values, and the foreseeable consequences of their choice.

What kind of reasons? Let us return to our T-shirts. I am about to choose the red one, when you point out to me that it contains nylon to which I'm allergic (say nylon gives me a painful rash). Like most people, I have a strong preference to be free of pain. I now have a reason not to choose the red T-shirt. Let us call this a **prudential reason**. It would be imprudent of me to buy the red T-shirt, given the facts about its composition and my allergy, along with my preference to be free of pain. One meaning of 'should' or 'should not' relates to this kind of prudential reasoning: I shouldn't choose the red T-shirt because doing so would be bad for me.

I will use the term 'prudential' to refer to these kinds of self-interested reasons. Very often, when philosophers are debating whether we should choose to live forever, they cite such prudential reasons. They argue, for example, that if you lived forever, you would inevitably be terribly bored, then conclude that if you don't want to be terminally bored, you should therefore not choose to live forever. Spelled out, the argument looks like this:

1. Living forever would inevitably be boring for you.
2. You do not want to be bored.
3. Therefore you should not choose to live forever.

Prudential reasoning is about what a person should do, or should want to do, given their underlying goals or preferences. In this argument, the underlying preference features in line 2—the preference not to be bored, and the conclusion drawn from it is in line 3.

We mentioned above that when assessing the desirability of a scenario in which someone is purported to live forever, we should check if it meets the identity criterion—whether it really is the same person surviving through this period of time. We can now add that the scenario should also meet what we can call the **prudential criterion**—that is, whether the life offered by the scenario is compatible with this person's underlying goals and preferences. If not, they should not choose it.

There is another form of practical reasoning that is relevant. Take our T-shirts again. You are about to buy the blue one, when I point out that it is made by child labourers held in conditions close to slavery. You think making children work in such conditions is wrong. This isn't a prudential reason, in the sense we are using the term, as it is not self-interested—it's not about you and your welfare. Instead, it is about the welfare of people faraway whom you will never meet. Nonetheless, you think the right thing to do is boycott this kind of T-shirt. This is an instance of **ethical reasoning**.

Ethical reasoning is the other important meaning of 'should' or 'should not'. Whereas prudential reasoning relates to what is sensible, ethical reasoning relates to what is right or moral or just.[3] Needless to say, there are many different theories of ethics, from Confucianism to modern contractarianism, and from the Ubuntu philosophy of Africa to Aristotelian virtue ethics. These different theories take different approaches to many fundamental questions, such as the moral status of non-human animals, or whether and when war can be justified. But broadly speaking, what they have in common is that they are concerned with the impacts of our actions on others. In this book, I will use 'ethical' to contrast in a particular way with 'prudential': so whereas prudential reasoning is about what is in your interest, I will use the term ethical reasoning to mean what is in the interests of society as a whole. In later chapters, when we address some of the specific questions posed by the choice to live forever, we will look more closely at the answers given by different ethical traditions (for example, Hinduism and utilitarianism).

With this in mind, we can add a third criterion (to the identity criterion and the prudential criterion), which must be met if we are to say that we *should* want to live forever: **the ethical criterion**. To be met, the scenario in which we are living forever must be compatible with the interests of society as a whole (while noting that there are many different ways of interpreting that).

When people ask some 'should' questions, they are referring clearly to the ethical sense. For example, 'should you boycott clothes manufacturers who use child labour?' is unlikely to be about whether you personally would benefit from this action, and more likely to be about whether child labour is morally unacceptable and what should be done about it. Other 'should' questions are clearly prudential: 'should you go for a run before or after lunch?'. But some questions could be either or both prudential and ethical. For example, many would interpret the question 'should you eat meat?' as ethical. But at the same time, many others would consider it also (even primarily) a prudential question about whether eating meat is

---

3. I will use the terms 'moral' and 'ethical' interchangeably.

14 Stephen Cave

healthy or affordable. In a complex, interconnected world, many decisions have prudential and ethical elements, which frequently have to be weighed against each other.

I believe the question 'should we choose to live forever?' has both important prudential elements and important ethical elements. It will be easiest to give a straight answer to our question if these elements align—e.g., if it were both in my interests and society's for me to live forever. For example, if society collapsed because of overpopulation, that would be bad for society and very likely bad for me as an individual too. But it is possible that these elements will prove to be in tension—for instance, it could be that living forever would be good for me, but bad for society (e.g., if it leads to me acquiring immense power and wealth). In such a case, the prudential criterion would be met, but not the ethical criterion. We would then have to do some careful weighing and carefully qualify the answer we give to our question of whether we should choose to live forever.

Despite these interconnections, it is worth separating these two meanings of 'should' and considering the two criteria in turn. Therefore Section 3 of this chapter will deal with the prudential reasons for and against living forever, while Section 4 will then deal with the ethical reasons.

2.4 Why the Question Matters

Before we move on, it is worth considering what is at stake. After all, some people might consider our question frivolous, because they believe that we cannot live forever. To them, the question of whether we should choose to or not does not arise. Such immortality-sceptics might well be right. However, I think there are a number of good reasons for considering our question.

First, the majority of people alive today believe that they *will* live forever. As mentioned earlier, over one billion people believe in reincarnation. Billions of others—Christians and Muslims, for example—believe that they have a soul that will live on in another realm, or that they will be physically resurrected in a paradise on Earth. Many of them might believe they have no choice in the matter. That is, they believe in *true immortality*, whereby we will all live forever whether we like it or not.

In that context, the question of whether we should choose to live forever—and the related questions of whether and how immortality might be good or bad—takes on a different note. It becomes more like an inquiry into how we should try to imagine the eternal life that these religions promise, and whether it can really be as attractive as they claim. Theologians and other believers have debated these questions for centuries—indeed, the Gospels of the New Testament record Jesus debating this with the sceptical Sadducees two thousand years ago.[4]

Second, there are many who believe we can achieve much longer lifespans in this world. We live in an age of extraordinary scientific and technological progress, which has already brought breathtaking benefits to health and longevity. As a consequence, in the past few generations life expectancy in industrialised countries has doubled, from around 40—about the same as our most distant ancestors—to over 80.

This is an incredible achievement. Much of it is due to decreasing the chances of dying in infancy. But at the other end progress is being made, too, and diseases such as many forms of cancer that would once rapidly have been fatal can now be managed for long periods. The COVID-19 pandemic has shaken any idea that continued increases in life expectancy are inevitable (Santhanam 2021). However, optimists extrapolate from the trends of the past decades to argue that we can continue to live longer and longer (de Grey and Rae 2008). Some are also willing to put their money where their mouths are: healthcare has always been an enormous sector in modern economies, but now very large sums are going directly into anti-ageing research. Some of the richest people on the planet, such as Jeff Bezos (founder of Amazon) and Larry Page (co-founder of Google) are among those investing (Regalado 2021).

It is not clear whether these investments will radically transform human life expectancy. The upper-end projections, such as the idea that the first person to live to be 1,000 has already been born (de Grey 2004), seem unlikely. But breakthroughs are not impossible, and it is clear that many investors and scientists are determined to pursue them. We should therefore consider whether we as individuals or as a society want such breakthroughs. This in turn might shape public policy decisions: for example, whether to actively support anti-ageing research or not.

---

4. Matthew 22:23–33; Mark 12:18–27; Luke 20:27–40.

Techno-Optimism and Transhumanism

Techno-optimism is the belief that technology will make society better. Of course, 'better' means different things to different people. But one thing it is often taken to mean is that our lives will be healthier and longer. One version of techno-optimism that particularly focuses on longevity is **transhumanism**. Transhumanists believe we can and should use technology to radically improve ourselves—so much that we transition to being *post*-human. Numerous influential transhumanists, such as Nick Bostrom and Ray Kurzweil, have advocated for the possibility and desirability of using technology to radically extend our lives. Transhumanism has been defended by some as a natural extension of humanist and Enlightenment thinking, and criticised by others for ties to racism and eugenics.

Third, the question of whether or not we want to live forever can shape our attitude to the lifespan that we have. To take two extreme examples: someone who believed that they had an immortal soul, but who believed that immortality would be terrible, might live their lives in utter dejection. Or someone who thought earthly existence was all there was, but who desperately desired to live forever, might go through their days feeling thwarted and despondent. On the other hand, those who believe death is the inevitable and final end might find that belief easier to accept if they believe also that life without such an end would be a curse.

This first part of this opening statement has focussed on clarifying the question 'should we choose to live forever?'. We looked at what we mean by 'forever', what we mean by 'living on', and what we mean by 'should'.

To help make sense of 'forever', we distinguished between four different ways of living longer:

- *Moderate life extension:* extending life expectancy to somewhere between 120 years and 160 years.

- *Radical life extension*: defeating ageing and disease, so that people could live indefinitely, unless and until some outside shock put an end to them.
- *Contingent immortality*: being able to live indefinitely, but also being able to die if one so chooses.
- *True immortality*: not being able to die; not being mortal.

In our discussion of what it means to *live* forever, we noted that there were many different theories of personal identity—that is, theories of what living on for humans consists of. Some people believe we live on only through the continued functioning of our bodies; others that we can be uploaded onto computers; and others still that we survive because our souls survive. We do not have to decide now which one of these theories we find most plausible. But when examining a scenario which claims to be about living forever, we should check that it could plausibly meet the *identity criterion*. That is, we should be sure that the scenario convincingly describes an instance of the same person living on.

We then distinguished two different meanings of the word 'should':

- *The prudential criterion*: whether the life offered by a given account of living forever is good for a given person; whether it is compatible with their underlying goals and preferences.
- *The ethical criterion*: whether the scenario in which we are living forever is moral or just; whether it is compatible with the interests of society as a whole.

Finally, we identified three reasons why the question matters. First, lots of people alive today believe that they will live forever. It seems therefore worth examining whether that is a happy prospect. Second, some people alive today are actively pursuing much longer lives. We should therefore consider whether this is a good idea that should be supported. Third, we noted that our attitude to living forever could impact our attitude to death and the life we live now.

18 Stephen Cave

Next, in Part 3, we begin our enquiry in earnest, by examining the prudential reasons for and against wanting to live forever.

3 Prudence: Would Living Forever be Right for Me?

Often, if a person is wondering whether some option is the right one for them, they could try that option and see. Failing that, they could look at how others who have made that choice have fared. The oldest person alive at time of writing is 115 (some way from the age of the oldest person ever to have lived whose dates are well-documented: Jeanne Calment, who lived to be 122). Perhaps we could ask such 'supercentenarians', as they are called—people who are still going strong a decade or more after their hundredth birthday—whether such long lives are worth pursuing.

But while we might be able to learn something from polling such people, neither side in our debate would be content to leave matters there. If it turned out that supercentenarians were all miserable, the immortality-optimist could argue that this was due to their declining physical well-being. By contrast, in the futuristic scenarios they sketch where ageing and disease have been defeated, people aged 120 would still feel in their prime—and this would be a wholly different experience to that of the elderly today. Equally, if it turned out that this group was still full of the joys of spring, this would not convince the sceptics that we should pursue immortality. The age of 120 might seem extraordinary by current standards, but it is a small fraction of the thousand years some optimists promise, and an infinitely small fraction of forever. Perhaps despair sets in at a million?

So we cannot rely on experience—our own or that of others. We must therefore *speculate* about whether living forever is to be wished for. Fortunately, humans have been doing this for centuries. There is a rich tradition of myths, legends, stories, plays and other works, providing a wide range of visions, from gods bickering on mountaintops, to cursed undead roaming the earth, to those who have found bliss by eternal springs. They are, of course, only speculations. But the best of them have provided a toolkit for philosophers to think through the implications of unending life. In the discussion that follows, we will look at two stories that have been much debated in the literature: the 1922 play *The Makropulos Secret* by Karel Čapek, and the 1947 short story 'The Immortal' by Jorge Luis Borges. Alongside some speculations of our own, they will provide

Why You Should Not Choose to Live Forever 19

case studies for exploring the main worries regarding whether unending life would be good for any given individual: boredom, ennui, meaninglessness and procrastination. We will now look at each of these problems in turn, before drawing some conclusions.

3.1 Boredom

Karel Čapek's play *The Makropulos Secret* begins in 1919 with a century-old court case about who should inherit an aristocratic estate.[5] It so happens that a glamorous and exceptionally accomplished opera singer called Emilia Marty is performing in the city as the case comes to a head. When she hears of it, she intervenes, revealing an astonishingly detailed knowledge of the protagonists from a hundred years before, especially a singer called Ellian MacGregor. As the plot unfolds, it becomes clear that Emilia and Ellian are one and the same: a person whose real name is Elina Makropulos, born in Crete in 1585. Her father was court physician to Emperor Rudolf II, and was tasked to create an elixir that would grant those who drank it 300 years of youth. He first tested the elixir on his daughter, Elina, who fell into a coma, upon which the Emperor threw the physician in prison. But a week later, Elina awoke and escaped with the formula for the elixir. In the subsequent centuries she assumed various identities, always with the initials E.M., but also lost the formula. As three hundred years have passed, she is desperate to find it again—and does so, among the papers of the disputed estate.

The Makropulos Secret is a play about the desirability of radically longer lives. The case for taking the elixir is made by the lawyer Vitek:

> Let's give everybody 300 years of life! This will be the greatest event since the creation. It will be a liberation and a new beginning. God, what can be done with a man in 300 years! Fifty years to be a child and a student, fifty years to understand the world, a hundred years to work and be useful, then a hundred years to be wise and understanding, to rule, to teach and give example! Oh, how valuable would a human life be if it lasted 300 years! There would be no wars, no more of that

---

5. The Czech title, *Věc Makropulos*, literally translates as 'The Makropulos Thing'. It has been variously translated into English as 'The Makropulos Affair', 'The Makropulos Case', or 'The Makropulos Secret'.

dreadful hunt for bread, no fear, no selfishness. Everyone would have dignity and wisdom.

(Čapek 1990, 169)

E.M. herself, however, is not filled with such a sense of possibility. She has become cold and arrogant, indifferent to the ordinary mortals around her. She callously rebuffs their expressions of love. Nothing interests her, not even her profession: 'to sing is the same as to be silent', she says (Čapek 1990, 174). She is seeking the elixir only because she is, she admits, afraid to die. But in the end, she decides she cannot bear to live longer. She offers the formula for the elixir to the assembled characters, who all refuse, until one young woman takes it and burns it over a candle.

Philosophers have interpreted the story of E.M. as an argument that living forever would inevitably be unbearably **boring**, so much so that death would be preferable. Of course, no one has lived long enough to know whether this is really true. So the argument is based on certain claims about human nature and the nature of experience. It often runs like this:

The argument that living forever would inevitably be boring

1. There is a limited number of distinct pleasurable activities that a person can engage in.
2. No matter how pleasurable an activity, it will become boring if repeated often enough.
3. If a person lives long enough, they will eventually engage in all pleasurable activities to the point that they become boring.
4. Therefore anyone who lives long enough will inevitably become perpetually bored.
5. If a person is perpetually bored, their life is not worth living.

We can use this argument to look more closely at the case of Elina Makropulos. Premise 1 is that there is a finite number of different pleasurable activities a person can pursue. Presumably at some point E.M. loved singing—and other things too, the play suggests, such as dancing and lovemaking. But there is not an infinite variety of activities she enjoyed.

Of course, there is a *very* wide variety of activities that humans enjoy, from underwater cave exploration to tinkering with old motorbikes to flower arranging. But that does not mean that any particular individual, with their particular preferences and talents,

Why You Should Not Choose to Live Forever 21

will enjoy all these things. Perhaps E.M. tried underwater cave exploration and exhausted its possibilities—but more likely, given what we know of her character, she would have found it ridiculous or unpleasant.

We could imagine someone more open-minded and even longer-lived than E.M.. Such a person might find joy in a vast range of activities from motorcycle repair to opera singing. But there is not an *infinite* range of such activities. If we live long enough, we will eventually have pursued all kinds of music, all kinds of ball games, all kinds of outdoor exploration, and so on.

An immortality-optimist could reply that we are not looking closely enough, that in reality there is an endless variety of experiences to be had, of games to play, of artworks to be created or appreciated, of puzzles to solve—and a whole universe to explore. In a narrow sense, they might be right. Take the geometric paintings of Piet Mondrian, which consist of horizontal or vertical lines, with the lines themselves and the spaces they contain rendered in black, white or primary colours. Mondrian himself produced a great range of these works. Perhaps there is a potentially inexhaustible variety of such paintings waiting to be composed, with lines of different thickness, positioned subtly differently, on canvases of different sizes. But while each work might be technically distinct from the others, it is hard to believe that any given human would find interest in every possible variation. Ten variants might each contain surprises; perhaps even a hundred. But it is hard to believe that a thousand would, or a million.

Many other pursuits might be like this: perhaps it is possible to come up with an endless variety of cooking styles or board games. But this would only be possible through changes so subtle that they would no longer engender anything like the excitement of someone trying, say, ajapsandali (a delicious stew from Georgia in the Caucasus) for the first time. We are finite creatures: our nervous systems and sense organs, our characters and dispositions, are capable of recognising only a limited range of experiences. While that range might be immense, it is not infinite.

By itself, the fact that humans are capable of recognising and enjoying only a limited range of experiences is not enough to demonstrate that living forever would be boring. To demonstrate that, we need the further premise—Premise 2 in the argument above—that any activity will cease to be pleasurable after enough repetition. It would not matter that Elina Makropulos loved only singing if she found joy in singing forever. But she does not: after three centuries, she has tired of it.

This is probably the most disputed premise in the argument that living forever would be boring. In current lifespans of 70 or 80 years, many people find continued pleasure in the same pursuits: lifelong support of a local football team, for example, or eating annually a favourite festive dish. If a person has a wide range of interests and tastes, she need not return to the same thing every day, or even every month. She might enjoy listening to a song that she has not heard for years; she might re-read a novel and see in it new themes. She might alternate her favourite foods in a cycle lasting a year or more, so that each time she sits down to, say, Thai green curry, it is with eager anticipation.

It seems hard to prove or refute the claim that any activity will cease to be pleasurable after enough repetition. To some people it seems obviously true, to others obviously false. The sceptic might say to those who still enjoy green curry after 80 years, that this timespan is nothing compared to the millions of years that make up forever. Perhaps this is a question of personalities: some people will be bored of all their pursuits after a century—just as some people are easily bored today. As the novelist Susan Ertz put it, 'millions long for immortality who don't know what to do with themselves on a rainy Sunday afternoon' (Ertz 1943).

But the optimist could shrug this off and argue that the proper rotation of pleasures will keep them fresh. Christine Overall notes that other creatures do not seem to tire of certain simple pleasures: think of the pet dog that each day rejoices at breakfast and a nice walk (Overall 2003, 146). This is perhaps a telling analogy. Philosophers sometimes suggest that an immortal could happily spend eternity in contemplation of the universe. But perhaps it is more likely that it would be the simplest folk who would be easiest to please forever: those who are happy with breakfast and a nice walk, and who only dimly remember what they did the day before.

But it is worth noting that the stories the immortality optimists tell about how they can avoid boredom frequently feature entirely unrealistic assumptions about the world. They consist of fantasies in which their favourite food stuffs are available exactly when they want them, new partners—in love, work or play—are always available, creative expression can be pursued at leisure, and their chosen work is available as much or as little as they would like. Of the nearly 8 billion people alive today, very few if any could claim

Why You Should Not Choose to Live Forever   23

to lead such a life. Even for the tiny fraction who do currently have a life somewhat like this, it is far from guaranteed that it will continue so. History teaches us that civilisations rise and fall.

What is remarkable is that even when considering highly idealised, entirely unrealistic scenarios about what life might be like, still the question of whether boredom is inevitable or avoidable is hotly debated. Recall that our question is whether we should choose to live forever. In this section, we are considering this question in prudential terms: that is, whether for a given person, considering only their individual interests, it would be rational for them to choose to live forever. In the light of the boredom argument, we can draw the preliminary conclusion that this would be a highly risky choice, as even under the most favourable circumstances imaginable—circumstances highly unlikely to pertain—it is debatable whether terminal boredom could be avoided.

However, the seriousness of the boredom problem will vary according to the category of longer life we are considering. Recall that our four categories are: moderate life extension, radical life extension, contingent immortality, and true immortality. In scenarios with moderate life extension, people are living to between 120 and 160 years. In these scenarios, we can concede that boredom is unlikely to be a major problem for most people—or at least no more than it is with current life expectancies around 80. But we also noted above that 160 years can hardly count as a meaning of 'forever'.

We are taking radical life extension scenarios to be those in which people are immune to ageing and disease, but not to other shocks such as bomb strikes. In these scenarios, lifespans could vary widely, from 5 to 5,000, depending on the likelihood of those external threats. Given this uncertainty, few people offered an elixir might trouble themselves about a distant prospect of being bored centuries hence. Of course, terminal boredom might well set in among those who live long enough, but we currently do not have enough evidence to know when that would be.

However, in our radical life extension scenario, people are free to choose to die. Like Elina Makropolus, they could decide one day to refuse the elixir that kept ageing at bay. This 'exit clause' could make a difference to a person's deliberation about whether they should 'live forever': if living forever meant living a few centuries and having the choice to die if one wishes, then the problem of boredom might not dissuade someone from taking an elixir. The same argument could even apply to the case of contingent immortality—that is, scenarios in which people are able to live indefinitely, but could still choose to die. Even if someone felt that boredom was inevitable, but did not know when it would occur, they might choose to take an elixir, as it could mean a thousand years of fun before it all becomes stale. However, we will see in Chapter 3 that the 'exit clause' might be less helpful than it first seems for considering the attractiveness of immortality.

The literal meaning of 'forever' corresponds to what we are calling true immortality: living without end (whether one likes it or not). This is not a state we could aspire to through medical science and improved road safety. But as noted, billions of people around the world believe it is their fate. It is this category of living forever that is most threatened by the boredom argument. In scenarios of true immortality, living on is inescapable. If we therefore accept the first two premises of the boredom argument—that there is a limited number of pleasurable activities a person can engage in, and any pleasurable activity will become boring if repeated often enough—then in the case of true immortality, boredom does become inevitable.

Those religious belief systems that ascribe to true immortality attempt to deal with this in various ways. Islam would perhaps fare least well of the major religions, as it posits a paradise based largely on sensual pleasures, such as food, drink, and soft furnishings (Rustomji 2009). Christian accounts vary from equally sensuous interpretations, described by religion scholars Colleen McDannell and Bernhard Lang as 'anthropocentric', to accounts that are 'theocentric' or more focused on being with God (McDannell and Lang 1988). The theocentric accounts are partly a response to the problem that an eternity of fine wine and food might become insipid. But they largely try simply to wave the problem away, arguing that being with God just will be blissful, and not like any pleasure we know on Earth. Sophisticated theologians recognise that with our predispositions to envy, anger, boredom, etc., permanent bliss is not a state that ordinary humans can readily aspire to. So they suggest that we will be radically transformed, perhaps even merging with the Godhead, or in the words of Pope Benedict XVI, becoming part of 'the new 'space' of the body of Christ, the communion of saints' (Ratzinger 2007, 237). These accounts, however, seem to violate our identity criterion: that a person must genuinely live on.

That is the dilemma the boredom problem poses for those who believe in true immortality: as finite beings, humans cannot be happy for infinity; so to be happy for infinity, they must lose their humanity.

A state of permanent bliss for all is one in which we have no individual goals, no traits or quirks to mark us out from one another, no individual personalities at all. It is a state in which we are reduced to less than contented infants, one in which all identity is lost to the extent that it is hard to tell eternity apart from oblivion.

3.2 Ennui

For many people, the idea of boredom conjures something like standing in a long queue. It is a state in which we are temporarily unable to pursue our goals or interests. But after three centuries of life, Elina Makropolus's affliction is much worse than that. She tries to describe an affliction that will not go away:

> Boredom. No, it isn't even boredom. It is ... it is ... oh, you people, you have no name for it. No language on earth has a name for it.
>
> ... Everything is so pointless, so empty, so meaningless. You are all here? It seems as if you are not. As if you are only things ... or shadows.
>
> (Čapek 1990, 173)

E.M. is arguing that what she feels goes beyond regular boredom. It is an emptiness that never leaves her, wherever she goes, and whatever she does. She says that 'no language on earth has a name for it', but the English usage of the French word *ennui* might come close. **Ennui** is sometimes used to describe a state of listlessness, similar to some of the symptoms of what we nowadays call depression. If boredom is how you feel when waiting in the queue (for a movie, say), then ennui is what you are experiencing if you get to the end of the queue, watch the movie, and still don't feel any better. It is an inability to get excited about anything, or to enjoy anything, or to feel you can take part with any enthusiasm in any of the ordinary activities of life.

As we saw in the last section, the problem of living forever has often been framed as one of boredom. But ennui seems to be a better description of E.M.'s experience, and of the tedium of unending life. Imagine a future society that has conquered ageing and disease, and also developed wondrous pleasure domes to keep people entertained. These pleasure domes can simulate the most amazing experiences, with sensory stimulation, mysteries and puzzles, challenges and

26 Stephen Cave

battles, romances—whatever genre of adventure one favours. If an inhabitant of this society is bored, they simply go to the pleasure dome to experience the thrills. We can imagine the thrills are such that it is hard to be bored, in the usual sense, while on one of these adventures. But we can also imagine that after centuries of this life, the inhabitants nonetheless start to feel ennui. The pleasure dome might get the participant's adrenaline pumping for a while, but afterwards they might feel stale and empty. Despite the thrills, we can imagine that such a life would come to seem dreary and pointless.

This risk lurks also for the immortality optimist who believes that the proper rotation of pleasures would help them avoid boredom and stay perky for infinity. It might be true that after a century of other dishes, a person could again relish a Thai green curry. But it might also be true that ennui would set in after years of this hedonistic lifestyle, that the immortal would stop enjoying green curry, not because they have had too many green curries in the previous millennium, but because they are tired of eating three times per day, of dressing and undressing, of the subway ride to the pleasure dome, and so on.

This kind of ennui seems to be E.M.'s fate. It is a state that combines boredom with the sense that life has become pale and pointless. It seems to me a much more serious worry than that of boredom as it is usually conceived. We know that ennui, as we are calling it, is a very real condition. It was a major theme of late nineteenth- and early twentieth-century literature, where it was portrayed as a condition of the privileged classes—those who found their lives of leisure empty and tedious. Now in the twenty-first century, more people are comfortably off than ever, and more people are diagnosed with depression than ever.

I suggest we should take this worry seriously, although it would be hard to prove decisively that ennui would be inevitable for everyone after they had lived a certain amount of time. But other authors have made arguments that unending life would inevitably, in various related ways, become meaningless and thus intolerable. It is to these arguments that we turn in the next section.

3.3 Meaninglessness

The short story 'The Immortal' by Jorge Luis Borges claims to be a first-person account by Marcus Flaminius Rufus, an army officer of ancient Rome. Rufus hears one day of a legendary City of the Immortals, with a river that 'cleanses men of death' and sets off with two hundred soldiers to find it. Through disease, desertion and mutiny he loses his companions, and finds himself alone in a mountainous desert. Almost dying of thirst, he comes across a stream. Around it live people he describes as troglodytes—'naked, grey-skinned, scraggly' (Borges 1970, 138). On the other side of their dwellings—crude niches cut into the rock—is the city he seeks. But it is not what he expects.

The city's walls are impenetrable, but he finds a way in through an underground labyrinth. Inside, he finds a subtle horror: nothing in the city makes sense. Staircases are inverted, hanging upside down; corridors lead nowhere; grand doors lead only to pits. 'The gods who built it were mad', he concludes, as he escapes the city (Borges 1970, 140).

Waiting for Rufus outside is one of the troglodytes, who follows him about like a dog. Rufus calls him Argos, after the Greek hero Odysseus's dog, and tries to engage him in conversation, but to no avail.

> I thought that Argos and I participated in different universes; I thought that our perceptions were the same, but that he combined them in another way and made other objects of them; I thought that perhaps there were no objects for him, only a vertiginous and continuous play of extremely brief impressions. I thought of a world without memory, without time.
>
> (Borges 1970, 143)

Then one day it rains; Rufus and the troglodytes all rejoice, and eventually Argos speaks and the truth is revealed. The 'troglodytes' are the Immortals. They once built a magnificent city, but found in it no satisfaction and built instead its parody. Then they retreated to their current existence, removed as much as possible from the physical world: 'I remember one whom I never saw stand up'; recalls Rufus, 'a bird had nested on his breast' (Borges 1970, 145).

The man Argos is revealed to be Homer, composer of the *Iliad* and the *Odyssey*. At first, Rufus is greatly impressed. But then he realises:

> If we postulate an infinite period of time, with infinite circumstances and changes, the impossible thing is not to compose the *Odyssey*, at least once. No one is anyone, one single man is all men.
>
> (Borges 1970, 145)

28 Stephen Cave

After some centuries have passed, the Immortals hit upon the idea that if there is a river that makes humans immortal, there must somewhere be another that would make them mortal, and they disperse around the world to find it. Rufus, who had unwittingly become immortal on drinking the stream of the troglodytes, in October 1921 finds that stream's opposite.

The story is only 14 pages, but incredibly rich, containing many claims and arguments about the nature of living forever. Let us try to unpack some of them. Borges is suggesting that an immortal will eventually find the kind of pursuits that occupy us mortals to be **meaningless**. His immortals have wholly withdrawn from the world; they have stopped even perceiving it as we do—with engagement, interest and urgency. Why should this be? Because they have done everything there is to be done: 'in an infinite period of time, all things happen to all men' (Borges 1970, 144). This seems like one of the premises of the boredom argument, but Borges's point is a different one. As everyone eventually does everything, values start to become meaningless: everyone has performed 'all goodness' but also, he writes, 'all perversity'. Everyone's actions balance out, leaving them characterless: there are no heroes and villains among the immortals, but each of them is both and everything in between.

This makes the immortals indifferent to the world and each other. When one falls into a quarry, it is seventy years before the others help him out. No action seems worth taking, because:

> every act (and every thought) is the echo of others that preceded it in the past, with no visible beginning, or the faithful presage of others that in the future will repeat it to a vertiginous degree. There is nothing that is not as if lost in a maze of indefatigable mirrors. Nothing can happen only once, nothing is preciously precarious.
>
> (Borges 1970, 146)

We can see these immortals as beset by meaninglessness. For them, every action is meaningless precisely and literally because it has no *significance*, no meaning as part of a greater project or goal.

Compare this to a mortal life. The choices we make in our relatively brief lives have immense significance. We choose which projects to pursue; we strive after goals, and we decide which virtues to live by. In a life in which people have only one or two careers, a handful of hobbies, and an equally limited number of meaningful relationships, decisions about which careers, hobbies, and relationships etc., are enormously consequential. Those decisions not only give shape to our lives, but give each of us an identity; they make us who we are as individuals. These choices— whether to care for a child or open a cafe or fight for a cause—give us goals that drive us forward, and reasons to live well.

The message of Borges's story is that without the prospect of death, all this disappears. None of us will have a distinct identity, as we will all in time raise children—sometimes well, sometimes badly—*and* open a cafe *and* fight for a cause, and indeed do everything else under the sun. There will be no virtue, as we will all eventually do the right thing and the wrong thing. There will be no purpose, as all things will come and go, rise and fall. The philosopher Martha Nussbaum summed up the core of this argument: 'the intensity and dedication with which very many human activities are pursued cannot be explained without reference to the awareness that our opportunities are finite' (Nussbaum 1996, 229).

We could try to summarise this multifaceted argument thus:

The argument that living forever would result in meaninglessness

1. If a person lives long enough, they will eventually do an immense variety of things—even all possible things.
2. If a person does (and believes they will continue to do) a sufficiently immense variety of things, then individual projects will lose their significance.
3. If all people do a sufficiently immense variety of things, then they will cease to have distinct identities.
4. If all people do a sufficiently immense variety of things, then categories of virtuous and vicious, good and bad, cease to have meaning.

The immortality optimist might respond that a person is not required to do all things given indefinite time. They do not have to raise children, sometimes badly and sometimes well, or be a priest and a murderer, a street sweeper and a movie star. With sufficient determination, an immortal could carve out a distinct and delimited existence, by, for example, just staying in their apartment and playing the trombone.

There are many things to say in response to this, but let us focus on two. First, in arguing that every immortal will engage in all possible human activities, Borges is indeed making some strong assumptions about human nature and the way the world works. On the face of it, it seems theoretically possible that someone could spend eternity in their apartment playing the trombone. But I agree with Borges that that would not really be possible for any person who is anything like an ordinary human alive today. People need to get out and engage with the world, and the world is continually changing, sweeping people up in its movements and fads, from communism to Rubik's Cubes. While Borges might be overstating the case, given what we know of humans and human society, it seems to me overwhelmingly likely that an immortal will indeed engage in an immensely wide range of activities, many of which seem at opposite ends of the moral spectrum, or which in other ways seem contradictory.

Second, if an immortal tries to avoid the problem of meaninglessness by engaging in only a few activities, then they will fall foul of the problem of boredom. Recall that the problem of boredom arises when certain favourite activities are repeated endlessly. Eventually, anyone will grow weary of Thai green curry or playing the trombone. The immortal therefore faces a dilemma: if they restrict themselves to a few favoured activities, in order to give their life shape and meaning, they will encounter the problem of boredom. But if, on the other hand, they engage in a very wide range of activities in order to avoid boredom, then they will encounter the problem of meaninglessness, as their activities lose significance and their lives lose distinctiveness.

However, as with the boredom problem, the problem of meaninglessness will not impact all categories of immortality equally. Scenarios of moderate life extension—with people living to between 120 and 160 years—hardly seem long enough for meaninglessness to become *inevitable*. (Although again it is worth reminding ourselves that many people in industrialised countries today already suffer from apathy and gloom.)

In scenarios of radical life extension, wherein ageing and disease have been defeated, very long lives are imaginable—with some assumptions about continuing socio-economic stability, these could be more than a thousand years. This does seem long enough for a deep sense of pointlessness to set in. Borges thinks so: we are not given the year of Rufus's birth, only that his adventure began 'when Diocletian was emperor' (Borges 1970, 135), which would make Rufus about 1650 years old at his death. Of course, we are in the realm of speculation. Perhaps to some, the changes of the past thousand years would seem wondrous and inspiring, leaving their zest for life still strong. But we can equally imagine others for whom it would seem a wearisome cycle of venality and war.

Our next category is contingent immortality, in which unending life is possible, but so is ending it. Lifespans in such scenarios could stretch for millennia, which certainly seems to be long enough for meaninglessness to set in. When considering whether we should choose to live *forever*, I suggest the answer should be no, on the grounds that meaninglessness will become inevitable. But in a scenario of contingent immortality, the question might be more like: 'Would you choose to take an elixir of life that will make you immortal until you choose otherwise?'. Some people might say no, on the grounds that they would like to go before their lives became so boring and meaningless that suicide seems preferable. But others might think a few decades of miserable apathy at the end would be a price worth paying for centuries of good times (though, as noted above, we will discuss in more detail the usefulness of an 'exit clause' in Chapter 3).

As with the problem of boredom, those who should be most worried by the problem of meaninglessness are those who seek or believe in true immortality. They have no choice but to live for the kind of timespans at which Borges's worries become most plausible: they will witness all pleasures and all profanities; they will see the cycles of history churn endlessly. Not only will they, after some extraordinarily long time, have seen all these things, but in addition they must live in the awareness that they are condemned to keep seeing them. As Borges writes, 'what is divine, terrible, incomprehensible, is to know that one is immortal' (Borges 1970, 144).

As we have seen with the problem of boredom, religions that profess immortality tend to brush these challenges aside, rather than confront them. In the Christian New Testament, Jesus argues that the afterlife will be very different from this life: 'people will neither marry nor be given in marriage; they will be like the angels in heaven' (Matthew 22:23–33). But it is not clear what it means to be like the angels.

Elsewhere, the Bible suggests that people will undergo a radical transformation on entering the afterlife—that they will acquire new, spiritual bodies (1 Corinthian 15:42–44). But here the immortalist faces the same dilemma they encountered with the boredom problem. Imagine upon death, believers are transformed into incorruptible angelic beings who never tire of worshipping at the throne of God for eternity. Perhaps we can imagine such beings, but they don't sound much like any actual people I know. In other words, this scenario would violate the identity criterion—the requirement that the desirable immortality we are imagining for a person genuinely counts as that person continuing to exist. But if, on the other hand, a person continues to exist much as they are, then they will be susceptible to the problem of meaninglessness.

The problem of meaninglessness is partly backward-looking in time—that is, it concerns what a person has already experienced. But it is also partly forward-looking. That is, it partly concerns the daunting prospect of endless years to come. Such problems of looking forward to an indefinite future are less explored in the literature, but also important. It is to those that we turn next.

3.4 Procrastination

Those immortals who succumb to meaninglessness could be both weary of the cycle of events that they have already experienced and also thrown into despair at the prospect of endlessly repeating them in the future. But there are other problems arising from the prospect of an endless future. One of them we will call the **procrastination problem.**

Above, I argued that the constraint of finite time makes our decisions matter—these decisions, because they are limited, define who we are. But the constraint of finite time has another effect on us: it galvanises us to action. Knowing that we are mortal and our time is limited shapes our every decision. We cannot postpone indefinitely the things that are important to us; or if we do, we risk lying on our deathbed filled with regret.

In other words, death is the source of all our deadlines. If we live forever, these deadlines disappear. There is an idiom: 'life is too short to [x]', where x can be 'grumble', or 'hold grudges', or 'stay in bed for weeks watching TV and eating cold pizza'. But if we lived forever, life would not be too short for these things. It would be impossible to waste time, because there would be an infinite amount of it. As a rule, the value of a thing is related to its scarcity. If it were infinite, time would therefore have no value.

Yet the value of time is a crucial consideration in our decision-making. To take an example: imagine you have found the elixir and are working hard to save for a fantastic holiday to celebrate your good fortune. You are thinking of packing your bags when your employer says to you that if you work one more week she will give you a bonus of $1,000. If you were mortal, in making this decision you would have to weigh the value to you of the money with the value to you of your limited time. But as an immortal, you have all the time in the world—if you worked an extra week, you would still have an infinite amount of time ahead of you in which to take your holiday and do everything else you have ever dreamed of. So by sacrificing a week, you lose nothing. But money you still need: and the more you have, the longer you can enjoy your holiday— after all, you are only limited by the amount of cash you have; time you have in abundance.

It is therefore rational for you to accept your employer's offer: you get much-needed extra money, yet lose nothing. Next week, however, she offers you the same deal. As you still have infinite time ahead of you, it makes sense for you again to take the cash. But the week after that she offers you the deal again ... and again ... forever. Your dreams of seeing the world have turned into an eternity chained to your desk.

That example might seem rather contrived. But the point is that knowing our time is limited permits us to rationally decide how we wish to spend it. One of the Psalms in the Bible has us sing 'Teach us to number our days, that we may gain a heart of wisdom' (Psalm 90:12). Understanding that our days are numbered allows us to make wise decisions about how to allot them. Because they are numbered, there comes a time, as the Bible also says, to put away our childish things (1 Corinthians 13:11). But would a child who had drunk the elixir ever become an adult? We mortals spend roughly the first quarter of our lives preparing for life's labours, and the last quarter enjoying their fruits (if we are lucky). But infinity cannot be divided up into neat portions: there is no such thing as a quarter of endlessness. Yet our lives are shaped by such questions: How much education is enough? How much leisure is enough? How much time spent earning is enough? When time itself has no value, these questions have no answer.

It is a common enough problem today already that people waste their lives, forgetting that they are finite: whether it is spending their time in idleness instead of pursuing their dreams, or doing a job they dislike instead of spending time with their loved ones. Those who experience brushes with death frequently comment on the renewed appreciation it gives them of the preciousness of each minute

34 Stephen Cave

(Lipsenthal 2012). But for the immortal, each minute is not precious; indeed, it has no value at all, because endless more will follow.

Like those problems we examined earlier, the seriousness of the problem of procrastination will vary depending on which category of 'living forever' is under consideration. In cases of moderate life extension (120–160 years), the problem will be only a modest amplification of what it is today. That is, we could expect plenty of people to waste plenty of time. But the problem should not be paralysing. No one would be expecting to literally live forever, so it would not be the case that time loses all value.

In cases of radical life extension, wherein lifespans could vary enormously in length, the problem takes on a different character. We saw above that it becomes impossible to rationally apportion one's time when it is infinite. In cases of radical life extension, it is not infinite, but could be much longer than today—thousands of years perhaps. But it also could be very brief—recall that this scenario imagines only immunity to ageing and disease, not drive-by shootings and riding accidents. It would certainly be very hard to properly apportion one's time when it could stretch to millennia. Procrastination would surely reach new levels, as any sense of wasting one's time would diminish in proportion to the increase in its availability.

But apportioning one's time would also be made difficult by the uncertainty. Of course, we live with uncertainty today. But in industrialised countries, the chances of reaching around 75 years of age are good. It is therefore prudent to follow the well-established model of two decades of education, four decades of work and saving for retirement, and so on. The uncertainty increases enormously, however, when considering lifespans that could last centuries, given the possibility of radical societal and environmental upheaval in that time. It would therefore be very hard to make a rational decision about, for example, how much time to spend in education, or how much to save for retirement, and so on.

Cases of contingent immortality are different in this regard, as we are assuming in these scenarios that the immortal could live forever if they so choose. They are therefore not faced with the same degree of uncertainty. But they are faced with the prospect of endless time. Of course, we are allowing that they could choose to end their days. But we can presume for the majority that they are not planning on doing so at a fixed point in the future, and that they must therefore make their decisions based on the possibility of infinity stretching before them. (Perhaps an infinity in which there is little to do, if everyone is procrastinating, instead of engaging in creative, productive pursuits.) The true immortal, who is obliged to live forever, must also make their decisions in the knowledge of an unending future. As we have seen, making any kind of rational decision about how to spend one's time when it is infinite is extremely difficult, perhaps even impossible. In this light, Borges's portrayals of the immortals—lying in shallow pits, watching the passing of the celestial bodies above them—seems as reasonable and realistic as any.

3.5 Weighing the Prudential Arguments

Recall that our focus in this part of the book is whether living forever would be the right choice for a given individual such as you or me, considering only what is good for that individual. We have called this the prudential criterion: whether living forever would be compatible with that person's underlying goals and preferences. From the prudential point of view, there must be a strong presumption in favour of living on—of not dying. The great majority of most people's goals require that they are alive: whether that goal is getting a black belt in karate, teaching a child to play the piano, or seeing a favourite football team win the trophy. To argue that it would not be in a person's interests to live forever is to argue that there will come a point when they are better off dead: that is, when dying is more compatible with their underlying goals and preferences than living.

We can imagine two scenarios in which someone might conclude that they were better off dead, one more focussed on preferences, the other on goals. In the first scenario, some of a person's core preferences are not being met. These core preferences could include wanting to be happy, to enjoy life, to not suffer, and so on. If these core preferences are not being met, and have no prospect of being met, then a person might consider that their life is not worth living. In the second scenario, someone might simply lack any goals that require them to be alive, anything that propels them positively into the future. Such a person might therefore conclude that their life is not worth continuing.

The first three worries about unending life—boredom, ennui and meaninglessness—could all contribute to a scenario where someone felt some significant number of their core preferences were not being and could not be met. Any of those three problems at their most

36   Stephen Cave

severe would undermine any prospect of happiness, as they did for E.M.. And any of them could be considered not only obstacles to happiness, but unpleasant states in their own right. A life of ennui is one we could imagine many people would prefer to end.

Similarly, all three of these worries could bring about the second scenario, in which someone loses all goals that propel them into the future. It would be hard to maintain positive goals if all activity seems boring; all the more so for someone plagued with ennui. Most of all, a state of being in which all activity seems meaningless is exactly that state in which all positive goals have become impossible. The four problems we have considered therefore do seem serious enough to ground a decision that it would be better not to go on living.

If someone is considering whether they should choose to live forever from a prudential viewpoint, they would therefore want to know how likely they would be to encounter these problems. I have tried to argue above that if we are really considering someone living *forever*—that is, the case of the true immortal who cannot die—then it is inevitable that they will encounter these problems. But even if you are not convinced by *all* of the arguments above, then it is worth considering that *any* of boredom, ennui, and meaninglessness (for eternity) would likely be bad enough for death to be preferable. Similarly, if you are not completely convinced by any of the arguments above that these problems are *inevitable*, then I suggest that there is at least a *very good chance* that each of them will come to pass. I therefore conclude that, from a prudential point of view, no one should choose to live literally forever. Admittedly, this is not a choice open to ordinary humans here on earth. But if you meet a genie who offers to transform you into an immortal spirit, I recommend that you politely decline.

At the other end of the 'forever' spectrum is moderate life extension to between 120–160 years. I argued above that the problems of boredom, ennui, meaninglessness and procrastination would likely apply to a person with this lifespan only a little more than they do to ordinary people today. Some people in this range might become bored and goalless; some, on the other hand, would likely flourish, and consider dying at the age of 160 to be far too early. I suggest, therefore, that from a prudential point of view, these arguments do not speak strongly against the kind of moderate life extension that anti-ageing researchers are pursuing today.

The difficult cases are the two in between: radical life extension and contingent immortality. The latter is highly speculative, if not wholly

Why You Should Not Choose to Live Forever 37

fantastical: it assumes that a person could genuinely live forever, yet also choose to end it all. We noted above that an immortal with a get-out clause might worry less about boredom or meaninglessness. Though we also saw that they would likely be beset by the problem of procrastination, and could easily become stuck in an endless rut.

The question of whether it would be rational to pursue 'living forever' in the form of radical life extension is perhaps the most interesting. This is partly because it is potentially a this-worldly decision. It is highly speculative that humans will have the option of an elixir that could defeat ageing and all disease. But it does not seem impossible, and many people with large amounts of resources are pursuing it. Unlike the more mystical scenarios, radical life extension is a goal whose achievability could be affected by policy decisions made today (about research spending, for example, or tax incentives). But is it, on balance, something an individual should want for themselves, considering their interests?

It is very hard to say how probable it is that someone with an elixir of radical life extension would experience boredom, ennui, and meaninglessness, given the great uncertainty about how long their lives would be, and the general uncertainty about when these three problems might set in for different people with different personalities and dispositions. In a society with a high risk of war and other catastrophe, it might well be rational to take such an elixir, which cures a person of ageing and disease, in the ex-pectation that one will anyway be dead by other causes well before one's thousandth birthday. Equally, it is easy to imagine circumstances in which it would not seem rational to take such an elixir: for example, where millennia-long lives are secured only by extreme risk-aversion, and people are kept in highly safe surrounds (nuclear bunkers, say, deep under mountains) that all but guarantee boredom and meaninglessness.

Of course, scenarios of radical life extension are far from 'living forever' on any literal interpretation of that term. It is therefore perhaps not surprising that arguments for why living forever would be bad do not necessarily apply to these scenarios. But I have ar-gued that they *could* apply: the radically life-extended person could experience the procrastination problem, or any of boredom, ennui, and meaninglessness. I suggest therefore that whether it would be prudent to pursue this course will depend very much on the particular circumstances, and anyone offered such an elixir would do well to read the small print.

In this part of the book, we first noted that deciding whether we should want to live forever would bring us into the realm of speculation, as there are no (reliable!) firsthand reports of immortal lives. We then resolved to focus on two speculations in particular, both often discussed by philosophers: Karel Čapek's 1919 play *The Makropulos Secret*, and Jorge Luis Borges's 1947 short story 'The Immortal'.

We used these texts to explore four problems with immortal lives:

- **Boredom**: there are a limited number of pleasurable activities that a person can engage in, and all of them will become boring if repeated often enough. Therefore if a person lives long enough, they will eventually engage in all pleasurable activities to the point that they become boring.
- **Ennui**: even before every possible pleasure has become boring, the repetition involved in an endless life will lead to staleness and depression; a sense that life has been drained of its colours.
- **Meaninglessness**: if a person lives long enough, they will eventually do an immense variety of things, including things that contradict, counteract, or repeat other things they have done. As a consequence, individual projects will lose their significance; each immortal will cease to have a distinct identity; and categories of good and bad would cease to have meaning.
- **Procrastination**: many of the decisions we make require us to weigh the value of our time. But for an immortal, time is infinite, and therefore has no value. This makes it impossible to make rational decisions about how to spend one's time and would lead to a range of traps, contradictions and ruts.

We saw that people in our four different categories of living forever will experience these problems to very different degrees. At one end, people in scenarios of moderate life extension would hardly experience them more than people do today. These problems are therefore not arguments against trying to progressively increase human lifespans in the way that has happened in the past two centuries. At the other end of the spectrum, true immortals, who cannot cease to exist, would encounter these problems to a very serious degree—to the extent that we might consider true immortality to be a curse.

We saw that someone who was contingently immortal would be likely to encounter these problems. But they have a get-out clause—they could choose to give up their immortality—and this could change the balance of whether it would be prudentially rational to pursue this option (although we will discuss this more in Chapter 3). Finally, we saw that someone whose life had been radically extended would face a difficult choice, as their likelihood of encountering any of the four problems would depend very much on their particular circumstances: their personality, their society, and how history unfolded around them.

4 Ethics: Would It be Right for Society for People to Live Forever?

In the previous part of this chapter, we looked at the prudential criterion—whether living forever would be the right choice for someone considering only their own interests. In this part, we will zoom out to look at the interests of society as a whole. This is the other important meaning of 'should' or 'should not': whether it is the moral or just choice—what we are calling the ethical criterion.

We will look at two main worries: that people living forever (or significantly longer) would lead to catastrophic overpopulation, and that people living forever (or significantly longer) would exacerbate social injustices.

4.1 Overpopulation

Overpopulation is often the first worry that springs to people's minds when they consider what would happen if we could live forever. As a rule, this is a worry that relates to living forever on this planet (or at least in this physical universe), not in some other-worldly realm. The thought is a simple one: if humans continue to be born, but cease to die, then the population will keep growing until at some point the planet is too full. However, behind this intuitive thought are a number of claims that are plausible but contested. For example, one assumption is that immortal humans will continue to have children; another is that this planet (or the reachable physical universe) can support only a limited number of humans. In this subsection, we will examine the claims behind the overpopulation problem, as well as its ethical consequences.

We can spell out the argument for the overpopulation problem like this:

1. If humans continue to be born, but no longer die, the population of humans will continue to increase indefinitely.
2. This planet (and any other reachable parts of the physical universe) can support only a limited number of humans comfortably and sustainably.
3. Therefore if humans continue to be born, but no longer die, the population of humans will eventually exceed the number that can live comfortably and sustainably.

Let us first consider premise (1), that if humans can live forever, the human population will grow indefinitely. First, this assumes that immortal (or very long-lived) humans will continue to have children. This is a reasonable assumption, as having children is a very important part of many people's lives. For example, one recent survey of 'what makes life meaningful' across 17 countries found 'family and children' to be a clear winner (Silver et al. 2021).

But some people disagree with this assumption. They point to the fact that the average number of children per woman (the **fertility rate**) has gone down as life expectancy has gone up. Replacement fertility rate—the number of children each woman needs to have to keep the population stable—is about 2.1 in the US. The '2' is to replace the woman and a corresponding man. The extra—0.1 in the US—is to reflect that some children die in infancy, and so will vary depending on infant mortality rates in a given time and place. In the half century from 1960 to 2010, worldwide average fertility rates halved from around 5 to around 2.5 (The World Bank 2021). But this worldwide average of 2.5 hides wide discrepancies: in many countries of Sub-Saharan Africa, fertility rates in 2021 remained around 5. But in many wealthy, industrialised countries fertility rates have dropped below replacement levels: for example, in 2021, the rate was 1.1 in Singapore and 1.2 in Spain (ibid.).

Why You Should Not Choose to Live Forever   41

There are many reasons for this, such as adults choosing to invest more resources in fewer children (a strategy that makes sense only when infant mortality is low), the availability of contraception, more opportunities for women, and changing cultural norms. It is notable that these factors are present in wealthy, industrialised countries, which are just those countries likely to develop and have access to life extension technologies, at least initially. Perhaps if people become even wealthier, even better cared-for medically, and even longer lived, they would have even fewer children: that is, many people would be content to have none at all, and those who did have children would be content with one or two.

This is possible. I personally belong in the camp of those who consider raising children to be one of the most meaningful aspects of life, and one I would not want to do without. But I recognise that many people might see this differently, and that my own preferences are products (at least partly) of a particular time and place. However, a decrease in fertility rates will not be enough to stop a planet of immortals from becoming overpopulated. If people are not dying, then *any* number of children being born will contribute to an indefinitely increasing population. This looks somewhat different, though, if people are merely living longer rather than forever.

Recall our four categories of living forever. In two of them—true immortality and contingent immortality—living forever is guaranteed. But these are mostly other-worldly or fantastical prospects, and the problem of overpopulation is a very real this-worldly one. The likelihood of achieving even contingent immortality (immunity to ageing and disease *and* other physical shocks) in this universe is so remote that it hardly seems worth asking ourselves what its implications would be for the very practical problem of overpopulation. However, overpopulation *is* an important consideration when contemplating either moderate or radical life extension. But in these scenarios, people are still dying—only later. What are the implications of this for overpopulation?

Philosopher John K. Davis and demographer Shahin Davoudpour have explored the implications for population levels of a range of different life extension scenarios (Davis 2018, chap. 6). In short, they conclude that overpopulation is a serious risk in these scenarios, even though people are still dying. Indeed, overpopulation would be a serious risk in the short term if people lived longer, even if fertility rates were lower than replacement levels.

The reason is that more generations would be alive at any one time. Whereas today it might be common for three generations to overlap (children, parents, and grandparents), even under conditions of moderate life extension (up to 160 years) five or six generations could overlap—that is, be alive at the same time. Eventually, the population would stabilise, once the number of people dying again roughly equaled the number being born. But before this happened, the population would increase hugely because of these overlapping generations. Davis and Davoudpour calculated that if people lived to an average of 150 years and women had on average two children each, then the population would *triple* before stabilising (Davis 2018, 107–10). The current world population is approaching eight billion; if everyone had access to life extension technology, and the fertility rate was two, then the global population would rapidly increase to 24 billion.

Davis and Davoudpour have run calculations for variations on this, including smaller and larger fertility rates. To simplify their conclusions: if the fertility rate is less than replacement levels (that is, less than around two), then there is still a boom in population as more (albeit smaller) generations come into existence, while older generations stick around. But after a time, the population begins to decline. Such scenarios could therefore lead to a temporary over-population crisis. On the other hand, if the fertility rate is greater than two, then the population rapidly booms and keeps booming! Additionally, if life expectancy is even greater than 150 years—such as in scenarios of radical life extension—then the population boom is correspondingly greater, as more generations co-exist.

Another important variable is the number of people with access to life-extension treatments. The calculations above all assume that everyone has access. In reality, any significant life extension technologies that are developed could be complex and expensive, perhaps requiring regular costly treatments. We could imagine that this would only be affordable for wealthier countries, or we could even imagine that this would only be affordable for a few super-rich individuals. Clearly if only a few of the world's nearly eight billion people have access to life extension, then the impact on the global population would be negligible. But at the same time, it could seem to many people to be unjust that access to such an important technology be so restricted. We will deal with this concern in the next section. But we can see already that this poses a dilemma: the more people have access to life extension, the higher the risk of overpopulation; the fewer people have access to life extension, the more unjust this will be.

We have so far been examining premise (1), that if humans can live forever, the human population will grow indefinitely. We have seen that even if humans are not living forever, but just moderately longer (150–160 years), there will still be a very significant population boom. But how bad a prospect is this? Premise (2) of our argument is that this planet (and any other reachable parts of the physical universe) can support only a limited number of humans comfortably and sustainably. Presumably, if the population boom exceeds the number of people who can live comfortably and sustainably, that would be a very bad thing. But the assumptions behind this premise are also contested.

Some people think that the current population of humans on this planet already exceeds the number that can live comfortably and sustainably. They cite the fact that, while many people live prosperously, many others do not; and at the same time current population levels are generating unsustainable amounts of greenhouse gas emissions, using up limited resources, and despoiling the environment in ways that could have dramatic impacts on, for example, agriculture and fisheries. It is therefore hard to imagine how a much larger population could live comfortably and sustainably. A 2012 United Nations report surveyed expert predictions of the Earth's maximum sustainable population, and found the most common estimate to be eight billion—about the current population (Pengra 2012). However, even without life extension technologies, we are set to exceed that, reaching 10 billion sometime this century.

Others are more optimistic and believe that the maximum sustainable population could be much higher. They argue that the use that humans are able to make of the Earth's resources depends on the state of technology. Earth's current population levels would have been unthinkable a few centuries ago and are only possible today because of revolutions in agricultural technology (among other innovations). Perhaps, the optimists argue, future technological revolutions in sectors like renewable energy will permit further human expansion. However, in response, we might say that technological revolutions are indeed hard to predict, and so are their long term impacts on the environment. So while it is possible that the Earth's carrying capacity will increase, it seems unwise to bet on it.

44 Stephen Cave

But the optimists don't stop there. Some dream that we will not only conquer ageing and disease, but also other planets. The carrying capacity of Earth will then no longer matter, as our expanding population could spread across the Solar System. This is a story propounded by countless science fiction adventures and currently enjoying popularity among some very rich people, such as Elon Musk (founder of Tesla and the rocket company SpaceX) and Jeff Bezos (founder of Amazon and the rocket company Blue Origin). However, it is little more than a fantasy: nowhere in our solar system is nearly so hospitable as the least hospitable places on Earth. The top of Everest, the South Pole or under the sea are all more conducive to human settlement than anywhere in space. I am not suggesting that there will never be human settlements of any kind on other planets, but I am suggesting that they would be a very bad bet for getting us out of an overpopulation crisis.

On balance, I therefore suggest that there is a limit to the number of people this planet can support comfortably and sustainably, and furthermore that there is a decent chance that we are at or close to that limit. Any major breakthroughs in life extension technology are therefore likely to cause a crisis if they are available to any more than just a few. Whether that crisis is catastrophic and long-lasting or less bad and shorter will depend on how many people have access to life extension, how long their lives would then be, and how many children they have. What are the ethical implications of this?

For the ethicist or policymaker, the choices are tough. One could choose not to do anything and just let the drama unfold. But knowingly allowing an overpopulation crisis to develop does not seem like a responsible choice. The consequences could be terrible: starvation, mass migrations, war, the collapse of ecosystems (while any of these might seem unlikely to those living in countries that are currently prosperous and stable, it is worth remembering that such events have all been staples of human history). But taking action means intervening either in how many children people can have, or how long people can live, and both would be extremely controversial. Consider the following options:

1. The eight billion people who are alive when the elixir is discovered live indefinitely. They are not permitted to have children. Let us call this scenario: *the first generation inherits the Earth*.

Why You Should Not Choose to Live Forever   45

2. The eight billion people who are alive when the elixir is discovered are permitted to have children, but must die at the age of 100, to make room for their descendants. The next generation, however, is permitted to live indefinitely but not have children. Let us call this scenario: *the second generation inherits the Earth*.

3. The eight billion people who are alive when the elixir is discovered are permitted to have children, but must die at the age of 100, to make room for their descendants. The same rule applies to all subsequent generations. Let us call this scenario: *the century-long carousel of generations*.

4. Exactly as (3), but each generation is permitted to live for 1,000 years. Let us call this scenario: *the millenium-long carousel of generations*.

5. The eight billion people who are alive when the elixir is discovered are individually permitted either to have children or to live indefinitely. Let us call this scenario: *the children or longevity choice*.

In the first scenario, the generation that is alive when a life extension breakthrough occurs (let us again refer to this as the discovery of 'an elixir') are all able to have it. But an overpopulation crisis is averted by banning them from having children. While many might recognise the logic of this position, it would likely be highly unpopular. As noted above, many people (including myself) see raising children as one of life's most meaningful activities. Many also see it as a fundamental human right. It is hard to imagine the people of any democracy voting to deny themselves the right to have children. Such a policy would also be extremely difficult to enforce, requiring any of mass sterilisation, forced abortion, and infanticide. In short, while on the surface this option might seem plausible, in reality it would likely be horrific and unsustainable.

There is another kind of objection to the scenario in which the generation alive when life extension is invented inherits the Earth. Until now, history has been a cycle of one generation passing on the baton of life and opportunity to the next. Countless generations lie behind us, and have made our lives possible. And if this pattern continues, then countless generations will also lie ahead of us. But in scenario (1), this pattern stops: a single generation calls an end to the cycle, and declares itself lords of the Earth forever.

46 Stephen Cave

To some this might seem quite natural. Many humans have pursued longer lives, even an elixir that would stop ageing and disease for good. Surely no one could blame the lucky generation that succeeds in this pursuit for wanting to enjoy the benefits? But while understandable, I do not think this would be blameless. Consider scenario (2) above, in which the second generation (after the discovery of the elixir) inherits the Earth. Some of you might have wondered why I introduced this scenario, which seems morally the same as scenario (1). The answer is that scenario (2) emphasises the arbitrariness and unfairness of one generation choosing to live at the expense of all future ones. I hope that your reaction to scenario (2) is something like: *why them*? Why should the second generation be the one that lives indefinitely? But then, why the first, or the third? As philosopher Christine Overall put it: 'On what ground could we claim that we have earned the right to become the gods? It would not be because we deserve to be, but because we can' (Overall 2003, 135).

The next scenario, the century-long carousel of generations, takes seriously the ethical and political challenges of banning children, and instead aims to avoid an overpopulation crisis by allotting everyone the same finite lifespan. On the face of it, this might seem fair: everyone, including future generations, gets an equal shot at life. But it might not seem fair to you if you are a healthy 99-year-old, still feeling like you are in the prime of life, with much to give and much you want to do (including, in this scenario, being with your children and grandchildren). Yet you would be required to forfeit your life. Presumably (except in the incredibly unlikely event that the effect of the life extension treatment stopped on your 100th birthday), you would need to be killed. That is, the state would be obliged to engage in continuous acts of mass murder. Bioethicist John Harris describes this option as 'generational cleansing' (Harris 2000).

Again, it is hard to imagine people in a democracy voting for this (particularly the older ones!). The practical implementation of such a policy would likely be as horrific as the banning of children, only this time it would be older people who would be hunted and killed. It would also require very significant changes to our moral values. We currently think that people have a range of duties and responsibilities towards their children—but not a duty to die. For example, if a child needed a heart transplant, and only their parent

Why You Should Not Choose to Live Forever   47

was a compatible donor, neither the law nor society require that parent to be killed and their heart donated.

Scenario (4), the millenium-long carousel of generations, faces just the same problems; it will just take longer to reach them. At first, it might seem like an attractive option, as there will still be future generations, but each generation gets a good, long go at life. Perhaps, by the age of 999, some of the problems of boredom and meaninglessness that we examined earlier will have set in, and people will go willingly to the euthanasia chamber. But perhaps not, and they will instead need to be hunted and killed. It is also worth noting that, while this scenario does permit people to have children, they would have to do so only at the very end of their lives if an overpopulation crisis were to be avoided. Otherwise, the number of generations overlapping with lifespans of one thousand years would be immense, and the starting population would increase manifold. But from the point of view of the individuals in this scenario, this would be terrible: surely one of the advantages of living so long would be seeing one's children and grandchildren grow up, and enjoying their companionship. In other words, people in this scenario would have to die just as they had acquired a new reason to live.

Scenario (5) presents a slightly more nuanced option: individuals can choose whether to live indefinitely (or for a specified very long period) or instead to have children. On the face of it, this option seems to better respect people's autonomy (in giving them a choice) and its proponents could therefore hope for more buy-in from society. But in reality, I think it is likely to suffer from the problems of both scenarios (1) and (2), and (3) and (4). That is, if people choose the elixir, then draconian measures would be needed to ensure they do not have children; or if they choose children, then draconian measures would be required to ensure they do not live beyond their allotted years.

In summary, an overpopulation crisis would be a very serious threat if we find a way to live forever—or even for a few decades longer than we currently do. It behoves the advocate of longer lives to propose a solution. But the main options all seem unattractive, morally and practically—that is, if we assume that life extension treatment is widely available. If access to such treatment is tightly restricted, then overpopulation would be much less of a problem. However, many would regard this as deeply unjust. Let us now turn to that challenge.

4.2 Social Justice

We mentioned earlier that there is a good chance that life extension technologies would be very expensive, perhaps requiring ongoing costly treatments. They might therefore be available only to the rich. Many would regard this as a nightmarish scenario. Philosopher John K. Davis sketches why:

> Imagine: a world in which the wealthy few live on and on in endless youth, an elite gerontocracy of near-immortals who use their extra centuries to gather up the reins of property and power. They look down with indifference as generation after generation of short-lived ordinary people come and go in a passing spectacle of mortality, like ranchers watching a herd of cattle whose members change with the years.
>
> (Davis 2018, 143)

We already live in a deeply unequal society with gross wealth disparities. The 10 richest men in the world own more than the bottom 3 billion people (Ahmed et al. 2022). These disparities translate to the opportunities people have, and many other aspects of life, including access to health care. Consequently, life expectancy at birth in the Central African Republic is 53 years, whereas in wealthy Switzerland it is 83 years (The Global Health Observatory 2022).

Life extension for the wealthy threatens to exacerbate this in two ways. First, it will give them more time to acquire 'property and power', as Davis put it. We can see plenty of examples of how both can be accumulated over time: as I write, Vladimir Putin, for example, has been alternately President or Prime Minister of Russia for over twenty years, in which time he has changed the law to allow himself to continue in these roles and consolidated his grip on the state apparatus. At the same time, it is the nature of capitalism that wealth accrues to those who already have it. Warren Buffett epitomises this and is the idol of many other investors: in 1962 he became a millionaire at the age of 32, and now as I write in 2022 his wealth is valued at over $100 billion.

Ethical and political philosophies differ in the extent to which they tolerate inequality. But measures to address its extremes are close to a universal in societies around the world, with the primary measures being taxation and redistribution of wealth. Many people are upset at how unequal society is already, as evidenced, for example, by the Occupy Movement that swept across the US and beyond in the 2010s. The world's societies would therefore likely consider it unacceptable for this inequality to be exacerbated by a ruling elite gaining further in power. Although such an elite would, of course, be well-placed to repress any attempts to displace it, conjuring the prospect of further shifts towards authoritarianism.

These are worries about how life extension for a minority would be unjust because of how they could exacerbate existing imbalances in wealth and power. The second way in which it would be unjust to have a long-lived elite arises because time is itself a good. Equality of opportunity is a widespread moral principle underpinning the approach of many states. But all opportunities—to work, to have relationships, to pursue leisure—require time. Someone with more decades of life therefore has significantly more opportunity. Here in the UK, divides in life expectancy are frequently reported—between North and South England, between different ethnic groups, between rich and poor—always with a sense that this is wrong, and must be addressed. The UK Government responded to recent news of growing disparities with the statement that it 'will drive the mission to tackle health inequalities to ensure everyone has the chance to live longer and healthier lives' (Campbell and editor 2021). If current discrepancies of up to a decade in the UK are considered unacceptable, I am sure society will not tolerate differences in life expectancy of many decades or even centuries.

A variant of these worries about social justice arise even in scenarios where *everyone* has access to life extension technology. The political scientist Francis Fukuyama argues that we are status-conscious animals, drawn to creating hierarchies. These can be seen everywhere: schools and universities, sports clubs and businesses, politics and so on. Those at the top have more power—including over who gets to go up and down the ladder. Such systems are fine when those at the top naturally step down due to age and ill health, or are compelled to retire. But if people are living much longer, then their working lives will correspondingly be much longer. Consequently, those who get to the top of these hierarchies could be there for decades—or more (Fukuyama 2002, chap. 4).

This could cause immense personal frustration, as younger generations could be confined to lowly positions for years on end. This in turn could fuel intergenerational conflict—particularly if, as is increasingly the case, older generations hold property and wealth in addition to influence and prestige. It could also cause social, political and intellectual stagnation. As Fukuyama points out, social and political change often happens at generational intervals, when a new age cohort takes power: think of the sexual revolution of the 1960s and '70s, or the rapid improvement in LGBTQ rights this century. New ideas, new theories, new art and music—these all tend to come with the rise of new generations. Longer lives for all could therefore mean stagnation, conservatism and restricted opportunities for many.

Optimists—or those keenly aware of their own clock ticking—might try to wave away these problems. They could argue that problems such as wealth inequality are theoretically solvable, and that society has faced upheavals and challenges before. They might argue that society will find new ways of ensuring that older, life-extended people do not hog the top spots. Indeed, we can imagine solutions to all these problems. But it is telling that societies around the world are failing to solve problems of inequality now. In the two years since the start of the COVID-19 pandemic (that is, from March 2020), the wealth of the 10 richest men doubled, while the incomes of 99% of humanity worsened (Ahmed et al. 2022). We should not believe those who say that they will solve the problem of increased inequality that would arise from life extension unless they show us that they can solve the problems of inequality today.

> This part of the opening statement has been about the ethical problems that could arise from people living forever, and we have looked at two main kinds: those arising from overpopulation and those related to increasing social injustice.
>
> If people live forever and continue to have children, there will be a population explosion. More surprising, if people live longer (but not forever) and continue to have children, there will still be a population explosion, because more generations will co-exist. We asked whether very long-lived people would still have children, and concluded that (a) at least some would want to; and (b) that even a relatively low (below replacement level) fertility rate would cause a significant short-term population increase.
>
> Overpopulation is a real threat: the population of humans on Earth already seems to be about at the limit of what is sustainable. Dreams of colonising other planets in the Solar System (none of which are hospitable) are not realistic solutions.

If a society pursues significant life extension, it will be faced with very unpalatable moral and political choices: to face the consequences of overpopulation; to restrict people's right to have children; to enforce an age limit for people; or to make people choose either to have children or to have a longer life.

Aside from overpopulation, there are a number of other worrying impacts that living forever (or much longer) would have on society. First, if access to life extension technology was restricted to the wealthy (or some other elite), existing inequalities would be exacerbated. Second, even if everyone had access to life extension technology, there is a risk that those in power would be able to entrench their positions to the detriment of the powerless and younger generations.

5 Preliminary Conclusions

Should we choose to live forever? I have argued that there are both prudential and ethical reasons why we should not choose to. I have also argued that the problems with living forever have some interesting interrelationships, such that solving one problem could simply land us with another. Here are three dilemmas that we have encountered in our discussion so far:

- **Boredom, ennui, and meaninglessness versus identity.** In Sections 3.1 to 3.3 we encountered the problems of boredom, ennui and meaninglessness. We saw that there have been attempts to solve these problems (or to wave them away) with claims that eternal bliss could be manufactured for an immortal being, perhaps by a god, or perhaps by engineers. But I argued that such beings would not retain any of the characteristics distinctive of a particular human individual. Humans, as complex but finite beings, cannot be happy for infinity without being transformed into something else. Solving the problems of boredom, ennui, and meaninglessness for an immortal would therefore come at the expense of failing the identity criterion.
- **Boredom versus meaninglessness.** In Section 3.3, we saw that a sufficiently long-lived person would engage in such a wide range of activities that their life would start to lose distinctiveness,

52 Stephen Cave

shape or meaning. An immortal could attempt to avoid this by restricting their activities. But doing so would of course lead them straight to the problem of boredom, which would result from endless repetition.

- **Overpopulation versus injustice:** In Section 4.1, we saw that if people lived forever, or significantly longer than present, this would likely cause an overpopulation crisis. But only if large numbers of people had access to life extension technology. If, on the other hand, only a few could access this technology, overpopulation could be averted. But this would come at the expense of exacerbating injustice.

It is important to emphasise these relationships as they make clear how difficult it is to construct a coherent and satisfying account of a happy forever for anyone recognisably human. While it might be possible to address individual problems associated with living forever, it is much harder to do so in ways that don't just lead to further problems.

In conclusion, I want to highlight an additional dilemma. In Part 3, we concluded that *the prudential problems of living forever were most problematic for anyone who was genuinely immortal.* So if various religious accounts are correct, and we have immortal souls that ensure we will live on infinitely, then we will encounter the problems of boredom, ennui, meaninglessness, and procrastination. But if instead we are merely living longer, but not forever, then these problems look less bad. In scenarios of radical life extension, we saw that the extent to which these problems would arise would be very dependent on specific circumstances. While in scenarios of only moderate life extension, we probably do not need to worry about them any more than we do already. But then we turned in Part 4 to look at the ethical problems with living forever. We did not think that ethical problems such as overpopulation would be a problem in scenarios of true or contingent immortality, as these are usually posited to be happening in other-worldly realms.[6] *But the problems of overpopulation and injustice are very real for those proposing life extension in this world*—even if that life extension is relatively modest.

---

6. At least, these days. But see (Cave 2012, chap. 6) for an account of how the Christian heaven started in this world.

This is not an argument against research into killer diseases such as cancer, or indeed into slowing ageing itself. A gradual increase in healthy life expectancy could bring more happy years to millions of people and therefore be very welcome. And while it would throw up challenges for society, these could be managed if the change is gradual, and measures are undertaken to combat the unsustainable use of the Earth's resources and social inequality. But what I have presented is an argument against choosing to live forever: if it were an option at all, it would be the wrong one for individuals and for society.

Chapter 2

Why You Should Choose to Live Forever

John Martin Fischer

Contents

1	Introduction: The Human Desire to Live Forever	55
	1.1 Legends and Stories	55
	1.2 A Thought-Experiment	60
2	What Kind of 'Immortality' Do We Want?	61
	2.1 Living	62
	2.2 Forever: True Immortality vs. Radical Life Extension	63
	2.3 Radical Life Extension Under Favorable Circumstances	66
3	The 'Forever' Wars and the Rejection of Immortality	69
	3.1 Apologist Legends and Stories	69
	3.2 Objections to Living Forever: Preview and Teaser	71
4	It Wouldn't Be Me	74
	4.1 The Self Constructed from Memories	75
	4.2 The Basic Self as Subject of Experiences	77
5	Motivation and Values	78
	5.1 Why Get Off the Couch?	78
	5.2 Our Value Framework	81
6	Stories and Stages	83
	6.1 Our Lives Correspond to Narratives	83
	6.2 Our Lives Have Stages	85
7	Would an Immortal Life Necessarily Be Boring?	89
	7.1 What Is Boredom?	89
	7.2 The Circumstances of Boredom	91
	7.3 Bernard Williams: Chairman of the Bored	92

DOI: 10.4324/9781003105442-3

7.4 Initial Replies to Williams	93
7.5 Repetition and Boredom	94
8 Summary: The Last Words (for Now!)	103

I Introduction: The Human Desire to Live Forever

I.I *Legends and Stories*

In Shakespeare's *Measure for Measure*, Claudio, who is facing death by execution, reflects:

> 'tis too horrible.
> The weariest and most loathed worldly life
> That age, ache, penury, and imprisonment
> Can lay on nature is a paradise
> To what we fear of death.
> (Act 3, Scene 1, lines 143–47)

Human beings are afraid of death. Some are literally *terrified* by their future death. 'Terror-management theory', which gets its inspiration from Ernest Becker, claims that much of what we do is to manage our terror about our own death (Becker 1997). If we are terrified by our death in the future, does this imply that we wish to live forever? Not quite. I might be anxious about the process of dying, and even about death itself—the state of being dead—but also not want to live forever. That is, I might have the not-so-cheery view that dying and death could reasonably be feared, but also that living forever would not be desirable for human beings. (To get an even gloomier package of views, one might add that it would have been better never to have been born at all—but why start this optimistic chapter in this way?)

Still, many of us do want to live longer, even much longer, than we actually do. For now let's call the 'much longer' in question 'immortality'. Our usage of the terms 'immortality' and 'living forever' will thus not entail living an *infinite* number of years in the future, although it will be compatible with this interpretation. In any case, these terms will imply extreme longevity—living considerably longer than we actually do or can envisage for the near future. Further, although I shall sometimes use them in this way, I will introduce a more precise terminology below, in part so that Stephen and I are consistent.

56 John Martin Fischer

Human beings have always yearned for immortality. We can trace this basic desire back to ancient Mesopotamia in the *Epic of Gilgamesh* (Anonymous 1800 BCE/1960), the early emperors in the Han Dynasty in China, through the centuries to the present, where we see people opting for cryogenic preservation (freezing) at death, the use of medications and supplements of various kinds, and all sorts of fitness and dietary means to increase longevity. Interest in 'anti-ageing medicine' and research, both mainstream and fringe (as well as in-between), is increasing. We are searching for longevity in innovative ways. You could say that immortality is 'big business'.[1]

People have different interpretations of immortality, and we will distinguish some of them in the next section. Begin however by noting that one of the most prevalent and powerful terror management strategies is religion. Different religions posit different sorts of existence (or even 'life') after death, but they all hold out the hope for immortality in a certain sense. Some religious views present the possibility of highly desirable forms of immortality in an afterlife.[2] The almost universal presence throughout the world and human history of such religious views is testimony to the human desire for immortality (of some kind or another).

Although I cannot give a detailed history of thinking about immortality here, I will begin by following Gerald Gruman in pointing to three kinds of themes in positive immortality legends: 'antediluvian', 'hyperborean', and 'fountain' (Gruman 2003, 29–42). The 'antediluvian' theme is that people lived much longer in the past.

---

1. The classic work on the history of human efforts to achieve immortality is Gruman (2003). For helpful discussions that include more recent approaches, see Weiner (2010); Cave (2012); Davis (2018). Fascinating scientific and medical research on ageing and longevity is being done by people too numerous to mention throughout the world. I'll simply highlight a few focal points of this work: The Stanford University Center on Longevity, The Buck Institute for Research (Novator, CA), The Paul F. Glenn Center for Biology of Aging Research at Harvard University, and The MIT AgeLab.

2. Not all religions do, and some (such as Judaism and Christianity) have evolved since their inception to incorporate positive views of the afterlife. Early Judaism and Christianity had more emphasis on an unattractive, rather than an attractive, afterlife. Further, it is unclear that even paradigmatic doctrines of Christianity posit an afterlife *for the same individual*—a continuation of *their* life in Heaven, rather than a second life (or mode of existence). Consider, for example, Paul: 'We will not sleep but we will be changed'.

In the Hebrew biblical tradition individuals were said to live for almost a thousand years, although the meaning of 'year' here is contested. There are also depictions of extremely long lives in the Greek, Roman, and Indian traditions.[3] **Antediluvianism** is often coupled with '**primitivism**', the view that things were much better at some point in the past. (Gruman 2003, 30–31). As the saying goes, 'Things just ain't what they used to be'. This thought has been around for a long time!

The 'hyperborean' theme is the idea that in some very remote part of the world people live immortal lives. The word goes back to the ancient Greek idea that people live into 'extreme old age' in a land 'hyper' (beyond) 'Boreas' (the north wind). Greek folklore depicts 'Isles of the Blest', in which individuals who are in-between natural and supernatural creatures live long lives 'untouched by sorrow'. There are Persian, Teutonic, Japanese, Hebrew, and Chinese versions of the abodes of the blest. For example, in the Teutonic 'Land of Living Men', there is no ageing or death at all; the inhabitants of this land are a race of giants who welcome daring human beings.

Lost Horizon, a novel by James Hilton (made into a motion picture [1938] directed by Frank Capra, also director of the holiday classic, *It's a Wonderful Life*), is a relatively recent example of **hyperborianism**. (Hilton 1933). The analogue of a territory of the blest (a heaven on earth, you might say) is 'Shangri La', a peaceful land in the Himalayas where the residents live very long lives. Hugh Conway, a member of the British diplomatic service, survives a plane crash in the mountains of Tibet and seeks shelter at the nearby lamasery of Shangri-La. He receives an invitation to stay in this remote land, with which he wrestles. A resident implores him:

> Think for a moment. You will have time to read—never again will you skim pages to save minutes or avoid some study lest it prove too engrossing. You have also a taste for music—here, then, are your scores and instruments, with Time, unruffled and unmeasured to give you their richest savor. And you are

---

3. Throughout my discussion of the legends, stories, and historical treatments of ideas of immortality in this and following sections, I am indebted to Gruman (2003).

58 John Martin Fischer

> also, we will say, a man of good fellowship—does it not charm you to think of wise and serene friendships, a long and kindly traffic of the mind from which death may not call you away with his customary hurry?
>
> (Hilton 1933, 161)

The key inducement of Shangri La is more time to do what one cares about and enjoys: more time for joy, friendship and love, play, striving to achieve big things, and much more. Who would not be enticed? Time is short in our lives, so more of it is highly attractive. This explains the wide appeal of the Shangri La story, along with other stories of beautiful but remote abodes of the blessed and 'lands without sorrow'.

On a less exotic, but still inspirational note, Dr. Seuss [Theodore Geisel] wrote:

> Oh, the places you'll go! There is fun to be done. There are points to be scored. There are games to be won. And the magical things you can do with that bat will make you the winningest winner of all.
>
> (Seuss 1990)

The third through-line of the legends and stories is the Fountain Theme. Just as we search for Shangri-La, we seek the Fountain of Youth. This is highlighted in depictions of the Spanish explorer Ponce de Leon's quest for a famous rejuvenating fountain. Although he did not find it, he discovered Florida in 1513 for the Europeans. (Note that many in Florida continue to seek the fountain of youth, in one form or another!) The idea of rejuvenating substances, in particular water and other liquids, can be found throughout history, going back to the Hindu fable of the 'Pool of Youth' and the Hebrew legend of a 'River of Immortality'.[4]

History is replete with the use of substances—not necessarily liquids—thought to enhance longevity. We can trace this effort back to the original Chinese emperors, who sought immortality via herbs, through the manual of Francis Bacon (1638/2005) that describes various means for trying to gain more years of life, to the

---

4. For a discussion of the Fountain Theme and its historical roots, see Gruman (2003, 35–40).

contemporary proponents of anti-ageing medicine (Gruman 2003; Weiner 2010; Davis 2018).

Some of these past attempts strike us as somewhat far-fetched and even amusing now. For instance, Bacon recommended (among other things) wearing red long johns to increase longevity, and various scientists in the late nineteenth and early twentieth centuries proposed injecting fluids extracted from the testicles of young dogs and guinea pigs into human beings, or even transplanting ape testicles into human beings. This was all part of the 'rejuvenation' movement (Weiner 2010, 39–40). Today 'rejuvenation' is a ubiquitous part of anti-ageing medicine and aesthetic treatments, although, fortunately, in a range of different and updated forms.

Continuing the Fountain Theme, playwright Karel Capek and composer Leos Janacek discuss the situation of a woman whose father has developed an 'elixir of eternal life'.[5] In the play and opera, the elixir gives a person the possibility of three hundred years without biological ageing. The woman, Elina Makropulos, took the elixir at thirty-seven years of age, and she is now 337. The play and opera discuss her decision whether to take it again and thus gain three hundred more years. (This is just a brief introduction to Elina's story, and we will return to her difficult choice below.)

Recent actual, non-fictional attempts to achieve greater longevity have employed the 'ultimate' biological elixir: blood. Blood from younger mice has been transfused into older mice. The hope is that the fountain of youth would pulse through their veins, and some researchers are hopeful about insights from this research (Hoffman 2018). They believe that there is something in blood that would unlock the key to understanding and preventing ageing.

The three main themes, and countless others, resound through human history from the very beginning. The fear of death is a basic human concern, and the desire for immortality equally fundamental. We see it in the terror-management strategies of all major religions, which posit continued existence (and, in some views, *life*) after the death of our current bodies. We also wrestle with our finitude in science, music, sculpture, architecture, fiction, philosophy, and just about every area of human imagination and effort.

---

5. The play *The Makropulos Case* was first performed in 1922. Capek (1990). The opera of the same name by Janacek was adapted from the play.

60 John Martin Fischer

To dismiss or diminish our desire for immortality, or the importance of terror management in some form or other, is to deny a fundamental reality of human existence.

1.2 A Thought-Experiment

Suppose someone comes to you and asks whether you would like to live comfortably—in no significant pain, in want of none of the material and psychological bases for well-being, in a relatively nontoxic environment, and so forth—for one more week. A stipulation is that you are in relatively good physical (and psychological) condition and there will be no physical deterioration or biological 'ageing' during this week. You would no doubt say 'yes'. Now the individual asks you to imagine being asked the very same question, with the same background assumptions, in a week. Given that you gave the overwhelmingly plausible answer, 'yes', to the question asked in the first instance, surely you would answer 'yes' in the second.

The individual points out that you would certainly give the same answer every week in the future (holding fixed the assumptions with which we began). What, however, is the difference between recognising this fact about a series of hypothetical questions and choosing *now* to live forever, under the favorable and fanciful assumptions of the thought-experiment? The answer might seem to be 'None'. Thus, why would you not choose *immortality* under the stipulations in question—that you are not biologically ageing, that you live in comfortable surroundings, and so forth?

The idea that one could 'age' chronologically but not biologically is, of course, science fiction, at least relative to current science. It will be increasingly difficult to meet the assumptions of favorable external circumstances embedded in the thought-experiment, given the current trajectory of environmental degradation. An important issue is about what is happening to one's friends, loved ones, colleagues, team-mates, and so forth over time. How will one relate to them and ongoing projects undertaken with them? We will have to leave these worries aside for now (returning to them later) and assume that at least some others will have the same opportunities for immortality as you do, and relationships with them and joint projects can be sustained indefinitely.

Let's call the imaginary scenario just described, '**Nagel's Thought-Experiment**', because it is based on a similar hypothetical choice-situation presented by Thomas Nagel (Nagel 1986, 224). If not downright optimism, Nagel expresses an open-mindedness to the potential for attractive immortality.

> To sum up, in this section we noted that human beings both fear death and yearn for immortality. The drive for immortality is expressed in legends and stories about living forever that go back millennia. These stories typically exhibit three themes: 'antediluvian' (the idea that there were attractive immortal lives in the past), 'hyperborean' (the view that there are places far away—lands of the blest—where people live appealing immortal lives), and the 'fountain theme' (according to which there are substances—typically, although not exclusively, liquids, that can enhance longevity significantly). We also offered a thought-experiment that suggests that we would—and perhaps should—choose to live forever under certain specific circumstances: if we would make the envisaged choice every week, then we ought to conclude that we should choose the envisaged sort of immortality in a 'one-shot deal'.

2 What Kind of 'Immortality' Do We Want?

Why do we wish to live forever? A plausible answer is that it is more likely that we will have more good things in an immortal life than a mortal life, on the favorable assumptions about immortal life presented above. The more time you have, the greater the probability of having more valuable experiences, engaging in worthwhile and rewarding projects, achieving great things, and so forth. This gives rise to a reason to prefer immortality. Who wouldn't want more joy, pleasure, rewarding friendships and collaborations, play, love, and so forth? We prefer mortal lives with more of these good things. Why not then prefer immortality, given that it is probable that such a life will have even more of what we desire? Think of all the adventures you could have! ('Oh, the places you'll go!')

It will be helpful to clarify the sort of 'immortality' at issue. It is not as easy as one might think to answer this question, and we won't be going into all the possibilities. Suppose we say that immortality is living forever. This raises several questions, including, 'What is meant by "living"?' and 'What is meant by "forever"?' Also, 'Does one simply in fact live forever or *must* one live forever, invulnerable to death by one's own hand or others'?

62   John Martin Fischer

Finally, 'Does one *know* one's longevity-status, e.g., that one is immortal'? Answers to these questions will bear importantly on the desirability of 'immortality'.

2.1   Living

Let's take 'living' first. We don't need a fully adequate definition of life; we just need a tolerably clear grasp of what living is for a human being. As a rough approximation, we can say that living is engaging in certain basic biological processes, such as metabolism and cell repair. Metabolism involves the transformation of nutrients into biological energy. The concepts of 'life' and 'living' are very complex, and human beings function biologically in many ways in addition to metabolism.[6]

Several questions arise about this simple characterization of human life. For example, it is controversial whether human life can only take place in creatures with biological constituents and processes like ours. Might we still be alive if we were resurrected in heaven but not embodied in the same way as we are here in our earthly existence? After all, some religious views hold that we have eternal 'life'. Might we be alive if we were 'uploaded' to a computer? (Most would say that, even if we would continue to 'exist', we wouldn't be alive.)

To have a manageable project here, we will focus on human life as embodied and functioning in roughly the 'normal' way in which we are currently embodied and function—with (overall) biological constituents of the sort we actually have. This is compatible with having *some* artificial or mechanical parts. Further, the immortality in question is living forever without having died (in the sense of 'bodily death'). I interpret this assumption as ruling out 'eternal life' in an 'afterlife', even where one's own body or a similar body has somehow been reassembled—or assembled from scratch, so to speak—in another realm.

---

6. For an excellent discussion of the concept of life, especially but not solely as it applies to human beings, see Feldman (1992, 60–71). Feldman goes through many proposals for an account of 'living' and considers objections. He concludes that we don't have a fully adequate definition of life, although we can nevertheless think about it based on its uncontroversial features. This is the approach we'll take in the current book.

In short, we are evaluating living forever as biological creatures of the sort we are on our planet Earth. This is not to say that questions about immortality in an afterlife are not interesting and important. Our main question here, however, is about whether you should choose to live forever in the secular sense.

2.2 Forever: True Immortality vs. Radical Life Extension

Immortality is living 'forever', in some sense to be specified. We've briefly considered 'living', but what about 'forever'? Let's begin by supposing that it is not just that immortal beings would live forever, but they would *know* this. After all, a human being couldn't help but notice that she is living a *very* long time when she is one hundred, two hundred, five hundred, a thousand years old, and more. It wouldn't escape her attention! She observes that implausible coincidences or surprising physical events (perhaps 'interventions') occur that keep her living, and she becomes aware that she is not 'ageing' biologically: she is not subject to biological deterioration or fatal diseases that afflict others. She must come to the conclusion that she is in fact immortal, at least in a very robust sense.

Relatedly, it is not just that she *actually* lives (or will live) forever. This is not the notion of immortality of interest in the literature on its potential desirability. Rather, we are concerned with individuals who know they are *invulnerable* to death (at least in certain ways). They know this in the sense that they are not subject even to the *possibility* of death by 'natural causes', such as organ deterioration and failure, disease, and so forth. Unfortunately, however, there are other ways of dying: murder, being run over by a truck, falling off a cliff, a drug overdose, and so forth. (I'll spare you the full list!) One can die of suicide, assisted by another—such as a physician—or not.

Consider first a version of immortality in which you are invulnerable to death from *any* cause. Stephen Cave calls this '**true immortality**', and I will follow him here (Cave 2012, 267–8). Here you simply *cannot* die, no matter what happens to you. This concept is difficult to imagine or picture concretely. It implies that even if you were incinerated or pulverised (for instance, by a building collapsing directly on you or a nuclear warhead landing on your head), you could somehow be put back together and rendered a functioning human being, embodied in such a way as to underwrite your continuation as the same person. (It is obviously contentious whether you would be the *same* person, given this catastrophic process.) It is a secular version of resurrection, with scientists and medical doctors playing the role of God.

Even if it were possible to coherently conceive of true immortality—and it is an extremely far-fetched possibility--most would not deem this sort of immortality worthy of choice, in part because it would be extremely risky. One would have no 'exit strategy'—no possibility of ending life (for *any* reason that might emerge over the centuries). Even with prospects for pain control, reconstructive surgery, and so forth, it would be risky to opt for an immortality from which one would have, as in the title of Sartre's play, no exit (Sartre 1944/1989).

I do not claim that it is literally impossible to imagine true immortality, or that it would *necessarily* be unworthy of choice in virtue of its riskiness. The more imaginative and adventurous among us might choose it. It is however much easier to wrap one's mind around a different sort of immortality, which Stephen has previously called '**medical immortality**' (Cave 2012, 63). He defines medical immortality as 'immunity to ageing and disease' (Cave 2012, 16). In past work I have borrowed Stephen's term (Fischer and Mitchell/ Yellin 2014; Fischer 2020).

We could just stick with this term and definition here, but Stephen and I think it would be helpful to employ 'radical life extension' for this notion, and I'd like to specify it a bit more fully (although not completely). For simplicity's sake, in some contexts where 'life-extended' is an adjective, I'll use the term 'life-extended person', to refer to individuals who have *radically* extended lives. It is important to remember that, whenever I use the term, '**life-extended person**', I mean '*radically* **life-extended person**'. I wish to carve out a notion of radical life extension that would rule out dying not just from ageing and disease, but catastrophic events such as cardiac arrest and strokes. It doesn't seem that all such events are due to ageing or disease. The life-extended individuals we will be considering know that they won't die of a sudden and unexpected heart attack or stroke or similar event, where these 'spontaneous' events would not necessarily be the result of 'ageing or disease'.

I grant that this is just a sketch of an account of radical life extension, and many questions remain. We do however have an intuitive grasp of the concept, as opposed to true immortality. If you can die, however, how can you really be immortal? The answer is that true immortality does not capture the only reasonable interpretation of 'living forever'. According to radical life extension, 'forever' is not understood as infinite time in the future, but as extreme longevity (*way* more than any human being has ever enjoyed). Note that ordinary usage of the term 'forever' need not imply infinite time, as in 'I'll love you forever' or 'Diamonds are forever'. (Regrettably, diamonds often last longer than love, but even the 'forever' of diamonds is not *infinite* time.)

Some of the most salient discussions in the literature surrounding the potential desirability of immortality presuppose radical life extension, and not true immortality as the subject. This is so in contemporary debates. For example, Elina Makropulos's choice of the elixir would give her radical life extension, not true immortality. Further, radical life extension, as opposed to true immortality, is 'thinkable' as a feasible possibility realizable by medicine in the future, even if the very remote future. Our primary focus here will be radical life extension, although we'll also refer to true immortality, especially in contexts in which the contrast will be illuminating. We'll see that many (but not all) arguments for the potential desirability of radical life extension would apply to true immortality.

When we ask, 'Should you choose to live forever?', do we mean, 'Should you, with your current physical status and chronic ailments, choose radical life extension'? On this view, you may continue to have this status (overweight, underweight, in-shape, out-of-shape) and chronic afflictions; you 'start' from this baseline. Now you might choose to adopt regimens to improve your health, including your weight, physical condition, and so forth. Further, you may over time make progress in addressing, or even curing, your chronic medical conditions. The main point is that, although you may still have some or all the chronic maladies and diseases, they will not kill you.

Alternatively, are we asking, 'Should you choose radical life extension, imagining that you 'start' from here *without* any chronic diseases and in excellent physical health?' This is different, and both are legitimate and interesting questions. For simplicity's sake and to focus the debate, I will adopt the assumption that if you choose radical life extension, you will start at the 'baseline' of your current medical condition. Given this, some (especially those with significant chronic and debilitating health conditions) will reject it. Our discussion will further assume that whatever chronic medical issues you have do not get in the way of leading a happy and

66 John Martin Fischer

meaningful life (although they may present challenges that must be addressed).

Note that this way of interpreting the question, 'Should you choose to live forever?', points to a difference from the more general question, 'Should *any* human being choose to live forever, simply in virtue of being a human being?' To address this question, we would not need to hold fixed any individual's health status or even age. Of course, this is closely related to our question, but it is different in an interesting way (even if we interpret our question as allowing us to 'subtract' our current diseases, etc.), since it allows for adjusting the age and other physical and mental attributes.

2.3 Radical Life Extension Under Favorable Circumstances

How long on average would radical life extension last? Of course, this will change over time, and we hope it will continue to increase as medicine advances, assuming favorable environmental and social conditions. How long before you fall off a cliff? Have a terrible accident? A longevity researcher has estimated—and of course it can only be a rough guess—that radical life extension in (say) the United States is currently about six thousand years (Cave 2012, 74). Six thousand years is not an infinite number of years, but it is indeed way longer than any human being has ever lived. It is *three times* the number of years since the life of the historical Jesus! Unless otherwise specified, we will interpret living 'forever' as living, on average, six thousand years. This implies that some will live significantly fewer, and others many more, than six thousand years. You won't know exactly when you will die—it could be tomorrow or (say) ten thousand years in the future.

It is important to keep in mind that radical life extension does not rule out significant impairments and suffering (physical and emotional). Having radical life extension does not usher us into a 'land without sorrow', and certainly not a land without risk. We are asking about immortality in a recognisably human life, as similar to the lives we actually lead as is compatible with the supposition of immortality. We are not asking about superheroes or individuals with super-human powers and total immunity from death by causes of *any* sort. It is perhaps an interesting question whether we would prefer to be such characters (if that were possible), but it is not *our* question.

Risky behavior in our actual lives can have bad consequences, including death. Risky behavior in an extended life could also have bad consequences. Assuming radical life extension, if we were to decide to go skydiving and something goes terribly wrong, we could die from the fall—this is not death by ageing, diseases, or *spontaneous* catastrophic biological events. Same if one ingests heroin that is laced with fentanyl, and so forth.

We would also be subject to a range of other bad consequences of risky behavior, accidents, and unpredictable events. If you fall in rock-climbing, you may injure a limb or even become paralyzed (if you don't die). If you eat too much, or too much of the wrong foods, you may develop diabetes. You would not *die* of complications, but you would need to take medication and perhaps insulin injections. No more ice cream or chocolate chip cookies: ugh!

We can imagine that treatments for various self-imposed maladies are better in our imaginary scenario that posits radical life extension, but one could still suffer consequences. A mortal human life can involve great triumphs and joy, but also difficult decisions about uncertain paths into the future, some of which bring pain and suffering. So too with a radically extended life.

It is not enough for a good human life that certain 'internal' conditions are met, *e.g.*, that you will not biologically age. We also must assume (among other things) that you have adequate resources, including good housing and food, enough money to be comfortable, and a relatively clean environment. This is just a sketch, but it could be filled in considerably, if need be. The assumption of a clean environment is for our philosophical question, and it is not intended to indicate a likely prospect.

It is hard to imagine a good human life without companionship, friendship, and love. How can an extended-life person live a good life, if she is the only one? We'll assume that there is a group of extended-life human beings with whom she can interact and form collegial and loving relationships. In a radically extended life, as with mortal lives, friendships and marriages and other personal and professional relationships will sometimes end, and new ones begin.

Could marriages last forever (like those lovely diamonds on wedding rings)? Many are skeptical, perhaps extrapolating from

68　John Martin Fischer

the challenges of marriage in mortal lives. Consider this rather bleak passage from *Gulliver's Travels*:

> If a STRULDBRUG happen to marry one of his own kind, the marriage is dissolved of course, by the courtesy of the kingdom, as soon as the younger of the two comes to be fourscore [eighty]; for the law thinks it a reasonable indulgence, that those who are condemned, without any fault of their own, to a perpetual continuance in the world, should not have their misery doubled by the load of a [spouse].
>
> Swift (1726/1997, Part III, Ch. 10)

Others however find a loving spouse or partner can reduce whatever misery life throws at us. Maybe a marriage could last forever (in the sense of a radically extended life). Even in our ordinary lives we must 'spice up' our marriages from time to time, and the loving bond often becomes stronger and stronger over time: sometimes a spouse will die 'of heartbreak' shortly after the other member of the couple dies. 'Walking away' from a marriage of hundred (or thousands) of years can't be easy!

Of course, not all marriages last in our ordinary mortal lives. Some people have two or more marriages due to divorce or the death of a spouse. Some never re-marry. (Some never marry in the first place.) None of this renders their lives without meaning or joy. It would be unfair to count the challenges of very lengthy marriages against radical life extension, since marriage already poses a set of challenges in our mortal lives.

We could 'rethink' the institution of marriage (or romantic partnership) in a radically extended life. Perhaps 'open marriages', or open long-term romantic partnerships, would become more popular. Your marriage has ended, and it is probable that you'll have lots more time (although one doesn't know for sure, even in a radically extended life). Maybe you'll want to live a single life for a while, or perhaps find a new partner for marriage or a committed long-term intimate partnership. Have you considered multiple romantic partners? You could try it, if you'd like. Those who believe that we human beings are just not 'wired for' monogamy might find the possibilities opened by immortality enticing!

The 'until death do us part' qualification in the marriage ceremony would presumably be deleted or revised, in exchange for a promise of a loving and honest commitment. The couple would decide on the nature of their relationship (whether it is 'open' or not, and so forth) and the length or endpoint need not be specified explicitly. Surely some will find the romantic adventures allowed by radical life extension exciting, and although marriage and partnership wouldn't be *just like* those in our mortal lives, they would be sufficiently similar to recognise.

There are many conceptions of human immortality. Although we have just scratched the surface, we have identified at least the parameters of a specific sort of immortality that is sufficiently clear to be part of an interesting philosophical question: radical life extension. Should you choose radical life extension, if you could? I'll try to convince you that the answer is, 'Yes'.

> To sum up, in this section I put forward the working hypothesis that immortality is 'living forever'. We then explored the twin concepts of 'living' and 'forever'. Living is hard to define, but a live human being at the very least engages in certain basic biological functions, such as metabolism and cell repair. Of particular importance to us in this book is a distinction between two interpretations of 'forever': 'true immortality' and 'radical life extension'. True immortality is invulnerability to death from any cause, whereas radical life extension is invulnerability to death by natural causes. We will focus primarily on radical life extension under favorable conditions.

3 The 'Forever' Wars and the Rejection of Immortality

Alongside the human desire for immortality is a perennial rejection of it. Some spoilsports have found immortality, even just as radical life extension, unappealing, and others have been deeply ambivalent. Gerald Gruman (2003) traced the history (sketched above) of 'prolongevists', who embrace the desirability of immortality, and 'apologists', who reject it. Apologist legends and stories have co-existed with those of the prolongevists. For as long as human beings have thought about immortality, there have been 'forever wars'—deep and apparently intractable disagreements about the desirability of living forever.

3.1 Apologist Legends and Stories

As menioned above, *The Epic of Gilgamesh* (1800 BC) depicts the search for the secret to achieving immortality by Gilgamesh, who

70 John Martin Fischer

lost his good friend Enkidu. His search represents the human desire for immortality. On his journey he encounters an old man who suggests various ways to reach his goal, but in each case, Gilgamesh fails, although coming tantalisingly close. The main point of the epic is that, despite our drive for immortality, the attempt to achieve it is bound to fail. Another famous story that makes these points is Christopher Marlowe's sixteenth-century play, *Doctor Faustus*, adapted later by Goethe in *Faust Part A* (1808) and *Faust Part B* (1831). Dr. Faustus made a pact with the devil to achieve immortality, but this didn't work out so well: in the end the devil takes him down to hell.

The *Faust* story has resounded through the centuries: the human project of achieving immortality is deemed a presumptuous act of over-reaching and will inevitably result in bad consequences. It has a ring of truth when we observe that many of the means we choose to live our dream of immortality have side-effects, some serious. The sad story of the end of Francis Bacon's research on the possible longevity-enhancing effects of cold temperatures is an example. He was outside on a very cold night, experimenting with stuffing ice into an already-dead chicken (don't ask me why!), and he caught a cold that developed into pneumonia. It is interesting that in recent years we have discovered that cooling down the brain after a traumatic event can increase the possibility of saving the patient by slowing the physiological processes down to allow for the appropriate interventions.[7]

A few contemporary examples of such unfortunate results: the use of human growth hormone has been shown to increase one's chances of getting cancer, and some research suggests that testosterone supplementation may also be carcinogenic. Both interventions do not appear to be helpful. In general, even the most beneficial medications can have side-effects that are not conducive to health in the long-term. The use of hormones, dietary supplements, and prescription medications has not been proven effective—and can defeat the whole purpose of the efforts.

In contrast to the prolongevist's stories of voyages to distant lands of the blest, the apologist may refer to Jonathan Swift's *Gulliver's Travels* (Swift 1726/1997). In this famous book, Gulliver travels to Luggnag, located in the imaginary land of Lilliput. It

---

7. For excellent discussions of new developments in resuscitation medicine, see Parnia (2008; 2013).

Why You Should Choose to Live Forever 71

emerges that Luggnag is no Shangri La. Here the residents are immortal but biologically deteriorating, and are

> ... despised and hated by all sorts of people ... They were the most mortifying sight I ever beheld ... Besides the usual deformities in extreme old age, they acquired an additional ghastliness, in proportion to their number of years ...
> (Swift 1726/1997, Part 24, Chapter 10)

Biological deterioration goes against our assumption about medical immortality, but the passage illustrates the intuitive revulsion many feel toward living forever. The apologists' unfortunate travelogues are very different from the adventurous voyages of the prolongevists.

So also with the quest for the Fountain of Youth. Some of the legends of rivers of immortality and 'pools of youth' also depict unwelcome results. Some are filled with poison and 'pollution'. In the play by Capek introduced above, Elina Makroulos decided *not* to take a second dose of the elixir of eternal life, because after three hundred thirty-seven years she felt alienated from her life and hopelessly bored. We will return to Elina and the topic of boredom below.

In what follows I'll adopt a different terminology from Gruman's. I'll use the term '**immortality curmudgeons**' or, for short, '**curmudgeons**', for the apologists, and '**immortality optimists**' or '**optimists**', for the prolongevists. There are also views that don't fall neatly into the divide between curmudgeons and optimists. The sort of pessimist about living forever we will consider in this chapter bases her negative view on facts about human character, but others base theirs on political or environmental concerns.[8]

3.2 Objections to Living Forever: Preview and Teaser

People rarely explicitly state *why* they would prefer living longer, perhaps because they think it doesn't need explanation. Those on

---

8. In Fischer (2020) I dub the environment-degradation based pessimistic view 'Immortality Realism'. This view does not hold that immortality is necessarily unworthy of choice because of facts about human nature. It does however hold that it will probably (or even definitely) not be possible for our environment to support increasing human longevity. I'll revisit these issues in my first reply to Cave below.

the other side are very clear and confident about their objections. The literature on the evaluation of immortality thus often takes the form of considering—either defending or rejecting— objections to immortality (especially, although not exclusively, true immortality). In this section I will give an overview of the main objections. In the next sections I will go through each more carefully and present responses. In laying out the worries about immortality initially, I won't distinguish true immortality from radical life extension in this section, but this distinction will be important in the subsequent evaluation of replies to the worries.

The first objection is about personal identity over time. Put crisply, the worry is, 'It wouldn't be me!' More carefully, if I'm given a story that is allegedly about my living forever, it's got to be *me*, and not someone similar or a stranger. A story of a long life that is not mine might be of interest to me, but not in the special way I take an interest in a depiction of *my* future life. As one gets older and older, one's memories will fade and eventually one won't have memories of any individual who exists now. Additionally, one's values will certainly change substantially. How could a future person without any memories of me or any of my values be *me*? Why would I care especially about *that* individual?

Another worry is that our mortal lives are 'fraught'. We know that we have limited time, and thus our projects and concerns become more urgent—as in the saying, 'You snooze you lose'. In immortality, snoozing would not necessarily lead to losing. Why would we have any motivation to wake up and get off our couches and actively pursue meaningful and rewarding goals or personal relationships, if we will always have more time? Events in our lives, and loving relationships, become precious and special because of their finitude; immortality would rob us of all this, according to the objection.

Various philosophers have contended that immortality would destroy our framework of values and the normative judgments that guide us in our deliberations and by reference to which we interpret ourselves and others. For example, courage is steadfastness in the face of death, health is bodily functioning conducive to avoiding death, and so forth. Death sets the parameters and shapes of values. Without death, our value structure would collapse, and we would be confused and unmoored.

Another concern stems from the idea that the meaning of our lives is given by our 'stories' or '**narratives**'. Our mortal lives can be described as narratives, and a narrative has a beginning, middle, and end. If an immortal life has no ending, it follows that an immortal life could not be describable by a narrative, and thus could not be recognisable as a genuinely human life.

Some curmudgeons point out that lives that are recognisable to us as distinctively *human* lives have *stages*. They have a specific set of stages, even if they cannot be characterised precisely or always take exactly the same amount of time. One of the stages is old age (or perhaps 'being elderly') in which an individual seeks to bring together and make sense of her life, and to prepare for death. Often people at this stage are models of preparation for death—its acceptance or denial—for their families, loved ones, and friends. Such a stage would not exist in an immortal life, and 'adulthood' would be radically extended. The stages of our mortal lives form a framework by reference to which we understand human life, and that immortality would dismantle in various ways.

Finally, perhaps the most frequent objection from the curmudgeons is that immortality would be boring. Forever (no matter how interpreted) is a long time! How could we continue to be engaged in the projects we currently have, or even find them interesting? How could we enjoy any kind of activity in which we've engaged indefinitely many times already? Doesn't everything get boring eventually, and if 'eventually' is forever, wouldn't our projects and interests inevitably run out at some point? Who would choose a life that is relentlessly alienating and inescapably boring?

I pause here to return to Nagel's thought-experiment about the weekly choice of an additional week of life (or not), and my suggested extrapolation to a 'one-off' choice for radically extended life. It is important to note a major difference between Nagel's weekly choice scenario and a one-off choice. A reiterated choice of one more week of life essentially *renders irrelevant* all the objections above, since what is envisaged is just one more week of life. This then shows why the *extrapolation* from an envisaged weekly choice to a one-shot choice for radical life extension is unwarranted; the potential problems are ruled out by stipulation, so to speak. Elina's choice is thus immortality different from your choice in Nagel's thought experiment. Although his thought-experiment is suggestive and might present an initial case for radical life-extension, we need to address all the objections 'head-on', lest the analysis be question-begging.

The curmudgeons thus have a suite of weapons in their arsenal. The 'Forever' Wars are engaged! In the following sections I will lay

74 John Martin Fischer

out each objection in more detail and sketch strategies of response to these worries on behalf of the optimists. You won't find philosophical pacifism here.

> To sum up, in this section we have begun to consider 'the other side of the story', i.e., the rejection of radical life extension. Gruman called proponents of this view 'apologists', and I use the term 'curmudgeons'. Just as with prolongevism (which I dub 'optimism') there are legends and stories that express this position that go back for millennia. We have noted a set of objections to living forever: it wouldn't be me, our lives are 'fraught' and precious, our mortal lives correspond to narratives (and thus have endings), mortal lives have 'stages' that render them recognisably human, and immortal lives would necessarily be boring. We will go into each of them in more detail in the following sections.

4 It Wouldn't Be Me

Someone gives me a description—as colourful and detailed as you could imagine—of 'my' living forever in the future. The individual referred to as 'John Fischer' has many adventures: his life takes twists and turns, as any extremely long life would, and eventually—say a thousand years down the road—he has no memories of the John Fischer of today and shares none of the current John Fischer's values. Why should I—the John Fischer who exists now, as I'm typing diligently on my computer—care at all about that future individual? Here we are going to abstract away from certain complexities and simply assume, for the sake of discussion, that the notion of 'same person' lines up with 'person I care especially about in the way I typically care about myself'.

I care about others. I would be sad to hear that you will suffer pain tomorrow, and happy to know that you will experience joy. Even so, I would be disturbed in a *special* way to be told that *I* will suffer tomorrow—perhaps tortured. I would also be happy in a distinctive way to know that I will experience joy tomorrow. The point is that we care about what happens to ourselves in special and distinctive ways, even if it is controversial how much weight to give this fact in our moral reasoning.

The issue now is whether the individual who will be referred to by 'John Fischer' one thousand years in the future is really me. If not, the story is not the depiction of an immortal life for *me*. The proponent of the 'It wouldn't be me' objection points out that it seems intuitive that I wouldn't care about the future individual in the special way I care about *this* John Fischer, and thus that future individual just would not be me. The question of whether I would choose such a life makes no sense—it wouldn't be *my* life. Further, it seems that *any* story of an individual with extreme longevity could not be a story of me.

Personal Identity

It is important to keep in mind that we are discussing me—the particular individual I am—and not someone similar to me. I want to know whether I will continue to exist, whether I am immortal in the story, not whether someone who is very similar to me is immortal. When philosophers analyse 'personal identity', they are trying to figure out what makes me the particular person I am at a time and over time. When psychologists discuss these issues, their inquiry falls under 'personality theory', where they seek to understand how the personalities of particular persons change over time. That is, they assume that they are focusing on particular individuals over time, and they ask how their personalities (personality traits) are acquired and change over time. I recognise that I may change my personality traits or other properties over time, but I care in a distinctive way about myself. For good introductions to philosophical theories of personal identity, see (Perry 1975, 3–30, and Perry 1978).

4.1 The Self Constructed from Memories

Is this correct? Is the story that depicts a human individual's extreme longevity—a radically extended life--incoherent? It is always difficult to apply a concept like 'same person' to hypothetical scenarios that depart from the facts about reality in significant ways. Perhaps the concept, which works well for us in our lives, doesn't apply in such scenarios. The difficulty of applying our concept of 'same person' in contexts of big departures from our ordinary lives makes it difficult to evaluate whether we could coherently prefer immortality.

I grant the difficulty, but nevertheless hold that such stories *can* depict extreme longevity *for me*—for the individual who is the subject of the story. Let's think of persons as defined in terms of memories and values. On this sort of view, the individual referred to by 'John Fischer' in a thousand years must be connected in the right way—*via* memories and values—to the current John Fischer. What is this 'right way'? Does it require that the referent of 'John Fischer' in the future have memories of the John Fischer currently typing on his computer? Any of my liberal and compassionate values, including my passion for freedom of inquiry and expression? My love of cats?

I don't think so. Note that we lose memories all the time and often don't have *any* memories of our lives in the remote past. For example, I was born in Cleveland, Ohio; I know this because my (trustworthy) parents have told me so, my birth certificate confirms it, and I've seen photos of myself at three years of age bundled up to keep warm in the snow, and so forth. I don't however have any memories of this time in Cleveland. (None of us has memories of our births, and almost none of us has memories of our lives before [say] three years of age.) And yet that was me in Cleveland, and that was you all those years ago. As I grow older, I don't remember much about certain times of my life, and eventually I assume I'll remember nothing about them. I hope this won't be because I will have developed Alzheimer's Disease or another form of dementia; it is normal. Those previous periods are nevertheless parts of *my* life.

Given this fact about all our current lives, why not say the same thing about a radically extended life? Why apply a double standard to mortal and radically extended lives? The same point applies to values; in our ordinary lives, we often change our values over time and sometimes eventually have a totally different set of values. We can even have sudden and radical changes due to epiphanies of various sorts. When an individual has a sudden 'conversion'—religious, moral, political, and so forth—they typically are considered the same person. We should eschew a double standard when evaluating our ordinary and radically extended lives.

What exactly is the 'right' way the memories and values must be connected over time in order to support sameness of self? It is very difficult to say exactly, but the general idea is that they must fit together like links in a chain. A link at one point in the chain need not be directly connected to one at a different point, but they must be 'indirectly' connected via a chain of intermediate links. We can think of the links as metaphors for the mind of an individual at a time. Each of the intermediate links—the state of the individual's mind—is directly related to the previous link by sharing memories with the previous link. The subsequent link will have almost all the memories of the previous link, and some additional ones. Similarly, each intermediate link is directly related to the previous link by sharing values and possibly having some new values that are present as a result of reflection on those of the previous link. This is the way it works in the case of memories and values gluing us together as persons in our mortal lives. Nothing about immortality would weaken or dissolve the glue.

4.2 The Basic Self as Subject of Experiences

We have assumed that the person or self is not 'basic', but it gets 'constructed' out of—or analysed in terms of—more fundamental ingredients, such as memories, values, and their connections through time. This 'reductive' picture is reasonable, but another is available, according to which there is a **'basic self'** that does not get reduced to any other ingredients or relationships.[9] I *have* memories and values, and my memories and values are connected in the right ways to support my identity over time. I am not however *identical* to this stream of memories and values, nor am I defined in terms of it. According to this view, I might have had a totally different set of memories and values—a completely different stream of consciousness. I am the *subject of consciousness*—more like the riverbed than the stream.

For example, I could have been adopted at birth and raised by a different set of parents, had different siblings, a different education, and so forth. I could have been inadvertently 'swapped' with another baby in the hospital and brought home by a couple who was not my biological parents. It happens! It would still have been me—the very same subject of consciousness—if my biological parents had brought me home. If later in life I were to discover what had happened, I could wonder about what *my* life would have been like, had *I* grown up with them.

---

9. Note that the basic self need not be conceived of as a 'soul' or anything non-physical. It is simple and irreducible, but not necessarily non-physical.

78 John Martin Fischer

Just as I could have had a different history, giving rise to different memories and values, there is no reason I— this subject of consciousness—could not continue forever. At the very least, the fact that the *contents* of the consciousness (memories and values) change over time does not in itself imply that the *subject* does not continue. The water in the river changes but the riverbed may remain the same.

> To sum up, in this section we have addressed the worry that alleged stories of my living forever are not really such stories, because the individual referred to by 'John Fischer' would not be the same throughout. The story would thus not be about me—the very same person—living forever. I considered two main replies. First, one might think of the self as constructed out of overlapping sets of memories like a chain built out of links. We understand memories to work this way in gluing us together in our mortal lives, and we should not adopt a double standard when evaluating mortal and radically extended lives. Alternatively, one might think of the self as simply a subject of experiences. As such, none of the experiences is essential to the self. Either way the story could indeed be the story of a particular human individual living forever in the sense of a radically extended life.

5 Motivation and Values

5.1 Why Get Off the Couch?

Time is in short supply in our lives—hence the appeal of Shangri La and the Fountain of Youth. Imagine what we could do if we had much more time! Some, however, worry that 'forever' is *too much* time, even interpreted as a radically extended life (as opposed to true immortality). Given the constraints of limited time, our lives are fraught. Our failures can be devastating, but our accomplishments and triumphs especially sweet. Wouldn't immortality drain life of much of its vivid colour? If we had an extremely large amount of time, what motivation would we have to attempt to start and build relationships and to pursue projects in a timely way? Why would we do anything at all that requires active efforts, e.g., getting off our metaphorical and even literal couches?

Here's an illustration of some of the worries:

IMMORTAL LOVER 1: All I'm asking you to do is to commit to being with me for the rest of time.

IMMORTAL LOVER 2: I fully intend to commit to you, but I just don't understand why you're rushing me and I can't spend 2,000 years doing something else first.

IMMORTAL LOVER 1: Call me greedy if you want, or just head-over-heels in love, but I want as long of a period of time to spend with you as possible!

IMMORTAL LOVER 2: How many times do I have to tell you? Whether I commit to you now, one year from now, or 2,000 years from now, we will have the exact same amount of time to spend together: ℵo years!

IMMORTAL LOVER 1: I feel like every 2,000 years when I ask for your commitment you always say the same thing ... (Gorman forthcoming; online 2/16/2022).

Does radical life extension weaponise procrastination? There will always be time (assuming true immortality), so why bother? Similarly with radical life extension: it is reasonable to expect more time. Although the issues are complex, I think the general worry about motivation and timely action fails to recognise an important fact about us: the importance of 'now', or less elegantly, the importance of the temporally proximal. We live in the present, and we strongly prefer that current bads, especially experiential bads, be eliminated as quickly as possible. Similarly, we want to enjoy our future goods as soon as we can. We do not *just* wish to maximise total time with our beloved, no matter how it is distributed, and, specifically, we would be extremely disappointed with an *avoidable* wait of 2000 years for the many and tremendous goods of love. Not only would we be disappointed, but it would also be very disturbing to know that a putative lover would not mind—or would even prefer—such a delay!

LOVER 1 would justifiably feel that LOVER 2 is not really a 'lover', at least of them. A genuine lover would not spend 2000 years dabbling in other projects and experimenting with other people. It is one thing

80 John Martin Fischer

to sow your wild oats, getting them out of your system; but does this apply even after a loving relationship is established? How long does it take? The dialogue presents the two as at least putative or 'wannabe' lovers, but one who *still* needs to sow those oats for thousands of years is not *yet* a lover. One of the inescapable, and sometimes devastating, characteristics of romantic love is the strong desire to be with the loved one *now*. This is why LOVER 1 would be so disappointed, and not just because they have been put off before.

Radically extended life would be no different from our mortal lives with respect to the importance of now (and the temporally proximal). Suppose you (in an immortal life) are in terrible pain from an accident. Pain would certainly be present in immortality. Suppose a member of the emergency medical team on the scene says, 'Don't worry. I see your *Medical Immortal* ID around your neck. We won't give you the shot of morphine now, because eventually you will heal and won't be in pain. In either scenario—the morphine-now scenario and the no-morphine-now scenario—you will live approximately the same number of pain-free years, so why bother'? Surely, you are likely to say, 'It DOES matter, because *I hurt now*. I want it to go away as soon as possible, and the point about the total number of pain-free years is quite beside the point. Give me the shot'!

There are many reasons to rein in our tendencies toward sloth and procrastination in ordinary life. In a radically extended life, there would be similar reasons to get off the couch—the threats of anxiety, depression, loneliness, boredom, and a myriad of other lamentable conditions. I will want to take action to prevent the onset of them. If I am suffering *now*, I will want to alleviate the suffering as soon as possible. If the enjoyment of a good, or the elimination of a bad, must be delayed, I have to deal with the situation with patience. This is true in our mortal lives, and it would be equally so in a radically extended life; in either sort of life, *unnecessary* delays are the problem. Death is not the only thing that motivates us.

Recall that we've narrowed our subject to a certain sort of radical life extension, rather than true immortality. Although this implies that I would probably have about six thousand years, I do not know for sure that I will not be run over by a truck tomorrow. Of course, I'll take precautions and can be relatively certain that I'll have more time, but unpredictable fatal events occur, and this will give me additional (and strong) motivation to take advantage of the time I have. Many participants in the discussions of living forever presuppose true immortality, and some of the objections (including the motivation worry) are more pressing, with this assumption. Note however that many of my responses will pertain to *both* radical life extension and true immortality.

The 'fraughtness' of life concern is not only about the problem of motivation in a radically extended life. It is also about the 'precious' nature or quality of our life. Some worry that this exquisite aspect of our lives would be lost in immortality. But experiencing compelling pleasures—say from attending a concert by your favorite band or appreciating art or enjoying sex—does not involve awareness of death at all. It is not as though I'm enjoying my delicious meal or beautiful music because I know (consciously or unconsciously) that there will only be so many such experiences in my life: they are compelling and precious, but not because they are accompanied by intimations of mortality.

You love pasta primavera with homemade pasta, fresh vegetables sauteed in olive oil, a touch of garlic, and a sprinkling of herbs. Perhaps you'll pair it with a lovely glass of wine. Maybe you love cheeseburgers with French fries and a soda. Imagine the experience of really appreciating and enjoying your food—noticing its textures and flavors and enjoying each bite. You immerse yourself in the experience, and the compelling quality of it has nothing to do with a recognition of mortality. It is not as though you especially enjoy the pasta or cheeseburger because you know that your time eventually will run out, and there will be no more pasta, no more cheeseburgers, and so forth. You enjoy them because they are delicious.[10]

5.2 Our Value Framework

Death is unnecessary to provide motivation, and I hold that it is also unnecessary to shape a recognisable human value framework. Samuel Scheffler writes:

> ... the concepts ... loss, illness, injury, harm, risk, and danger ... derive much of their content from the standing recognition

---

10. Nora Ephron has written, 'You should eat every meal as though it were your last, because just before your last meal, you probably won't feel like eating!' This is of course a (somewhat dark) joke, and she is not literally imploring us to eat every stir-fry as if it were the last.

82　John Martin Fischer

that our lives are temporally bounded, that we are subject to death at any moment, and that we are certain to succumb to it in the end.

(Scheffler in Kolodny, ed. 2013, 97)

In my opinion none of these value concepts requires human mortality. Loss can be loss of just about anything, and loss of something significant—a marriage, friendship, job, and so forth— can be devastating. Illness and injury can limit us in pursuing our projects and cause suffering. Harm is the unjust setback of an interest, but we have interests in a wide variety of things that do not presuppose death. For instance, I have an interest in freedom of inquiry and speech, participation in a democratic political society, freedom to practice (or not) a religion, and so forth. I can be harmed if any of these (and other) interests are set back unjustly. Harm need not be understood in terms of death, and neither must loss. We can experience financial loss, the loss of an important relationship, and so forth.

Consider health. It can be understood as proper functioning of the body—functioning that makes it possible for us to lead good and meaningful lives. This interpretation of the concept of health would need to be elaborated and refined, but it does not appear to require mention of death. Similarly, illness can be understood in terms of impairment in bodily functioning; we don't have to include the notion of death. Think also of courage. Some instances of courage are cases of steadfastness in the face of death. Others however are manifested in the face of other threats and dangers: humiliation, injury, defeat, and so forth. It can take courage to face a challenging competitor, your boss, or a sexual abuser, or to admit failure or bad behavior, but the required steadfastness is not necessarily in the face of death.

Death does not *appear* to be essential to the content of our value framework. Scheffler, or another proponent of the 'necessity of death for value concepts', might contend that at a deeper level these notions presuppose death in some way or another. So, for example, on this view the loss of a marriage or other personal or business partnership is significant only because our time is limited and thus, we cannot rekindle the relationships or find others.

Just as in our discussion of motivation above, however, there are other reasons why the loss of a relationship can be significant. The loss of a long marriage or intimate partnership can be extraordinarily difficult, leading to loneliness, guilt, depression, and a whole suite of terrible emotions. This is how human beings are—we grieve loss, whether to death or not, and it doesn't help to know that we have more time to heal and try to recover the relationship or start another. You hurt *now*, just as when you have physical pain from a terrible accident.

In our mortal lives as we live them currently, we are often *not* consoled when we know we have time to seek reconciliation or find new partners. Would the knowledge that you have much longer make things any better? I don't think so, because this challenge has nothing to do with an awareness of limited time, or death, and everything to do with present suffering.

> To sum up, in this section we have noted parallel challenges about motivation and values in an immortal life. If we know we will live forever, why should we act now rather than later? That is, without death it seems there would be no motivation to act in the present. Similarly, without death, how can there be value concepts such as health, illness, risk, and danger, and virtues such as courage? The answers are also parallel. There are reasons for action now rather than later in an immortal life: the threat of death is not the only motivator. Similarly, value-ideas such as 'loss' need not be defined in terms of death. There are devastating losses short of death, and they can help to shape a human value framework.

6 Stories and Stages

6.1 Our Lives Correspond to Narratives

We can tell the story of a tree or automobile or cat. These are 'stories' in a broad sense. There is, however, a stricter way of understanding the relevant concept: '**narratives**'. Narratives have specific features, among them having an ending by reference to which we understand the development of the plot. Narrative understanding is through the lens of the ending—we understand the characters and plot in ways we hadn't prior to the ending. The ending makes sense of the twists and turns of the plot—and the development of the characters—in a distinctive (sometimes called 'totalizing') way. How could an immortal life provide narrative understanding?

Here we should again recall that we are focusing on radical life extension. Such a life will have an ending, even if the life is extremely

84   John Martin Fischer

long. The objection based on narrativity thus does not apply to radical life extension, although it might take a long time to get the narrative understanding. (Note that even with an ordinary mortal life, conceived of as involving narrative meaning fixed at the end, the meaning will not emerge or be grasped *during* their life.)

I do not think the objection is persuasive even as regards true immortality, but I'll focus on radical life extension. We can understand such a life as analogous to a *set* of novels or narratives. Perhaps the novels are like the *Harry Potter* books or your favorite series of mysteries. The individual books stand alone and have endings, but they are also interrelated in having some of the same protagonists acting within the framework set by the previous books. The protagonists typically develop and change over the course of the series. Why couldn't there be a very long *series* of free-standing narratives—a long set of *Harry Potter* books, mysteries, or, for that matter, television shows? In many types of television shows, each episode can stand on its own and has a narrative structure (and thus an ending), but the episodes also are interconnected via certain characters (with personal characteristics that may change over time), settings, and themes.

Why couldn't radically extended lives be like this? Just as in our mortal lives, radically extended lives have an ending. There are also endings to the parts of the life, and the different parts can contain the same protagonist having further adventures. We could say, then, that after the endings to specific parts (books), the individual's life (and episodes in it) have 'tentative' or 'presumptive' meaning, which can be adjusted in light of events in later books. Again, this is not so different from the situation in a mortal life. (Note that this point applies also to true immortality.)

This sort of life could have the kind of narrativity that would render it recognisably human. An immortal life— true or radically extended—would not be *just like* our mortal lives in all relevant respects. (A truly immortal life would have no 'totalizing' ending, and a radically extended life might be best understood in terms of an extremely long series of interconnected novels.) This is not at issue. The question is whether an envisaged immortal life would be *similar enough* to be a recognisably human life. This is a quite general way of thinking about the debates in the 'Forever' Wars. The optimist will concede that the envisaged immortality is different from our ordinary lives in various respects, but the question is whether they are *so different* as not to be recognisable as possible human lives. The optimist will insist that we not adopt a double standard in evaluating mortal and immortal lives.

6.2 Our Lives Have Stages

Some curmudgeons contend that our lives have particular stages of specific durations (within a range), and that only lives with this sort of structure can be recognisably human. Samuel Scheffler defends this position:

> Consider ... the fact that we understand a human life as having stages, beginning with birth and ending with death, and that we understand each of these stages as having its characteristic tasks, challenge, and potential rewards. ... [T]he fact that life is understood as having stages is, I take it, a universal response to the realities of our organic existence and our physical birth, maturation, deterioration, and death. Our collective understanding of the range of goals, activities, and pursuits that are available to a person, the challenges he faces, and the satisfactions that he may reasonably hope for are all indexed to these stages.
>
> (Scheffler in Kolodny, ed. 2013, 96)

A radically extended life would lack the stages that characterise ordinary human life, and their relative durations would necessarily be different. It would thus not be recognisably human.

Of course, such a life would have *most* of the stages of our current lives. The one that would be absent would be the last stage of recognition of, and preparation for, impending death. (The point of death will generally be unpredictable, given radical life extension.) Also, the 'adult' stage would be considerably longer in a radically extended life. These two differences—the absence of the final stage (as currently understood) and the elongation of the adult stage—would change the structure of stages by reference to which we currently understand human life.

Let's say that in our ordinary lives adolescence is one of the stages, and that it lasts about four years. Now let's say that 'adulthood' is also a stage, and that it typically lasts about 32 years, to keep the math simple. (Adulthood is between young adulthood and old age.). The ratio of the durations is eight to one. In radical life extension adolescence will last the same length, but adulthood would on average be much longer. We have assumed that adulthood is on average about 6000 years. The ratio will now be astronomically high compared to eight to one—approximately 1,500 to one. The change in average lifespan is not envisaged as an expansion of the length of *each* stage. (As a parent, I don't even want to imagine a much longer period of adolescence—say 1000 years!) Rather, adulthood is expanded significantly, yielding very different ratios between the stages.

I do not see why we need to have *all* the current stages or maintain the current structure of duration ratios to recognise a life as human. Radically extended lives would have all our current stages up to adulthood, and their duration ratios would remain the same. In my opinion, a life with these similarities to ours could be recognisably human. Recall that an envisaged immortal life does not have to be *just like* ours in order to be recognisable as a human life.

Over the centuries the average human lifespan has increased dramatically. At the turn of the twentieth century, average lifespan in 'first-world' countries was roughly 40 years, whereas it was almost 80 at the turn of the twenty-first century. With obesity, COVID-19, and opioids we have lost some ground, but the expectation is for further increase of the average human lifespan (assuming that we can avoid environmental devastation.) This increase will imply a change in the duration of human adulthood and a corresponding change in the duration-ratios of the stages. We could however still recognise ourselves as living (longer) human lives in the future, just as those living in 1900 could have recognised us with our current average lifespan, if our situation had been described to them.

A pioneer in developmental psychology, Erik Erikson, mapped out eight stages of human life. Each stage has a typical duration with corresponding physical and psychological constituents. His iconic book was *The Life Cycle Completed* (Erickson 1982). Some years after his death, his wife Joan Erikson published a new and 'extended' version of the book, in which she added a ninth stage to reflect ever-increasing longevity (Erikson and Erikson 1997). Thus, even a standard understanding of our life-stages has been altered already (a stage has been added). We might even come to understand human life-stages in a different way, with even more stages and different duration-ratios. There is nothing fixed about the framework of life-stages by reference to which we recognise human life.

In fairness, Scheffler does concede that the circumstances of human life might change so that we individuate stages differently or even add new ones. He claims, nevertheless, that 'the fact that life is understood as having stages is, I take it, a universal response to the realities of our organic existence and our physical birth, maturation, deterioration, and death' (Scheffler 2013, 96). (Eric Erickson also claimed that the particular stages of life are accompanied by physiological changes, in a roughly Freudian way.) This may be so, but the point is that we would *still* have stages, even if our 'organic realities' were different and there was no deterioration leading to an impending death. Life circumstances would have changed, and the new stages would be a response to the realities of the new circumstances. I hold that the resultant stages could connect a recognisably human life. Such changes (and perhaps others) might require us to think of our lives in new ways but would not necessarily imply that the lives, reconceptualised, are not *ours*.

We could even envisage becoming a member of another species, as Gregor Samsa did in Franz Kafka's story, *The Metamorphosis*. He awakened as usual, but when he happened to look down at what he expected would be his (good old) body, it was that of an insect! Similarly, the protagonist of James Cameron's film, *Avatar*, becomes a member of an alien species at the end of the film. Embracing these sorts of examples as coherent possibilities is to think much more expansively than necessary to make my point, but they are nevertheless worth considering.

This is because they suggest a basic and important point: what we are really interested in is whether the envisaged future possibility would involve *me*—the very same *self* or *person*. The assumption that I am *essentially* a human being, introduced into the contemporary discussions by Bernard Williams, may seem plausible, but I simply mark here the possibility that it is gratuitous. I can imagine waking up as an insect, distressing as that would be. After all, religious views that posit reincarnation are committed to the coherence of the persistence of the same individual person (interpreted in a certain way).

Let's return from the dizzying heights of the philosophical stratosphere. Suppose someone had made the argument in 1900 that any extension of adulthood would 'blow up' our ordinary framework of stages and thus our understanding of human life, rendering such lives unrecognisable as human. They would have been wrong, and we have benefited greatly from the extension of

88 John Martin Fischer

average human lifespan. Who would prefer to go back to 1900, where the average lifespan was half of what it is now?

Similarly, why should we defer to those who now argue that any significant extension of adulthood would render such a life so different from our ordinary lives that they would be unrecognisable (because the stages and their relationships would be very different?) Why does this point have more plausibility now than in 1900? It doesn't seem that there is a natural stopping point in our capacity to recognise human lives with different frameworks of stages. To stop seeking longevity extension in 1900 would have been disastrously conservative, and to do so now might be as well.

The point is that there is no reason to suppose that we must stop seeking greater longevity simply because our current lives have a specific framework of stages. People in 2200 might look back at the curmudgeonly arguments of 2023 based on our allegedly limited capacity to recognise lives with different stage-frameworks as quaint and unduly conservative.[11] In a nutshell: why stop here?

Gruman's term, 'apologists', is particularly apt here. Those who contend that a significantly longer life would not be recognisable as a human life are unduly pessimistic and conservative. They are apologists for the status quo. Why not aim higher, as did our predecessors at the turn of the twentieth century?

> To sum up, in this section we began by considering whether an immortal life can correspond to a narrative, since some contend that a narrative must have an ending. I pointed out that radical life extension does indeed have an ending, and even a truly immortal life might be interpreted as an interlocking series of

---

11. The distinguished physician, Sherwin Nuland, M.D., is too conservative in precisely this way in Nuland (1994, 253-4). Other physicians and philosophers have put forward similarly conservative views. See, for example, Gawande (2014) I think it is important however to distinguish attempts to increase average human longevity from attempts to keep people alive for extended periods in hospitals and other institutions long after their quality of life has diminished to zero or almost zero. That's a different proposition altogether, and I agree with Nuland, Gawande, and others that this is not the direction in which we should go. An aversion to immortality might result from conflating the two propositions: the extension of life primarily by lengthening the adult stage and extension of the length of the very last stage only (yielding indefinite says in sterile institutions.

narratives. We also considered whether a radically extended life would have stages. I pointed out that such a life would have most of the stages of a mortal life, and that requiring exactly the same stages of the same lengths (and thus) length-ratios is too conservative. Such a requirement would have implied that in 1900, in which average lifespan was 40 years, we could not have envisaged human lives that were on average double that number. Most however would not trade now for then—we are grateful to live in a time in which average lifespan in industrialised countries is close to 80 years. One wonders, then, why stop here; that is, why are we now incapable of recognising human lives of 160 years? And ...

7   Would an Immortal Life Necessarily Be Boring?

7.1   What Is Boredom?

Perhaps the most frequently mentioned obstacle to the idea that you should choose to live forever is the notion that immortality, including radical life extension, would be boring. We might even add to the human fear of death and drive for meaning in life a third basic concern: the fear of boredom and drive to avoid it. Kierkegaard wrote that boredom is the root of all evil, giving it pride of place over the usual culprit—money (Kierkegaard 1843/1994). The English poet Byron called it 'That awful yawn which sleep cannot abate' (Byron 1819/1966, canto 13, stanza 101, as quoted in Healy 1984, 27).

We might think of the fear of boredom as a special case of the fear of death, insofar as boredom has been called a 'pallid' version of death. Death, on the secular view, contains *no* experiences at all, and boredom can be thought of as experience without *engagement*. In both cases there is *nothing of interest* (for different reasons). Boredom—intractable boredom from which it seems you cannot escape—is a lot like death, and it fills us with a similar sort of terror. One does not want to be 'bored to death'. Many of the strategies for managing the terror of death are also employed to manage the fear of boredom—actively engaging in projects and staying busy.

What exactly is boredom? Often the philosophical discussions of the relationship between immortality and boredom simply presuppose that we know what boredom is, rather than seeking to define it.

90 John Martin Fischer

We can at least make some progress toward getting a firmer grasp of the concept of boredom. We need to distinguish a temporary state of boredom from a chronic (or even inescapable) state of boredom. When the chronic state is also severe, it is sometimes referred to as 'hyperboredom'.

How do we characterise the state of boredom itself? Cheshire Calhoun writes:

> Typically, boredom is marked by the absence of either desire or aversion. It is a state of indifference, disengagement, inability to pay attention, and lack of motivation—what Frankfurt describes as the absence of 'psychic liveliness'.
>
> (Calhoun 2018, 120)

We'll adopt this account of boredom. It is not necessarily that one has no content to one's experience ('experience without qualities', as it has been called)—a blank screen. It is also not akin to there being no screen at all (and no observer), as in death. It is that you simply don't care what is on the screen—it doesn't interest you. You couldn't care less, because you don't care at all.

Fernando Pessoa makes a similar point: 'Tedium is not the disease of being bored because there's nothing to do, but the more serious disease of feeling that there's nothing worth doing" (Pessoa 2002, 365; as quoted in Svendsen 2005, 34). Boredom is not the absence of cognitive content or options for action. Rather, it is an affective and motivational deficit. Nothing interests you enough to engage with it.

It is as if you are in the back seat of the family station wagon on a very long trip for the annual summer holiday. My kids used to get so bored that they would 'unravel'. I can still hear them plaintively asking, 'Are we there yet'? Or imagine the view out the window of your commuter train, which you have been taking for 40 years—the very same route, the same bleak scenery, and so forth. In both contexts the screen is not blank, so to speak. It's just that you are left cold by it all.

Walker Percy writes of being on a commuter train going through New Jersey for the thousandth time (a repetitive version of the seemingly endless ride in the station wagon): '… it is dense, sodden, impenetrable, and full of itself; it is exactly what it is, no more, no less, and as such it is boring in the original sense of the word' (Percy 1975, 87, quoted in Healy 1984, 61).

7.2 The Circumstances of Boredom

We get bored in various contexts (Calhoun 2018). Sometimes we get bored when we feel that our lives are 'stalled' and going nowhere. Perhaps we are blocked in successfully pursuing our most important projects and believe more of the same efforts will not take us on a positive trajectory. Another typical context of boredom is repetitive activities. Repetition *per se* is not necessarily boring, but repetition of activities one does not find meaningful in themselves can be extremely boring (Calhoun 2018, 16).

Think of Sisyphus rolling the rock up the hill, only to have it roll down, then rolling it up again, only to see it roll down—forever. This is not unlike the lives of certain factory or agricultural field workers, workers in meat processing plants, those doing menial clerical tasks, and so forth. Repetition of actions which in themselves are not interesting or meaningful can be, and typically is, boring.

Consider this quotation from Betty Freidan's famous book, *The Feminine Mystique*:

> Ye Gods, what do I do with my time? Well, I get my son dressed and then give him breakfast. After that I wash dishes and bathe and feed the baby. Then I get lunch and while the other children nap, I sew or mend or iron and do all the other things I can't get done before noon. Then I cook supper for the family and my husband watches TV while I do the dishes. After I get the children to bed, I set my hair and then I go to bed.
> (Freidan 1964, 23, as quoted in Calhoun 2018, 16)

When this is the daily routine, it is boring, not to mention sexist. Note that raising a child may be deeply meaningful, but here the *details* of it—the particular activities that serve the bigger purpose—are in themselves boring. Unfortunately, given the power relations between the sexes, women often had, and still have, boring lives. Jane Austen's novels are built around this theme, among others, depicting the challenges for women of finding engagement (and not just to men!). It is remarkable how Austen is able to write compelling novels about lives in which nothing interesting or striking happens. Patricia Spacks gives a detailed analysis of the relationship between women's lives, as they are portrayed in great novels (such as those of Austen), and boredom (Spacks 1995). She calls this boredom in uninteresting lives 'the consciousness of the dull' (Spacks 1995, 60–82).

92 John Martin Fischer

7.3 Bernard Williams: Chairman of the Bored

The fictional character to whom we have referred above, Elina Makropulos, is at the center of contemporary philosophical discussions of the relationship between immortality and boredom. Recall: in the play by Karel Capek (1992/1999) a woman named 'Elina Makropulos', who goes by various aliases, all of which have the initials, 'EM'. Her father has given her an elixir of 'eternal' life, which causes her to live three hundred years before she must take it again to ensure three hundred more years. The elixir also prevents biological ageing, giving her three hundred more years.

In the play, Elina is biologically 37 years of age but chronologically 337. She faces the question of whether to take the elixir again. This is a version of the question with which we started, in which you are asked to consider opting for another week of life in favorable conditions, then another week, and so forth—except Elina gets 300 more years. She has had many relationships and marriages, and she has become alienated from life. No projects interest her. Elina suffers from consciousness of the dull. She complains that 'everything is the same' and she chooses not to take the elixir.

The philosopher Bernard Williams has propelled Elina into the contemporary debates about whether immortality is potentially worthy of choice for human beings. He argues that Elina's choice was correct and that everyone should make precisely the same choice. Elina had only medical, and not true, immortality. Williams claims that immortality—even 'mere' radical life extension—would *necessarily* be boring. It is interesting that the scenario of Elina Makropulos, discussed so widely in the literature on immortality, is clearly a case of only radical life extension, and not true immortality. This fact is often overlooked by participants in the contemporary debates.

Recall that above we interpreted the question of our book, 'Should you choose to live forever?', as asking specifically about you, assuming that you would 'start' your period of radical life extension (under favorable conditions) with your current range of health issues. Williams's question is the more general question of whether *any* human being should choose radical life extension (under favorable conditions), and almost all the contemporary discussions have followed Williams's lead here. We can simply note this difference, and it should be obvious that if Williams and his followers are correct, then this will apply to the more specific case of you (and me).

Why You Should Choose to Live Forever   93

Because of Bernard Williams's role in arguing for a negative answer to the fundamental question of this book based on concerns about boredom, we might call him, 'Chairman of the Bored', to borrow a phrase from the otherwise forgettable song of Iggy Pop, 'I'm Bored'. The Chairman (or better, Chair) of the Bored is the undisputed leader of the contemporary immortality curmudgeons.

7.4   Initial Replies to Williams

Williams's key point is that inevitably EM would lose all her projects—everything that interested and energised her and gave meaning to her life. She couldn't even take pleasure in simply observing the unfolding of the parade of events in her life—she was totally alienated and indifferent. He extrapolates to the conclusion that you should not choose to be immortal under any interpretation or envisaged scenario, no matter who you are or desirable the scenario.

I am not however convinced that the boredom objection is fatal (sorry!) to a positive answer to our question. We can be bored in our current lives. Often this boredom is temporary, but sometimes chronic. It can even count as hyperboredom. All these boredom phenomena occur in our ordinary lives, and certainly not just in women. Franz Kafka struggled with feelings of 'absolute indifference and apathy'. He felt that he was 'a well gone dry, water at an unattainable depth and no certainty it is there. Nothing, nothing ...' (Kafka 1914-23/1949, 126; as quoted in Healy 1984, 35). So much for the Fountain of Youth!

Throughout history authors of fiction and philosophers have discussed the problem of boredom in our lives as we actually live them. The existentialist philosophers of the nineteenth and twentieth centuries made it a centerpiece of their works. Greater longevity is unnecessary to introduce the challenge of boredom into human lives. Even when we are not chronically bored, we must live with boredom at least some of the time. Why adopt a double standard with respect to our lives as we currently lead them and potential radically extended lives? In a puzzling passage, Bernard Williams writes that the defender of the potential desirability of immortality must point to 'something that makes boredom *unthinkable* ... something that could be guaranteed to be at every moment utterly absorbing' (Williams 1973, 94).

94 John Martin Fischer

Adopting the 'unthinkability requirement' would obviously be to adopt a double standard![12]

In her discussion of boredom, Cheshire Calhoun points out that boredom is unavoidable for human beings in the contemporary world, and we simply must learn to live with it (Calhoun 2018, 117-44). Even if one *believes* one cannot recover from extreme boredom, it does not follow that in fact one cannot. Boredom is intimately interconnected with depression (traditionally called 'melancholy'). Boredom and melancholy are sometimes hard to distinguish, if they are indeed different at all. Depression also presents itself as impossible to get past; the depressed person believes he will never get better. It does not however follow that he won't, and most (although not all) depressed persons do in fact get better, either due to the healing powers of time or medical and psychological interventions. Why would hyperboredom be any different?

Now you might say that an extended-life person may be chronically bored for an extremely long time—much longer than an individual living an ordinary lifespan could be. It would then be a huge risk to choose immortality. This is possible, but there would be many routes available to regain psychic liveliness in an immortal life. As just noted, not all bored individuals will succumb forever.

Note also that immortal people would have more opportunities to have joy in their lives and be engaged in compelling projects, and it is plausible that many will have much longer such periods than individuals living ordinary mortal lives. Surely this possibility will have at least as high a probability as the possibility that one will be hyperbored for extremely long periods, and it would balance off the relevant risks. Some will no doubt have *both* long periods of darkness and depression, and sustained bright, happy, and engaging periods. In any case, it is not at all clear that one should choose to sacrifice the potential gain to protect against the risk, or to assume that the challenges of the sad times will not be worth the joys of the good.

7.5 Repetition and Boredom

The main point of Williams and other contemporary immortality curmudgeons is that radical life extension is importantly different;

---

12. For a different and illuminating interpretation of the passage in Williams, see (Beglin 2017).

Why You Should Choose to Live Forever   95

such a long life would result in repetition that would inevitably cause alienation and extinguish psychic vitality. As Williams put it, everything that could happen to an individual with a certain character had happened to Elina. Recall that she complained that 'everything is the same'. Williams's point is that eventually Elina's character could not withstand the tedium. She would unravel, as did my kids in the station wagon. It would be the death of her character and identity. She would literally be bored out of her mind.

In a colourful passage, Samuel Beckett describes the hero of his first novel in a similar way:

> He was bogged down in indolence, *without identity* ... The cities and forests and beings were also without identity, they were shadows, they exerted neither pull nor goad ... His being was without axis or contour, its centre everywhere and periphery nowhere, an unsurveyed marsh of sloth.
> (Beckett 1993, 121 as quoted in Svendsen 2005, 19)
> [emphasis mine]

The curmudgeons extrapolate: they hold that *all* immortal individuals, including extended life persons, would eventually lose their projects and anything that could engage them—we would all drown in our own unsurveyed sloth marshes. This is a keystone of their pessimism. I just do not think the claim is true. It would not be true of all people, nor of most.

7.5.1   Would Pleasures and Agreeable Experiences Go Away?

Consider pleasures. Why think all pleasures would run out eventually? Think of the pleasures of eating delicious food, listening to music, reading compelling novels, enjoying poetry, having healthy sex, engaging in sports, pursuing hobbies, traveling, and so forth. Life can be full of pleasures, and I do not see how they would have to be extinguished in a radically extended life! Of course, they must be distributed in a sensible way. It would be foolish and self-defeating to eat the same food for breakfast, lunch, and dinner every day, or to listen to the same piece of music throughout the day and night *every* day and night, and so forth. That would wreck the pleasure. As Kierkegaard pointed out, the person interested in maximising her pleasures 'rotates' them just as a farmer would rotate her crops to maximise the fertility of the soil

(Kierkegaard 1843/1994). The undergraduate reader might find it unimaginable, but even sex can be boring if pursued morning, noon, and night for days on end (if possible at all!).

Some curmudgeons maintain that, even with a sensible distribution of pleasures (and without a single-minded obsession with a narrow range of them), one would eventually lose the capacity to experience pleasure. I disagree. Think of the pleasures of listening to your favorite music or eating your favorite food—why would they *have* to run out, as long as they were distributed appropriately and not mushed together obsessively? Bach's *Second Unaccompanied Violin Partita* is extraordinary, as is Beethoven's *Ninth Symphony*.[13] I do not see how I would ever tire of coming back to them after some time has passed. We often gain new appreciation of a work of art—a piece of music, painting, sculpture, cathedral—after we return to it, having had more experiences and attained greater maturity. Our appreciation of a work of art is never from the same perspective and need not ever become boring. The pleasure of eating a delicious meal, having healthy sex—these would not be extinguished, as long as they were distributed as part of a sensible mix.

It is as though the curmudgeon is thinking of a library with a very large (but finite) number of books. After a while, we will have read all the books worth reading. We will have got what we can out of them. There are at least two problems with this analogy. In a radically extended life, the number of books is continually expanding for one's entire life, and some will surely be worth reading. Further, you get something new each time you read a book: as above with works of art, our appreciation of a book is dependent on our perspective. New experiences and reflection on them can change our point of view, so that when we return to a book, we read it anew. The finite library analogy is not helpful to the curmudgeons' cause.

There are certain places of breathtaking natural beauty—the Pacific Coast, the Sierra Nevada Mountains, the Rocky Mountains, Yosemite National Park, the Grand Canyon, Glacier National Park, and so many others. There is extraordinary natural beauty

---

13. The music need not be 'great' by conventional standards, or 'classical'. Pick your favorite music—punk rock, folk, country, hip-hop, jazz, spa, heavy metal, ... It does not matter, as long as you love it. Some enjoy Max Richter as much as Mozart, others Sid Vicious as much as Elgar, and so forth.

Why You Should Choose to Live Forever   97

throughout the world: the English Lake District, the Alps, the Greek Islands, the Dolomites ... Think also of the lovely cities (London, Paris, Rome, San Francisco, etc.) with their parks, urban energy, architecture, and diverse populations. Why think the awe and wonder of experiencing all this beauty would go away? As with a book, one returns to these natural and 'human' spaces of extraordinary beauty with new perspectives, appreciating them in new ways.

Whenever I return to San Francisco, where I grew up, and I see the fog embracing the cypress trees in Golden Gate Park, the red bridge and sun peeking through the fog, I am transfixed anew by the magic of the place. It is never the same (nor am I), and it is always engrossing. Why think that eventually the beauty would fade, the experience become less engaging, eventually flickering out entirely? Why would the majesty of a sunset over the Pacific, a sunrise in the Grand Canyon, or a view of the snow-capped Alps on a brisk winter day, eventually become any less sublime?

Some pleasures are *self-exhausting*. The pleasure of doing something for the first time, experienced as such, is this sort of pleasure—it cannot be repeated. The pleasure of driving on your own for the first time or skiing down an advanced slope for the first time, are examples, as are the pleasures of completing something, such as a particular paper or a required course of study. It is a mistake however to generalize from these to *all* pleasures. Some pleasures are *repeatable*. Philip Bricker writes:

> ... there are pleasures [repeatable pleasures] that we never grow tired of, of which we can say: 'the more, the better'. Take, for example, my unflagging desire for Thai food: I want to eat it this week, and the week after, and so on ...
>
> (Bricker 2020, 315)

Bricker's love for Thai food (and other repeatable pleasures) makes him want to live not just for a 'piddling' alpha-zero number of years, but for higher and higher order infinities of years (Bricker 2020, 320). We'll stick with the even more piddling radical life extension here.

Similarly, Corliss Lamont reflects:

> I deny that repetition as such leads to 'monotony and boredom'. Consider, for instance, the basic biological drives of hunger, thirst, and sex. Pure, cool water is the best drink in

98 John Martin Fischer

> the world, and I have been drinking it for sixty-two years. ...
> Yet I still love water. By the same token, the average person
> does not fall into a state of ennui through the satisfaction of
> hunger or sexual desire.
>
> Lamont (1965, 33)

Pleasures and enjoyable experiences are parts of a good life, and there is no reason why they would have to disappear in a radically extended life. Spiritual experiences are compelling, but they do not necessarily constitute or lead to 'pleasures'. I'll call them 'agreeable experiences', and we engage in many activities that involve such experiences. We anticipate and welcome them, but often they are not the sole reason why we pursue the activities and projects.

Why would these spiritual experiences, such as meditation and prayer lose their compelling quality, especially when integrated into a life that contains other activities? Spiritual and mystical experiences induced by meditation, prayer, or even psychedelic substances can be profound and transformative. People can repeatedly have these experiences, and they can be extraordinarily and deeply meaningful throughout their mortal lives. Why can't this be so in in a radically extended life? The 'intrinsic' nature of the experiences—their sublime and transcendent subjective qualities—suggests that they could be sustained.

An exclusively ascetic and spartan life can certainly lead to boredom. For example, the hermetic monks of the 4th century in 'Lower Egypt' were plagued by what they called 'the Noonday Devil'—a kind of deep boredom and melancholy, which sapped their spiritual energies (Healy 1984, 16–17). We can however engage in spiritual practices as part of a more balanced life. It is not the practices themselves that are or must eventually be boring; it is the *exclusive* practice of them, as with the fourth-century monks, that can lead to an unwelcome visit by the Noonday Devil.

7.5.2 Would Projects Go Away?

We might value making progress in solving social issues such as poverty and homelessness, or improving people's mental health, financial well-being, and so forth. We may commit ourselves to improving the environment and preserving natural beauty. Again: radical life extension is not a land without sorrow or an isle of the blest, and many difficult challenges will remain. Even if the environment will sustain us, the air could be cleaner, and the places of beauty and serenity protected. Additionally, we do not just care about pleasures and enjoyable experiences, or about ourselves. We care about morality and justice. Of course, it can be rewarding and may involve agreeable experiences to do the morally right thing and to help to achieve justice, but we need not care about doing these things *solely because* we anticipate positive experiences. We want to do the right things for the right reasons.

Maybe you find math fascinating and avidly pursue it in your mortal life. Math is sometimes very difficult and frustrating, but often rewarding. You anticipate agreeable experiences, but this is not the only reason you study math—it is compelling and engaging to you. Why would you eventually lose your interest in it, if it is part of a suite of activities in a balanced life? Why wouldn't the same be true about an interest in history, astronomy, psychology, or philosophy? I don't see why your curiosity and passion would have to slip away.

The curmudgeons simply *assert* (apparently based on introspection) that we would eventually lose our ability to experience pleasure and agreeable experiences, as well as deep interest and engagement. It is the sentiment of a depressed, but not necessarily an extended life person. It is significant that Elina was depicted as having been psychologically abused by her father, and her bleakness could be attributed to depression due to an unhealthy upbringing, rather than radically extended life as such (Rosati 2013).

I do not see why we would stop caring about all these (and more) valued activities in a radically extended life. They can be *repeatably rewarding*. The pleasures of sex between loving partners, listening to a moving piece of music, or appreciating a striking piece of art are not *self-exhausting*, like climbing a mountain (or riding a bicycle) for the first time.

7.5.3 Tourists in Life or Being Here Now

Shelly Kagan, however, disagrees:

> Essentially, the problem with immortality seems to be one of inevitable boredom. The problem is tedium. You get tired of doing math after a while. After a hundred years, a thousand years, a million years, whatever it is, eventually you are going to say, 'Yes here's a math problem I haven't solved before, but so what? I've just done *so much* math, it holds no appeal for

me anymore'. Or, you go through all the great art museums in the world (or the galaxy) and you say, 'Yes, I've seen dozens of Picassos. I've seen Rembrandts and Van Goghs, and more. I've seen thousands, millions, billions of incredible works of art. I've gotten what there is to get out of them. Isn't there anything new?' And the problem is that there isn't. There are, of course, things that you haven't seen before—but they are not new in a way that can still engage you afresh.

Kagan (2012, 243)

I'm not convinced. He looks at many activities as valuable because of a *byproduct* not explicitly specified. In considering the visits to all those museums and seeing all those works of art, he writes, 'I've gotten what there is to get out of them. Isn't there anything new'? It is as if we are looking for something cognitive—a new piece of information or insight we get from the art, apart from our experience of it. Or perhaps he thinks we are trying to learn a fact about our experience: what it feels like to do mathematics or appreciate the art.

I do not, however, think this is the main reason we seek aesthetic experiences. It is not why one studies abstract algebra. Knowing a theorem is not nearly as important as the process of deriving it. Kagan's picture seems to be that we go through life attempting to *extract* something from our experiences. It is almost as if we were tourists, seeking out novelty and bringing home souvenirs.

Kierkegaard writes:

> ... everyone who feels bored cries out for change ... One tires of living in the country and moves to the city; one tires of one's native land, and travels abroad ... and so on; finally, one indulges in a sentimental hope of endless journeying from star to star.
>
> (Kierkegaard 1944, 287, as quoted in Healy 1984, 26)

This view of life leaves out much that is significant. The 'endless journeying' in search of novelty is ultimately futile. It is like being a tourist on a train to nowhere. Consider this from the French Sociologist, Emile Durkheim, who writes about an individual in whom

> a thirst arises for novelties, unfamiliar pleasures, nameless sensations, all of which lose their savour once known ... from

now on nothing remains behind or ahead of him to fix his gaze on ... he cannot in the end escape the futility of an endless pursuit.

(Durkheim 1951, 256, as quoted in Healy 1984, 32)

Decrying a similar personality defect, Samuel Johnson writes:

[Some] lie down to sleep and rise up to trifle, are employed every morning in finding expedients to rid themselves of the day, chase pleasure through all the places of public resort, fly from London to Bath and from Bath to London, without any other reason for changing place, but they go in quest of company as idle and as vagrant as themselves, always endeavoring to raise some new desire that they may have something to persue ..., changing one amusement for another ...

(Johnson 1758 to 1760/1927, in Bullit, Bates, and Powell, eds., 454, as quoted in Spacks 1995, 42–3)

Johnson thought this attempt to keep busy out of a fear of boredom is not restricted to the wealthy and privileged. We all know people who seem always to be 'busy keeping busy'. Kagan complains that eventually there would be nothing left 'to get out of life'. In my view, however, it would be better not to try to get more *out of* life, but to get more and more *into* life—to fully immerse yourself in the activities you love and learn to appreciate them more deeply. This is a significant departure from an *extractive* orientation toward life. We can aim to be fully present 'in the moment', mindful of the awesome beauty all around us. We can even sometimes achieve 'flow' states.

'**Flow**' was first explicitly characterised by psychologist Mihalyi Csikszentmihalyi. He described **flow states** as having these characteristics:

... action follows upon action according to an internal logic that seems to need no conscious intervention by the actor. He experiences it as if unified flowing from one moment to the next, in which he is in control of this actions, and in which there is little distinction between self and environment, between stimulus and response, or between past, present, and future.

(Csikszentmihalyi 1965, 32, as quoted in Calhoun 2018, 142)

102   John Martin Fischer

You cannot always be in flow states, but you can cultivate them and learn how to enter them while engaging in activities you love. You can learn methods for being more present 'in the now," such as various kinds of meditation, including '**mindfulness meditation**'. A life in which you appreciate the present moment and sometimes enter flow states is not the life of a tourist: you live here, so to speak. In Hegel's phrase, you are 'at home in the world'. It is more *immersive* than *extractive*. The extractive, but not the immersive, model leads to worries about what more you could 'get out of life'. Indeed, it suggests that, at a fundamental level, projects (activities directed toward a goal apart from the activities themselves) are the *only* constituents of a good and meaningful life.

Much philosophical discussion of meaning in life has focused on projects—their content, objectivity, staying power, and so forth. Williams contends that Elina's projects would run out, and therefore meaning would have been sapped from her life. Projects, however, are not all there is to meaningfulness in life. (Setiya 2017; 2022) In immersing yourself mindfully in life, you would not be seeking novelty in a superficial sense, but a deeper engagement in it. Your centered psychological self would be a solid platform on which to pursue the projects you care about. On certain occasions, you would put those projects aside for the time being. You would *not* be busy keeping busy. You would not just be stalled on a train going nowhere. Inevitably, you sometimes get stalled on life's train, but you stop to enjoy the scenery.

To sum up, in this section the focus is on whether radically extended human lives would have to be boring. The main worries are whether pleasures and agreeable experiences, and similarly projects, would eventually run out. We considered responses to the concerns. We noted that, as in our mortal lives, activities would need to be distributed appropriately ('rotated', as in Kierkegaard's metaphor), and that considerable boredom would exist. We should apply a single standard when evaluating mortal and radically extended lives. I contended that there is no persuasive reason to suppose that pleasures, agreeable experiences, and projects would all be extinguished eventually. Many pleasures are 'repeatable', rather than 'self-exhausting', and there are compelling spiritual and religious experiences that would seem to be repeatedly rewarding. I commended a reorientation of our approach to life-activities

> from extraction to immersion. An extractive model raises the question of whether 'that's all there is to get out of life', whereas an immersive model need not.

8   Summary: The Last Words (for Now!)

Human beings have always had a strong desire to live forever. Legends posit far-away lands of immortality, and voyages in search of Isles of the Blest, Shangri La, and the Fountain of Youth. The early Chinese emperors sought herbal means to immortality, the Taoists proposed various methods (including abstemious and somewhat bizarre sexual practices) for achieving it, and Francis Bacon recommended a whole suite of means to enhance longevity.[14] Contemporary Silicon Valley billionaires, Russian plutocrats, and many others—not nearly so rich or privileged—employ an arsenal of anti-ageing methods from supplementation with vitamins and minerals to the use of pharmaceuticals, human growth hormone, cryogenic preservation, and ... The list goes on! We have achieved extraordinary leaps in average longevity in industrialised nations in the last century or so, and the efforts to push toward immortality are undeniably accelerating.

Think of an immortal life filled with a sensible mixture of meaningful activities and projects that are rewarding and important to you, engaging in some of which involves flow states. You sprinkle in ways to fully immerse yourself in 'the now', perhaps through mindfulness meditation and other spiritual practices (Setiya 2017; 2022). You care about helping others and alleviating social injustice, and throw yourself into these efforts. You enjoy food, music, art, friendship, love, sex, and so forth—'rotated' in sensible ways. You sometimes experience boredom, frustration, and suffering—physical and mental, but you are able to escape the boredom and relieve the suffering. Overall, you live a life of passion and value. Would you choose to die very soon rather than living this sort of life? Really? I would decline the invitation! The French existentialist philosopher Albert Camus once wrote that the first challenge one faces every morning is whether to commit suicide or

---

14. For a description of Taoist sexual practices aimed at longevity, see Gruman (2003, 43–81). These illustrate (yet again) the extraordinary lengths to which people will go in search of immortality.

have a cup of coffee (a version of Nagel's thought-experiment, I suppose). I'd take the coffee—strong, please!

People disagree about this. Bernard Williams was English, and the condition of melancholic boredom has been called 'The English Malady'. (Evidently his stints as a professor at UC Berkeley didn't lessen his curmudgeonly attitude toward living forever, despite the cheery California sunshine!) As we have seen, he is on the side of Elina Makropulos, who refused the elixir. My interlocutor in this debate, Stephen Cave, is also both English and on the Makropulos team. (Sorry!). We could perhaps think of Thomas Nagel's thought experiment as bringing out (or illustrating) the point that, other things equal, we want more and more of the goods of life, whereas Bernard Williams's (based on Elina's plight) invites consideration of the problems.

Thomas Nagel sums up the case for radical life extension nicely:

> Couldn't [radically extended lives] be composed of an endless sequence of quests, undertakings, and discoveries, including successes and failures? Humans are amazingly adaptable, and have developed many forms of life and value in their history so far ... I am not persuaded that the essential role of mortality in shaping meaning we find in our actual lives implies that earthly immortality would not be a good thing. If medical science ever finds a way to turn off the aging process, I suspect we would manage.
>
> (Nagel 2014)

Would I choose to live forever, in the sense of radical life extension? Not if it involved physical and mental deterioration, significant and unrelenting pain, living in a dirty environment or without adequate food and shelter, and so forth. Not if no one else were extended-life persons, nor if I had no exit strategy. But this is not the sort of longevity we are considering. Many think of radically extended life in these ways and are not interested in seeking it, but how about such life under favorable circumstances? With a radically extended life, I would have an exit strategy: if things were to get bad enough, I could end the suffering. (This in itself would seem to assuage the worries about boredom, at least for those without objections to voluntarily ending one's own life.)

I would at least like to try it! Give me a thousand years and I'll let you know how it is going. I love my family and friends, I'm excited

Why You Should Choose to Live Forever 105

about my writing and teaching, and I am committed to working for social justice and a clean environment. I enjoy my hobbies, and as you have probably guessed, I love food (not only Thai). I am not averse to sex! *In a radically extended life, I could have more of all this.* As Nagel put it, I think I'd manage! It is a deep fact about human beings, one that frames our affective and motivational ecosystems at least as much as the fear of death, that we want more of what we deem enjoyable and valuable. Having much more time makes it likely that I'll have more of what I value. This fact is so obvious that it is rarely even remarked upon—hidden in plain sight. It is presumably the reason why we are attracted to immortality in its various forms and you would say 'yes' to an additional week, every week, in Nagel's thought experiment. More of what we love is better.

The immortality curmudgeons contend that we simply would *not* get more of what we value overall in radical life extension, even under favorable conditions. On their view, the appeal of radical life extension is a mirage. Although it *appears* as if you would get more of what you care about in immortality, this is in fact not the case. According to the curmudgeons, this disappointing fact is shown by the various curmudgeonly objections we have considered: it wouldn't be me, I would have no motivation for timely action, my life would not correspond to a narrative, it would lack the value framework central to how we live our lives, it would not have the stages required to be a human life, it would be boring, and so forth. The curmudgeons insist that radical life extension would offer '*too much* of a good thing (or things)'. We have considered each of these objections to choosing immortality, and I have contended that none of them is persuasive.

Return to the curmudgeons' analogies: the library, station wagon, and commuter train. They are all faulty. We've already noted that excellent books will continue to be added to the library, and life-extended individuals can re-read books and find them compelling from their new perspectives. A young person looking out the window of the station wagon cannot actively engage in the world outside her window. She is entirely passive. In contrast, someone with radical life extension would not be isolated from her environment and unable to interact with it; she would not necessarily be wholly passive. The commuter train takes the same route every day. During the time of the commute, New Jersey passes by in the window, and the commuter only passively takes it in (like the child looking out the window of the family station wagon). Radically extended lives would not have to be *repetitive* in this way, and they would not need to be passive. Such lives would allow for actively interacting with the world—pursuing hobbies, helping to achieve social justice, having friendships, love, and so much more. Radically extended life does not imply isolation, dreary repetition, or passivity.

The analogies fail to respect the diversity and breadth of the possible experiences and activities in radically extended life, and the opportunities for active engagement. No wonder you would be bored, couped up in an impenetrable bubble of relentless sameness—a train through the same scenery to the same repetitive job every day! Radically extended lives would not have to be like this. To infer that such life would be boring from the supposedly analogous scenarios would be a mistake; the library, station wagon, and commuter train are not relevantly like radically extended lives. The extrapolation from these supposed analogies is a spurious transition, just like an inference from the current decrepitude of many of the elderly to the undesirability of radical life extension under favorable conditions. We do not have to relegate ourselves solely to the New Jersey commuter train. We can take the Orient Express.

The 'Forever' Wars seem to go on forever. The prolongevists and apologists—the optimists and curmudgeons—have debated for millennia. I do not anticipate philosophical peace to break out soon, especially as we consider Stephen's contributions to this book. I have at least fired my first salvo. I end with a popular 'toast' in China, reflecting their dreams of longer life and an optimistic conception of radical life extension: 'Ten thousand years of age'!

Part 2

First Round of Replies

Chapter 3

Reply to John Martin Fischer

Stephen Cave

Contents

1 The Fear of Death and the Desire to Live Forever	110
2 Rationality, Favourable Circumstances, and the Exit Clause	113
2.1 The Question of Favourable Conditions	113
2.2 The Exit Clause	117
3 The Procrastination Problem and the Relevance of Present Feelings	120
4 Boredom and Extractive versus Immersive Views of Life	122
5 Life Stages and Adaptation to Longer Lives	125
5.1 Have We Recently Adapted to Much Longer Lives?	126
5.2 Life Stages, Finitude, and Being Human	128
5.3 Life Stages and Society	131
6 Summary	132

In this chapter, I will reply to John's first essay in which he eloquently defends a choice to live forever. His rich and lucid contribution gives much food for thought. In this reply, I will focus on a few key areas where I think there is more to say:

1. The fear of death and the desire for immortality.
2. The question of 'favourable circumstances' and the rationality of choosing immortality.
3. The Procrastination Problem and the relevance of present feelings.

DOI: 10.4324/9781003105442-5

110   Stephen Cave

4. Boredom and extractive versus immersive views of life.
5. The role of life stages when considering the impact of immortality.

1   The Fear of Death and the Desire to Live Forever

In Chapter 1, I quoted Susan Ertz's wry observation that 'millions long for immortality who don't know what to do with themselves on a rainy Sunday afternoon' (Ertz, 1943). This observation is funny because it is true yet paradoxical, juxtaposing the grand metaphysical dream of eternal life with the mundane reality of life on Earth. This paradox could be put another way: we do not want to die, but we are not excited at the prospect of living through endless Sunday afternoons either. Another great observer of human (and extra-terrestrial) nature, Douglas Adams, was also troubled by this paradox. Describing a man who accidentally became immortal, Adams wrote:

> To begin with, it was fun … But in the end, it was the Sunday afternoons he couldn't cope with, and that terrible listlessness which starts to set in at about 2:55, when you know that you've had all the baths you can usefully have that day, that however hard you stare at any given paragraph in the papers you will never actually read it, or use the revolutionary new pruning technique it describes, and that as you stare at the clock the hands will move relentlessly on to four o'clock, and you will enter the long dark tea-time of the soul.

In Chapter 2, John recognizes that the fear of death and the desire for immortality are constants in human history. I agree. He also notes that these two are not quite the same thing. I agree with that too, and in this section I want to briefly explore the relationship between them.

John mentions the fascinating and important work of Ernest Becker, an anthropologist much influenced by the theories of psychoanalysis. Becker summarised the thesis of his now-classic 1973 book *The Denial of Death* thus:

> The idea of death, the fear of it, haunts the human animal like nothing else; it is a mainspring of human activity—activity

designed largely to avoid the fatality of death, to overcome it by denying in some way that it is the final destiny for man.
(Becker 1997, p. xvii)

About a decade later, a group of social psychologists (Sheldon Solomon, Jeff Greenberg, and Tom Pyszczynski) set out to test Becker's ideas through a series of clever experiments. Put simply, in these experiments they would take two groups of people who were similar in relevant respects; then they would remind one group about their mortality and the other group about something unpleasant but not fatal (like going to the dentist); then they would examine the two group's responses to various prompts. They found that groups reminded of death would cling more strongly to belief systems that offered some kind of immortality (broadly conceived)—such as religion, nationalism, the pursuit of fame, or the desire to have children. They conclude that many major aspects of human society and belief systems exist to help us manage the fear of death—a view they call 'terror management theory' (as John mentioned). This ground-breaking work, covering hundreds of experiments by the authors and other colleagues, is summarised in their book *The Worm at the Core: on the Role of Death in Life* (Solomon et al. 2015).

One way of putting the key finding of terror management theory is this: much of what humans all over the world believe about immortality, they do not believe because it is true (or well-evidenced, or well-reasoned), but because it helps them to manage the fear of death. The ancient Egyptians did not have good evidence that elaborate and hugely expensive processes of mummification would grant immortality—but it did help them to manage the fear of death; mediaeval Christians did not have good evidence for the belief that they would be bodily resurrected on an imminent Day of Judgement—but it did help them to manage the fear of death; Eugen Steinach, the pioneer of endocrinology, and his followers did not have good evidence for thinking that a vasectomy would reverse ageing, but it did help them to manage the fear of death. And so on.

Many beliefs about immortality are therefore instances of what psychologists call motivated reasoning, or what lay people call wishful thinking. What does this mean for our debate about whether we should choose to live forever? On the one hand, it offers a potential argument in favour of swigging an elixir. If the fear of death is indeed potentially paralysing, destroying the possibility of human happiness, then choosing to live forever could significantly improve our well-being by doing away with this dread.

However, this would only apply strongly to true immortality—a condition in which death is not possible. If you were a true immortal, whatever worries you might have, the prospect of dying would not be one of them. It might also apply to contingent immortality—a condition in which living forever is possible but not inevitable—depending on the circumstances. As we noted in Chapter 1, there are optimists who argue that such a state could be brought about by science: first by defeating ageing and disease, then by allowing us to create 'back-ups' of ourselves, then by allowing us to escape to other planets when the sun threatens to swallow the earth, then somehow averting the eventual heat-death of the universe, and so on. But these scenarios stretch the imagination, if not the laws of physics. Nonetheless, we could grant that if the contingent immortal is imaginable, such a person might also be free from the fear of death.

More plausible, in this world anyway, are cases of moderate or radical life extension. In these cases people would not be immune to death: they would be immune to ageing and disease, but still susceptible to catastrophes, such as fatal accidents or wars. Death would still be inevitable, and the fear of it would therefore continue to haunt people's minds. Indeed, it is imaginable that people in this condition would have an exaggerated fear of death, rather than an ameliorated one. In our present condition, wherein we can expect to live to between 60 and 90 (depending on how and where we live), death might deprive us of a few years or a few decades. But in a world with radical life extension, death could deprive us of centuries, even millennia. It would, in this sense, be much worse for us. Various authors have therefore argued that we would become more risk-averse in such a scenario, and more plagued by the fear of death, given we would have so much more to lose from it (e.g., Agar 2010, chap. 6; Kass 2003, chap. 4).

There is another way in which terror management theory relates to our debate about whether we should choose to live forever. Recall that the fear of death inclines people to believe stories about immortality regardless of the evidence for their plausibility. As seekers of the truth, we should be on our guard against such wishful thinking. This means we should be particularly sceptical of stories promising a happy ever after, and interrogate them with

Reply to John Martin Fischer 113

particular rigour. Of course, what we are debating in this book is the *desirability* of immortality, not whether we are likely to achieve it. Nonetheless, the two are related. My fear of death would be best ameliorated if I knew both that I would live forever *and* that it would be enjoyable. (The prospect of an eternity of suffering—a trope frequently deployed by religions to ensure good behaviour—would assuage my mortal dread much less well.) There is a risk, therefore, that wishful thinking is playing a role in how we conceive of living forever, and we should therefore take extra care in interrogating our intuitions.

2 Rationality, Favourable Circumstances, and the Exit Clause

Our debate is about whether we should choose to live forever. John argues that we should, but only under very, very specific circumstances. In this section, I will explore how the specificity of these circumstances affects whether the choice to live forever could ever be rational. I will be focussing on what I have called prudential rationality—whether the choice to live forever could be the right one for an individual considering only their interests—though we will see in subsection 2.2 that there is one issue that bridges the prudential and the ethical.

2.1 The Question of Favourable Conditions

In his essay, John concedes that true immortality would not be worthy of choice, because it would be extremely risky. Recall that true immortality means you could not die. So if you were condemned to hell, whether an otherworldly one or an equivalent on this world, you could suffer indefinitely, without even the possibility of ending your life in order to end the torment. Given there is always some risk of such torment, John accepts that we should not choose immortality. One might think that with this concession, the debate is won. After all, the most straightforward meaning of 'forever' is 'without end'. So if a life without end would not be worthy of choice, we should not choose to live forever. As I mentioned in Chapter 1, there are billions of people alive today who *do* think of living forever in these terms. A belief in true immortality is central to Christianity, Islam, and Hinduism, and some versions of Judiasm and other belief systems. Therefore, for

114 Stephen Cave

many people, the conclusion that true immortality would be a bad choice is an important one.[1]

However, John's arguments are more focussed on versions of 'living forever' (or, more accurately, 'living much longer') that do not posit otherworldly realms such as heaven or hell. In Chapter 2, he argues that we should choose to live forever in this world if certain conditions are met. These include having a good home, ample money, access to good food and drink, access to meaningful work and hobbies (potentially, to alleviate boredom, a very wide range of these), perfect physical and mental health, and friends and relatives who also have access to this kind of radical life extension. John and I are fortunate to live in countries that are also relatively safe, free, and politically stable (at the time of writing). An author writing from the many places in the world that do not enjoy such prosperity, liberty and stability might add other preconditions to John's list. These would probably include freedom from oppression and other rights, democratic government, the absence of war, civil or otherwise, functioning public services, and so on.

This is a long list of conditions. John and I, and some (but by no means all) of our compatriots in our respective countries, are lucky enough to enjoy something like these conditions at the moment. But there has been no point in human history when they prevailed for the kind of timespans that are relevant to radical life extension. Immortality optimists talk of living for a thousand years or more. A thousand years ago, the United States of America was centuries away from being founded, and what is now the United Kingdom was still separate, warring nations. In the intervening millennium, the world has been transformed in countless ways: empires have risen and fallen; radical movements such as fascism and communism have swept the globe; and catastrophic wars have been waged, bringing with them weapons of apocalyptic power that still exist in abundance. Given these facts, what are the odds of the preconditions for a happy immortality prevailing? I suggest that they are not high. Should we then choose to live forever, if doing so happily is predicated on these preconditions being met?

---

1. Although many believers might not believe they have a choice about whether they will live forever.

Imagine our question was 'Should we choose to build a great city under the sea?'. Someone—let's call him Professor Merman—proclaims confidently that we should, and enthusiastically goes from conference to symposium to city hall arguing that building a metropolis under the sea is a great idea. He points to all the enthusiastic snorkellers and scuba divers as evidence that humans really like being underwater, swimming among the sparkly fish. When questioned, Professor Merman concedes that we should actually only choose to build a great city under the sea if we solve a vast range of practical problems, such as how to secure reliable supplies of the necessary oxygen, freshwater, foodstuffs, metals and other materials; how to adapt the human body to life deep under the sea; how such a city could be protected against various onslaughts, natural or human-made; and so on. Professor Merman admits that he does not have solutions to any of these problems, and indeed he is not at all confident that they will ever be solved. He considers it highly unlikely that humanity will demonstrate the kind of far-sightedness required for such a project, or that the global political order will ever be sufficiently stable to guarantee the security and sustainability of such a new Atlantis. Furthermore, the Professor believes that building such a city would likely contribute to the despoliation of the oceans.

Given this, Professor Merman's claim that we *should choose* to build a great city under the sea becomes very hard to understand. With all the qualifications and conditions, and the worries about whether the circumstances could ever be right in practice, Merman does not seem to be arguing that we *should choose* to build the city at all. His claim seems to be a different one—something like that it is theoretically imaginable that we could live happily in a great city under the sea, that doing so would not be logically impossible, or contravene the laws of physics and what we know of human nature.

But even this claim might be stronger than what is justified by his arguments. The question of what is or is not 'imaginable' is not straightforward. Partly, this is because people have different intuitions: some people might consider it imaginable that humans will live in harmony with the rest of nature, while others might consider it inconceivable, because they have a different view of human nature. But also, something might seem imaginable only because the imagining is being conducted very superficially. For example, someone could say that they imagine a spaceship travelling faster than the speed of light. Perhaps they imagine this as part of a science fiction story about interstellar travel, in which Space Marines travel the 4.35 light-years from Earth to the nearest star, Alpha Centauri, in a single day to do battle with aliens. But of course the author has not really imagined any kind of underlying mechanism for how this could work. They have imagined travelling faster than the speed of light only in a very superficial sense, which tells us nothing about whether it might be possible. In the same way, Professor Merman's vision of a flourishing city under the sea is equally superficial, if he cannot imagine solutions to the many material and political problems that would have to be solved to make it possible.

Let us return to our question of whether we should choose to live forever. John has conceded that living forever would be desirable only if a long list of specific conditions are met—conditions that have never been met over such time-spans in all of human history. Indeed, John himself does not seem to have much confidence that some of them will be met, such as reversing the damage humans are doing to the planet. From the point of view of prudential reason (that is, reasoning about what would be in one's interests), this implies that we should therefore not choose to live forever. This argument can summed up thus:

- John argues that we should choose to live forever if (and only if) we can be sure that a long list of conditions will be met.
- We cannot be sure that this long list of conditions will be met. Indeed, the lesson of history is that it is highly unlikely that these conditions will be met.
- We therefore should not choose to live forever.

The debate therefore seems to be won.

However, the immortality optimist might have a few comebacks. First, they might concede that we should not choose to swig an elixir if offered one now, given it is unlikely the conditions for a happy forever will hold—but they might nonetheless argue that it is conceivable that the conditions for a happy forever could hold, and we should therefore work towards them. This is akin to claiming that a happy immortality is 'imaginable'. This is a much weaker claim than that we should choose to live forever. It is also much more vague. As we saw above, the claim that something is *imaginable* (a great city under the sea, or travelling to Alpha Centauri in a day) can be true in a weak sense that tells us nothing about whether that thing is really *possible* (e.g., I imagine the Space Marines being on Earth one day, then on Alpha Centauri the next, but I do not imagine the mechanisms for faster-than-lightspeed travel).

Is it imaginable that the conditions for a happy ever after will be met? In a weak sense, yes. It is easy to imagine myself living happily in Cambridge a millennium hence, enjoying my morning coffee, with little changed except which colours are in fashion and the year on the calendar. But does this vision imply that a thousand years of peace, progress and prosperity is possible? Hardly. There could be facts about human nature that make radical change and conflict inevitable—history suggests there might be. Until there has been a hundred years (or even ten, or even one) of peace on Earth, we have little reason to bet our happiness on it being possible for a millennium or more.

To this the immortality optimist could say: the only way is to find out. As long as we can stop taking the elixir of life at any point, and so end our lives, the right decision is to try it and see. If after a century we are terminally bored, or fighting for irradiated scraps in a post-apocalyptic wasteland, we can always make our exit. Let us now examine this idea more closely.

2.2 The Exit Clause

Journalist: 'What is your greatest ambition in life?'
Writer: 'To become immortal... ... and then die'.
Breathless (À bout de souffle 1960)

As noted above, John concedes that the condition of true immortality, in which we cannot die, is not one we should choose. His worry is that 'one would have no 'exit strategy'—no possibility of ending life'. He also writes that he *would* want to choose radical life extension (subject to the conditions mentioned above), exactly because there *would be* an exit strategy: 'if things were to get bad enough, I could end the suffering', he writes.

Many people would agree with this—indeed, I myself strongly sympathise with the sentiment. It is therefore worth exploring it a bit more fully. At first glance, one version of the argument is this: in my current mortal, non-extended state, I can expect to live 80 or 90 years. If I were to sup an elixir of life, I could perhaps live much longer—say, a few centuries. I recognise there are risks involved with living longer and that I might not enjoy it. But if I can end my life when it ceases to be enjoyable, I have nothing to lose. So if, say in my 200th year, life becomes intolerable (because I am impoverished and bored and there is nothing but bad news on the radio), then I can simply end it. Through choosing the elixir, I will have lost nothing but gained a century or more of pleasurable existence before it turned sour.

However, this argument makes some important assumptions about whether and when suicide or voluntary euthanasia could be rational. (I will use the term 'suicide' to mean a person intentionally ending their own life, and 'voluntary euthanasia' to mean a person asking someone else—a medical professional, for example—to end their life for them. Some people believe there to be important differences between suicide and voluntary euthanasia, even in cases where their motivations and methods are the same. But for the purposes of our discussion, we can consider them to be equivalent, inasmuch as they are both ways to voluntarily end one's life. For the sake of simplicity, I will largely refer just to suicide in the discussion that follows, but it applies also to voluntary euthanasia.)

Some people consider suicide to be always morally wrong—perhaps, for example, because it is forbidden by their religion. Others consider suicide to be always prudentially *irrational*—perhaps because they believe that all humans have a fundamental desire for life, and if someone wanted to end it, this would be evidence that they were mentally ill or in some other way temporarily confused. If someone held either of these views, then they would not be persuaded by the 'exit clause' argument; that is, they would not think that it would be rational to choose radical life extension on the basis that one could choose suicide if it turned sour. For people with these views, radical life extension would therefore be a much riskier option—indeed, in the light of the arguments in 2.1 above, it is hard to see how it could ever be the prudentially rational choice for them.[2]

However, let us assume that suicide or voluntary euthanasia can sometimes be rational. When? A common idea is that ending one's

---

2. Though a complicating factor is that people who believe suicide is always immoral or irrational might feel that refusing a life extension technology (were it available) would be a form of suicide, and so immoral or irrational. They would therefore be in a bit of a bind.

life can be rational for people who (in philosopher Steven Luper's words) 'find their level of suffering unacceptable, and who have good reason to believe that even with treatment their suffering cannot be reduced to an acceptable level' (Luper 2009, p. 179). Some people (but not all) believe that 'suffering' can include purely mental suffering—for example, prolonged depression with no other illness. This is of course highly relevant to our discussion, as the ails of immortality that we have explored are mostly mental ones—boredom, ennui, meaninglessness, and so on.

From either a prudential or moral point of view, would we consider suicide to be justified on the grounds that a person was bored? I think most people would answer 'no'. From a prudential point of view, there would always be the possibility that a new hobby or new job or some other change in one's life would pull one out of the blue funk. From a moral point of view, society might take a similar view, and not allow voluntary euthanasia on the grounds of boredom, because of the possibility that a person's life might pick up. After all, most of us know what it is like to go through a period of depression, drift or dissatisfaction with one's life, and to come out the other side of it.

Of course, in Chapter 1, I argued that an unending life might lead to a profound ennui or depression, from which we might never emerge. Surely in this case suicide might be justified? The problem, however, for the life-extended individual would be knowing when this moment had arrived. For how long would one have to be bored and depressed, for it to be rational to end it all? John writes that:

> Boredom and melancholy are sometimes hard to distinguish, if they are indeed different at all. Depression also presents itself as impossible to get past; the depressed person believes that he will never get better. It does not however follow that he won't, and most depressed persons do in fact get better, either due to the healing powers of time or medical and psychological interventions. Why would hyperboredom be any different?

If we take this seriously, then boredom and depression would never provide rational grounds for suicide, as there would always be the possibility (or indeed likelihood, in John's view) that they would pass. One might have a bad century, but still hope for a turn for the better. In the words of Douglas Adams's Marvin the Paranoid Android, 'the first ten million years were the worst' (Adams 2009).

This puts the immortalist—and society more broadly—in a difficult position. Recall that in the world today, both suicide and voluntary euthanasia remain highly controversial. Mostly in the form of physician-assisted dying, they are only legal in a handful of countries and a handful of US states (Rada 2021). The legal requirements vary, but they focus on either diagnosis of a terminal and incurable illness, or the patient experiencing unbearable suffering with no chance of it improving. In the scenarios we are considering of radical life extension, we are assuming that ageing and disease are curable, so no one would find themselves receiving a terminal diagnosis. We might also think that if it were possible to remedy all ageing and disease, it would be possible also to stop unbearable suffering from any physical cause.

So if the criteria for permitting suicide or voluntary euthanasia were anything like those today, they would require the patient to demonstrate that despite all these medical advances, they were suffering unbearably (e.g., from boredom) with no chance of improvement. But how could we know that there was no chance of improvement? In a life that could potentially run for millennia, how long would it be reasonable to wait to see if a person took a turn for the better—a year, or ten, or a hundred? With so much at stake—potentially centuries of life—it could always be more rational to wait for recovery. Which is to say, no one could ever rationally make use of the exit clause. In which case, its consolations are illusory.

3   The Procrastination Problem and the Relevance of Present Feelings

In Chapter 1, I argued that making decisions about how to spend one's time would be much harder—in some instances, perhaps impossible—if time was infinite. There are a number of aspects to this. One is that procrastination—already a problem for many—would become more widespread. This is because the knowledge that our time is limited to 80 years or so is the ultimate source of all our deadlines. Without that limit, the pressure to use our time wisely becomes much less acute. However, another problem is that it becomes difficult even for the well-motivated high-achiever, who would never dream of procrastinating, to make decisions about how to use their time when it is in abundance. This also has a number of reasons: one is the difficulty of dividing a life that is indefinitely long into different phases (such as education, work, retirement). Another is that the value of time falls as its availability increases, which makes it difficult to weigh its value in calculations about what to do.

In his first essay, Chapter 2 of this volume, John begins to address these worries. In particular, he argues that these worries about procrastination and indecision fail to take into account the relevance for us of temporal proximity—in particular, of the present moment with its present pains and pleasures. If someone is standing on my foot, I have a strong reason to ask them to get off, no matter how long I will live thereafter.

I agree that present pains and pleasures can provide strong motivations to act. All other things equal, it is rational to act to avoid pain or cause it to cease, and to pursue pleasure or cause it to continue. But often, all other things are not equal: they are complicated by our wanting a broad range of goals, some with immediate pay-offs (such as asking someone to get off my foot), and some with much longer-term pay-offs. Forgoing pleasures in the present for greater ones in the future is something we would consider paradigmatically rational.

Someone—let us call him Mick—might, for example, enjoy sitting in his pyjamas playing video games. However, Mick might realise that he will only achieve his long-term goal of becoming a medical doctor if he turns off the gaming console and turns instead to his textbooks. But here John's emphasis on 'the importance of now' works against him. If Mick is focussed on present pleasure and avoidance of pain, he will continue playing his favourite video games. What might stop him from doing that is a sense that time is short, that the clock is ticking, and that if he wants to spend a significant chunk of his life helping to heal others, then he had better start studying. In a much longer life, this sense of urgency would disappear, and a century from now, we might still find Mick playing on his console.

It might be helpful here to borrow a term from applied mathematics. Mathematicians contrast a 'local optimum', which is the best solution to a problem within a particular narrow range of options, and a 'global optimum', which is the overall best solution. Mick has attained a kind of local optimum solution for how to spend his time: he enjoys playing video games more than many other things, such as washing the dishes, watching television or studying medical textbooks. However, his *global* optimum would be practising as a medical doctor. In an 80-year life, it will become clear to Mick in his teens or twenties that if he is ever to attain his global optimum, he will have to undergo the relative pain of leaving his local optimum and picking up his textbooks. But for the immortal, it is much less clear when this would compel Mick to act, if ever. A 20-year-old video-game-playing Mick would believe that there would be many centuries ahead in which he could be a physician—and this would always remain true.

It is worth noting that this kind of problem could occur in scenarios of radical life extension as well as contingent or true immortality. It is clear that someone with a radically extended life will eventually die, because even though they would be immune to ageing and disease, purely statistically they will not be able to avoid accidents forever. However, all else being equal, death will not become more likely as they grow older. This is a stark contrast to our current situation: we know as we grow older that death by a wide range of diseases becomes more common, that we would be extremely lucky to live to one hundred and very unlikely to live much beyond that. But a life-extended person is not more likely to die at 1000 than 500 or five. If Mick thinks that, statistically, he has 500 years to live, this remains just as true when he is 520 as when he is just 20. His incentive to leave his local optimum therefore never increases.

In Chapter 1, we saw that it would be possible for the very-long-lived person to become stuck in a somewhat unpleasant rut: in that case, always choosing to work an extra week, because the extra money had value to her, whereas the time spent did not have value, because she had an indefinite amount of it. John has argued in Chapter 2 that this kind of case ignores the importance of our wanting pleasures *now*. But in Mick's case, this does not help: Mick does have pleasure now. As with many worthwhile things in life, such as getting fit, or mastering a musical instrument, his dream of becoming a medical doctor requires that he first *forgo* present pleasure. But in an infinitely prolonged life, there will always be time to do that in a tomorrow that never comes.

4 Boredom and Extractive versus Immersive Views of Life

In Chapter 2, John makes an interesting and subtle argument against the inevitability of boredom. He picks up on a phrase from the philosopher Shelly Kagan, that after a long enough period of time spent visiting enough museums and galleries, there would

Reply to John Martin Fischer   123

be nothing more to 'get out of' art. Kagan implies that this would be true of other aspects of life—that there would eventually be nothing to get out of studying maths, or cooking new dishes. This argument is of course similar to the one I make in my discussion of *The Makropulos Secret* in Section 3.1 of Chapter 1. John argues that this view is based on an 'extractive' approach to life, one that is only concerned with getting something out of different pursuits, rather than putting something into them. He contrasts this with what he calls an 'immersive' approach to life, which he believes avoids the problem of inevitable boredom. Taking the immersive approach means being more deeply engaged in activities and more fully present in the moment, like when one is in a 'flow' state or practising mindfulness meditation.

The distinction between these different approaches to life sounds intriguing, but does it hold up? Let us return to Elina Makropulos. When we meet her in the play, she has been an opera singer for three hundred years, and she has had enough of it. Do we have reason to believe that she took an extractive rather than an immersive approach to singing? The play makes clear that she is breathtakingly good at it—perhaps the best there has ever been. Clearly, she has spent many thousands of hours perfecting her art, and when she is on stage she delivers performances that are utterly transfixing. The play does not tell us how E.M. felt about opera singing when she was younger (a mere century old, say). But given the degree of her accomplishment, it seems reasonable to think that at one point she truly loved it, and immersed herself in it completely. Indeed, the idea that she is the greatest opera singer the world has ever seen is much more plausible if we imagine that she was once fully engaged with it than if we imagine her to always have been so cynical as when we meet her aged 300. And the notion that she *once* loved singing and fully immersed herself in it is completely compatible with her eventually falling *out* of love with it. In which case, immersion is no protection against eventual boredom.

Of course, E.M. is fictional. But coincidentally, I have a friend who used to be a world-class mezzo-soprano. She sang leading roles in most of the leading opera houses in Europe and beyond. However, after two decades of this, she had had enough: the joy of singing and excitement of performance declined until they ceased to outweigh the downsides—the physical demands, the relentless competition for the top roles, and so on. So she gave it up and became a teacher. I have no doubt whatsoever that she was once fully engaged in opera, that when she sang she was fully immersed—in the flow and focussed on the present moment. Nonetheless, after twenty years, she had nothing more 'to get out of it'.

I therefore do not agree that an immersive approach to life will make one immune to boredom in an indefinitely prolonged life. Of course, there are many benefits to immersing oneself in projects: finding activities that foster in you a flow state, or practising mindfulness are indeed good ways to get the most out of life (if you forgive my use of the phrase). Someone who can achieve such states will surely be able to pursue their interests without getting bored for longer than a flibbertigibbet would.

This is the main problem with the argument that immortality will inevitably be boring: it seems highly dependent on the particularities of personality and ability. It is hard to argue against someone who has, for example, been doing crossword puzzles enthusiastically for 60 years and is convinced that they could continue doing so with pleasure for eternity. Perhaps there are people alive today who could happily continue pursuing the same interests for eternity. Perhaps they are the most cerebral among us, keen to decipher the secrets of the universe; or perhaps they are the least—those who are content that each day provides a few good meals. Perhaps we could all be rendered capable of enjoying each day forever through the right tweaking of our genes, or the right drugs, or pleasure domes. In Chapter 1, I made clear my worries that such lives would collapse into ennui and meaninglessness. But reasonable people might differ. For this reason, I think the problem of inevitable boredom is the least serious of those facing the immortalist, even while it is perhaps the most discussed.

But before we leave the topic, I want to highlight an irony in John's conception of the immersive approach to life. As noted, he draws attention to mindfulness meditation and the importance of appreciating the present. Mindfulness is a concept derived from Buddhism. It involves a set of practices, including meditation, that direct attention to the present moment—though not just any aspect of the present moment, but specifically the thoughts, feelings and sensations that one is experiencing. Mindfulness encourages letting these come and go with acceptance and without judgement (Bishop et al. 2004). The short-term goal of mindfulness (and other forms of meditation) in Buddhism is the development of wisdom and morality; the long-term goal of these three aspects—morality, wisdom and meditation—is enlightenment, or **nirvana**. Nirvana

Reply to John Martin Fischer 125

literally means 'blowing out', as a candle is blown out (Keown 2000, chap. 4). Interpretations of this vary, but in essence this 'blowing out' is understood as the cessation of worldly desires and an end to the cycle of reincarnation—a person who has attained enlightenment is not reborn. As Buddhists do not believe in a real, abiding self or soul, this means the end of the person as an individual. The goal of mindfulness meditation is therefore not to help a person to continue their bodily existence on this earth indefinitely: it is, in fact, the exact opposite of that—to allow them to escape their bodily existence on this earth.

The Buddhist tradition, from which mindfulness comes, is completely opposed to the possibility of a happy, infinite life on earth. It is indeed profoundly pessimistic about life on earth: the first 'noble truth' of Buddhism is that life is suffering. But Buddhism does not respond to this by promising a heavenly afterlife. Instead, it suggests that the ultimate reward to be attained through dedicated practice and good behaviour is to cease to exist as an individual.

At first glance, this might sound very different to Christianity, with its very explicit promise of an afterlife in heaven (or hell). But this first glance is deceptive. Christian priests cajoling their parishioners might promise the kind of heaven where one could have tea with one's beloved, long-dead grandpa. But more sophisticated theologians, aware of all the problems that indefinite life brings, promise something more subtle: a kind of oneness with the godhead—an eternity of unchanging bliss with no awareness of self (McDannell and Lang 1988). The great mediaeval theologian Thomas Aquinas wrote that 'man is not perfectly happy, so long as something remains for him to desire and seek' (Aquinas 1266, Prima Secundæ Partis, Q.3)—a sentiment that would be immediately recognisable to any Buddhist—and he advocated for a vision of heaven as direct union with God. In short, the inevitable frustrations and limitations of indefinite life as a finite individual have long been well-known to wisdom traditions around the world, and are what lie behind practices like mindfulness. As we noted in the conclusion to Chapter 1, overcoming these frustrations comes at the expense of giving up one's identity as an individual.

5 Life Stages and Adaptation to Longer Lives

On to the final substantive point I want to discuss in this chapter: the question of life stages. It is relevant to both prudential and

126 Stephen Cave

ethical considerations of living forever. I hardly touched on the topic in Chapter 1, but in Chapter 2 John responds to an argument made by others that an indefinite life would lack the stages that make our lives recognisable and manageable.

The key premise of such arguments (which John does not dispute) is that our lives currently have distinct stages, such as childhood and adolescence, adulthood and old age. There are different ideas of how many stages a life involves, and such ideas vary from culture to culture. But there is a common basic structure that follows an arc of growth and education, followed by productivity (in the workplace and in terms of producing offspring), followed by retirement. The key question for us is this: if our lives were much longer (potentially indefinite), would this upset our life stages so severely that we should not choose longer lives, or would we be able to successfully adapt? I want to first rebut what is in my view a weak argument for adaptability; then I want to rebut a weak argument from the other side—i.e., that the upset would be too great. I will then lay out what I think the real challenges are.

5.1 Have We Recently Adapted to Much Longer Lives?

John argues that human lifespans have increased dramatically relatively recently, and we have adapted our life stages just fine. He points out that 'at the turn of the twentieth century, average lifespan in 'first-world' countries was roughly forty years, whereas it was almost eighty at the turn of the twenty-first century'. This doubling in human life expectancy is immensely significant—a revolution. He argues that it would have been 'disastrously conservative' for someone in 1900 to have argued against this revolution in life expectancy on the grounds that this would upset our idea of life stages. Clearly, John claims, we have successfully adjusted our conception of the shape of a human life. We therefore could do so again.

Broadly speaking, I agree with John that life expectancy has doubled in the past couple of centuries (in industrialised countries), and I agree with him that this is a very good thing, and that it would have been disastrously conservative for someone to have argued in 1900 against the relevant measures that enabled this. Where I disagree, is his claim that this doubling of life expectancy entailed a radical revision to our conception of life stages. It did not: it made almost no difference.

The reason for this is fairly straightforward, though it does warrant some unpacking. As a rule, the term **life expectancy** refers to *average* life expectancy *at birth*. That is, it is the average number of years a person (in a given population) will survive from the moment they are born. Throughout human history up until the twentieth century, a major factor impacting life expectancy was the fact that child mortality was very high. According to one recent meta-study (that is, a summary of a large number of individual studies): 'The average across a large number of historical studies suggests that in the past around one-quarter of infants died in their first year of life and around half of all children died before they reached the end of puberty' (Roser, 2019). It should be clear that this brings down average life expectancy immensely. It should also be clear that if half the population is dying very young, and the average life expectancy is around 40 years, *then the other half of the population is dying at a fairly ripe old age*. (For example, if, for the sake of simplicity, half the population dies at the age of five, then for the average life expectancy to be 40, the other half would have to die at 75.)

Many factors contributed to the huge reduction in child mortality that we have seen in the previous 150 years, including public hygiene (readily available clean drinking water, proper sewers, etc.), better nutrition, breakthroughs in understanding of disease that led to immunisation and more sanitary medical practice, and the discovery of antibiotics. Prior to these innovations, people had to accept the tragic reality that many of their children would die young. But those who did survive childhood could hope for a life with much the same duration and shape that ours do today.

There is abundant evidence of this from all cultures and all periods of history. For example, in his play *As You Like It*, William Shakespeare famously wrote that 'one man in his time plays many parts, his acts being seven ages': from 'the infant, mewling and puking in the nurse's arms' to the schoolboy; then the lover, then the soldier; 'then the justice, in fair round belly'; then into old age 'with spectacles on nose', and finally extreme dotage—'second childishness' (Shakespeare 1599, Act 2, Scene 7). Shakespeare was writing over four hundred years ago, but there is ample evidence that the conception of a normal human lifespan has been constant for much longer—thousands of years. The Bible's Old Testament, for example, says: 'The days of our years are threescore years and ten [i.e., 70]; and if by reason of strength they be fourscore years [i.e., 80], yet is their strength labour and sorrow' (*Holy Bible: King James Version* 1997, Psalm 90:10). In India, Hinduism has drawn four life stages (*ashrama*) for over two thousand years: the first is the student (although this actually starts between eight and 12, and so is preceded by a phase of childhood); then the householder—a time to acquire wealth and raise children; then the 'forest-dweller', who has passed on his wealth and pursues spiritual activity; then finally from an age of 70 to 75 onwards, the 'renouncer', or ascetic, pursuing liberation. While this might be quite different from modern Western ideals of retirement, it is clear that even centuries or even millennia ago, long before the innovations that recently doubled life expectancy, there was a conception of life ordinarily stretching to 70 or 80.

It is therefore a mistake to think that we have in recent centuries seen a radical shape up of our conception of life stages. There has been some change: in recent decades, life extension has continued to creep up because of better treatments for the diseases of old age. That is, it is no longer *only* the case that more people are managing to reach old age (which is what explained the huge jump in life expectancy from c.1850 to c.1960), but it is *also* the case (albeit to a much lesser degree) that extra years are being added to the lives of the elderly. This has had some social and economic consequences: for example, the institution of retirement with a pension has both become more widespread and come under financial strain as ages have crept up. But there has been no radical re-conceptualisation: the shape of our lives today would have been recognisable to Shakespeare or to an Indian priest a thousand years ago. We therefore cannot extrapolate from the experience of the past two centuries to conclude that future radical changes to life expectancy will go well.

5.2 Life Stages, Finitude, and Being Human

In laying out the position he is attacking, John quotes the philosopher Samuel Scheffler, who argues that a life having stages is 'a universal response to the realities of our organic existence', and that 'our collective understanding of the range of goals, activities, and pursuits that are available to a person, the challenges he faces, and the satisfactions that he may reasonably hope for are all indexed to these stages' (Scheffler 2013, p. 96). John infers from these statements a claim that an immortal life 'would not be recognizably human' and would therefore be undesirable. He of course disagrees with this, and argues that we might have to reconceptualise our life stages, but they would still be '*ours*'—and still recognizably human, just different.

I agree. At least, I do not think one can move directly from the premise that a longer life would shake up our life stages to the conclusion that this would render life inhuman and not worth living. But Scheffler's argument is subtler than that, and worth exploring more carefully. The point he makes about life stages is part of a broader argument that he builds towards the conclusion that an immortal life would undermine all our values. In this way, it is similar to the argument I developed from Borges's story 'The Immortal' in Chapter 1.

Scheffler starts with the point that our 'accomplishments and satisfactions' depend on their association with particular life stages, and 'the physical, mental, and social capacities' we have at those stages (Scheffler 2013, p. 96). He does not offer any examples, but perhaps we can relate this to the Hindu conception of life stages mentioned above. On this plan, the accomplishments of the 'student' phase, for example, relate to learning and discovery; the accomplishments of the 'house-holder' to material provision and contribution to society; and of the 'forest-dweller' to wisdom and spiritual growth. Scheffler argues that these phases and goals only make sense in relation to the organic reality of birth, maturation, deterioration and death.

It certainly seems right that our goals and ideas of accomplishment, etc., relate to our conception of life stages, and that these in turn relate to our conception of our lifespan. However, it does not follow from this alone that we cannot find equally meaningful goals and ideas of accomplishment, etc., in a longer life with different conceptions of life stages. Scheffler therefore develops his argument further. He argues that many of our values only make sense in view of our limited lifespans. He cites 'health, gain, security, and benefit' as examples of values that rely for their meaning upon the existence of their flipsides—'loss, illness, injury, harm, risk, and danger', which are in turn derived from the ever-present threat of death (Scheffler 2013, p. 97).

John has good answers to this too. He argues that there are many ways that we can be harmed short of death: if we are deprived of certain rights, for example, or if an important relationship ends. But to an extent, John and Samuel Scheffler are talking past each other. John's main concern is with extended, but not infinite lives, whereas Scheffler is talking mostly about true immortality. As we have seen throughout our discussion, it is crucial to distinguish between these different versions of 'living forever'. In Chapter 1, I suggested four relevant versions: moderate life extension, radical life extension, contingent immortality, and true immortality. In which of these versions would Scheffler's arguments have bite?

Recall that true immortality is a scenario in which one is immune to death. In most conceptions of this, the immortal is also immune to ageing and disease—indeed, people are not really physical bodies at all (though they might have them for certain periods). Rather, they are **souls**—some form of immaterial, incorruptible substance. In such visions—which, as we have noted, are very widespread around the world—it is indeed hard to imagine how many of the trials and tribulations to which we mortals are subject would apply. John argues that the immortal might still face loss (e.g., financial), or require bravery (e.g., to confront a mean boss). But as we saw in our examination of Borges's story, it seems likely that even these feelings would fade given enough time: would one still fear confronting a mean boss having done it a million times over a billion years?

Such timescales sound fantastical, but they are what is implied by true immortality. On these timescales, I think the argument that all our current values would be rendered meaningless is persuasive, and a desire for individual oblivion would eventually take hold, whether seen in purely negative terms (the cessation of all experience) or more positive ones (union with the godhead). The case of contingent immortality is similar: the contingent immortal can live as long as they want (but unlike the true immortal, can choose to end it)—and so presumably would also be immune to peril, and would undergo all possible experiences until they had all paled into a formless fog devoid of value.

But cases of life extension are very different. Even *radical* life extension, which would require immunity to ageing and disease, permits the possibility of pain, injury (even if always treatable), and of course death. In such scenarios, our lives are temporally limited (just in a very unpredictable way, as there would be no natural decline) and risk would be real. Our familiar concepts of loss, harm, risk and danger would therefore clearly still have meaning. In cases of *moderate* life extension (to 120-160 years), it seems likely that these fundamental values such as health or courage

Reply to John Martin Fischer 131

would hardly be impacted at all. However, life extension, moderate or radical, would impact our current conception of life stages. This impact might not be so severe that it would render a choice to pursue life extension prudentially irrational. That is, from the point of view of the individual, the upset to the ordinary flow of life caused by life extension might not be so extreme as to make death at 80 more preferable. But these changes do warrant consideration from a social and ethical perspective.

5.3 Life Stages and Society

Life stages do not just organise individual lives, they organise our entire society. By this I mean they inform widely shared norms and social expectations, public institutions, laws, the structure of the economy, and so on. Broadly speaking, we expect children to be in education and do not afford them much autonomy (they must be in someone's care, for example, and cannot vote); we expect adults between roughly 18 and 65 to be responsible for themselves and others (such as children) and economically productive; and we expect those who are older to be retired, with few responsibilities, and no obligation (and less opportunity) to be productive.

Contingent or true immortality would shake all this up to an unfathomable degree. But they are also rather otherworldly ideas, so we need not spend too much time dwelling on what they would mean for social structures in this world. However, it is worth briefly considering the impact that life extension would have. It should be clear that this impact would be profound. In Section 5.1 above I argued that we have *not* in recent centuries seen a revolution in our conception of life stages due to a doubling in life expectancy from 40 to 80. However, if life expectancy doubled again, from 80 to 160, we surely would. For example, an education received in the first twenty years of life would not stay relevant for over a century—particularly in this age of accelerating technological change. In the twentieth century, it was still common for people to have a 'job for life' and indeed a single partner for life. Both of these institutions are already coming under strain as people live longer—they would surely collapse if people were faced with the prospect of, for example, a hundred years at the same desk.

It is certainly possible to imagine solutions to these problems. We might start to take a more cyclical approach to life, with repeating phases of education and training, work, and break. A person might

132 Stephen Cave

expect to have three or four different careers over the course of their life, with gaps for raising a family, travelling the world or just tending the garden. They might have a number of different spouses. Many people might indeed see as one of the attractions of much longer lives this possibility of inhabiting a number of quite different identities over the decades.

However, we should not underestimate the challenges that these radical changes would bring. As we noted above, that a scenario is imaginable does not always mean that it is genuinely possible, let alone likely. For example: many people alive today strongly expect to retire at an age around 65, and would not be happy being told they had to wait until they were (e.g.) 100. If these older people did stay in the job market, they would likely hog the top spots, exacerbating existing problems of youth unemployment and causing immense frustration to those expecting to move up the career ladder. And so on.

To be clear: I do *not* think any of these arguments provide a strong case to stop research into ageing and disease that could extend lives. The arguments for extending lives are compelling, and I am sure when the time comes I myself would welcome more years than the expected 80. But these *are* arguments for carefully considering the potential consequences of breakthroughs in this area and being as prepared as we can be. Philosophers are too often content when it is 'imaginable' or theoretically possible that a course of action will go well. But when considering whether it is prudentially or ethically rational to pursue a course of action, our bar should be higher than that: we should want to know that it is *likely* that it will go well. Of course, this is partly in our hands, and by debating the question of longer lives now, we can become clearer on the steps we would have to take to make it desirable.

6 Summary

In this chapter, I have taken John's wonderful opening intervention as a springboard to explore in more depth some of the key considerations in deciding whether we should choose to live forever. To sum up:

- There is good evidence that the fear of death is an important factor in the development of human belief systems. While this fear might be eliminated for the true immortal, it might be exaggerated for someone in conditions of moderate or radical life extension. It can also lead us into 'wishful thinking' about the likelihood of immortality being possible and desirable.

- John argues that we should choose to live forever if (and only if) a long list of conditions are met. But we cannot be sure they will be met, and it seems unlikely that they will be. This suggests that we should not choose to live forever.
- It would help little to have an 'exit clause' in the form of being able to commit suicide: in a world in which ageing and disease could be cured and lives could be extremely long, it would never be rational to choose suicide over waiting in the hope of recovery.
- In longer lives, procrastination would be a serious problem. Someone having a pleasant but suboptimal life would never have a reason in the present to make the sacrifices required to improve their lives in the future.
- John claims that the argument that immortality would be boring is premised on an 'extractive' rather than an 'immersive' view of life. But there is no evidence for this. People immersed in certain activities for a period of time still get bored of them.
- Our lives are divided into stages. Despite changes in life expectancy at birth in recent centuries, these life stages have been stable for thousands of years. Life extension would force them to change, posing significant challenges for society. These challenges would need to be carefully addressed if longer lives are to go well.

Chapter 4

Reply to Stephen Cave

John Martin Fischer

Contents

1 Introduction	134
2 Prudential Reasons Not to Choose Radical Life Extension	135
2.1 Boredom	135
2.2 Ennui	138
2.3 Four Points from Borges	139
2.4 Procrastination	144
2.5 Value and Scarcity	146
2.6 The Perils of *Wanting* True Immortality or Radical Life Extension	148
3 Moral Reasons to Reject Radical Life Extension	150
3.1 Environmental Concerns: Overpopulation	150
3.2 Environmental Concerns: Optimistic Realism	154
4 Summary	157

I Introduction

I wish to begin by commending Stephen's initial chapter for its insights and elegance. We agree on many points, including the view that true immortality (with no exit) would not be worthy of choice by human beings. We both take seriously the various challenges to the potential desirability of radical life extension under favorable circumstances (although we come to different conclusions about them). Additionally, I agree with Stephen about the fact that environmental concerns pose significant challenges for the desirability of immortality—challenges an optimist needs to address. We do however disagree about my

DOI: 10.4324/9781003105442-6

contention that radical life extension under favorable conditions could be worthy of choice. Perhaps it is understandable that in a debate book, I'll focus on points of disagreement in what follows.

Stephen helpfully distinguishes between prudential and moral reasons for choosing radical life extension. He contends that both the prudential and moral perspectives yield reasons to reject radical life extension that are weightier than those that favor it. The prudential reasons pertain to certain alleged negative features of radically extended life: boredom, ennui, meaninglessness, lack of motivation to act in a timely manner (procrastination), as well as some "perils" of *wanting* such life. I have addressed some of these concerns in my initial contribution to this debate, but I will return to them (more briefly and in slightly different ways) here, considering Stephen's specific formulations of the worries. I will also discuss some of the ethical concerns he raises, especially about over-population and resulting pressures on scarce resources threatened by radical life extension. I will then turn to related issues of social injustice. I claim that when we weigh all our reasons for choice, we'll find that, all things considered, radical life extension under favorable conditions could well be worthy of choice.

2 Prudential Reasons Not to Choose Radical Life Extension

2.1 Boredom

A **reason for action** is a consideration that counts in its favor. A **prudential reason** is a reason of self-interest. Often this kind of reason is distinguished from a **moral reason**, that takes into account others' interests (in addition to one's own). Stephen argues that there are both prudential and moral reasons not to choose radical life extension. I'll start with his discussion of the prudential reasons and then turn to his presentation of the moral reasons.

Stephen finds considerable plausibility in the argument that boredom would inevitably ensue in an immortal life, including a radically extended one. He distills from various formulations of the argument a template that begins with two crucial premises:

1. There is a limited number of distinct pleasurable activities that a person can engage in.
2. No matter how pleasurable an activity, it will become boring if repeated often enough.

136   John Martin Fischer

He points out that these two premises, together with others, entail the conclusion that living forever (however interpreted) would inevitably be boring.

I have considered this conclusion in my initial chapter, but it is worth replying to Stephen's specific developments of it (and related views) here. He writes:

> Take the geometric paintings of Piet Mondrian, which consist of horizontal or vertical lines, with the lines themselves and the spaces they contain rendered in black, white, or primary colours. Mondrian himself produced a great range of these works. Perhaps there is potentially an inexhaustible variety of such paintings waiting to be composed ... . But while each work might be technically distinct from the others, it is hard to believe that any given human would find interest in every possible variation. Ten variants might each contain surprises; perhaps even a hundred. But it is hard to believe that a thousand would, or a million.
>
> Many other pursuits might be like this ...

Stephen has chosen a particularly unpromising example of something that could be endlessly engaging. Mondrian's work is perhaps not the sort of great art that calls one back to appreciate it repeatedly. One can only take so many abstract patterns of straight lines and boxes! This is not art that resonates deeply with human beings, illuminating and engaging our experience and the human spirit. The immortality optimist does not contend that *every* kind of activity, including *every* possible variation of a particular style of work (or kind of activity), would be possible to return to with interest. It is enough that there be *some* kinds of activities that contain enough instances, distributed appropriately over time, that are reliably and repeatably engaging. The Mondrian example does not really call this into question. Even if Cave's claim about Mondrian's works is true, it cannot be *extrapolated* in the way he suggests.

Next Stephen takes on premise 2. He writes:

> Christine Overall notes that other creatures do not seem to tire of certain simple pleasures: think of the pet dog that each day rejoices at breakfast and a nice walk (Overall 2003, 146). This is perhaps a telling analogy. Philosophers sometimes suggest

> that an immortal could happily spend eternity in contemplation of the universe. But I am not sure I have met many, or indeed any, people who would be happy in these circumstances ... Perhaps it is more likely that it would be the least intellectually sophisticated who would be easiest to please forever; those who are happy with breakfast and a nice walk, and who only dimly remember what they did the day before.

I am not sure what Cave means by "contemplation of the universe". I gather this is not the study of physics or astronomy. In any case, no one would suggest that such contemplation would be the *only* or even a *substantial* part of a life that could be engaging "forever". Again: it would be unfair to extrapolate from whatever one thinks about such a life (solely or largely contemplative) to a radically extended life in general. Further, I think intellectual activities (but perhaps not just "contemplating the universe") could be repeatably fascinating in a radically extended life. It is also plausible to me that human beings—even the most intellectually sophisticated—could reliably return to very simple activities and get pleasure. Recall that the philosopher Corliss Lamont proclaimed (as quoted in my initial contribution to this volume), "Pure, cool water is the best drink in the world, and I have been drinking it for sixty-two years. ... Yet I still love water".

How about a nice glass of wine? I can't imagine that enjoying a glass of wine (at appropriate times distributed sensibly over an immortal life, and perhaps a broad range of varieties, vintages, and vineyards) would inevitably become boring, no matter who you are (so long as you enjoy wine in the first place!). I love a sunset over the San Gabriel mountains, which I can see from my house in Southern California. You ask me: would you rather enjoy nice walks, a lovely glass of wine from time to time, and contemplation of *this part* of the universe—a sky ablaze with the colours of the sunset—during a radically extended life, or an immediate death that would cut off these experiences? It's a "no-brainer"! I would (and *should*) choose the continuation of these pleasurable experiences.

Stephen goes on to point out that optimistic scenarios in which we can keep from getting bored while living forever all make "unrealistic assumptions" and are "fantasies in which [people's] favorite foodstuffs are available whenever they want them ..." No doubt about it, the assumptions in question are unrealistic from our current point of view. Note however that the whole discussion

138   John Martin Fischer

in our debate here is "unrealistic" in the sense that it is obviously·
not feasible at this point (or even in the reasonably foreseeable
future) to make the medical advances necessary to achieve
immortality, even in the sense of radical life extension. We have
embarked on a philosophical journey in which we are considering
questions about unrealistic scenarios, given the medical and other
challenges of the contemporary world. In doing so, we have been
willing to suspend the constraints of "reasonableness", at least to
some extent. It is all part of our philosophical thought-experiment.

2.2   Ennui

Stephen proceeds to consider another--and deeper--form of boredom,
which he calls "*ennui*". Ennui corresponds to what I called "hyperboredom" in my initial chapter. He writes:

> Imagine a future society that has conquered ageing and disease,
> and also developed wondrous pleasure domes to keep people
> entertained. These pleasure domes can simulate the most
> amazing experiences, with sensory stimulation, mysteries and
> puzzles, challenges and battles, romances—whatever genre of
> adventure one favours, if an inhabitant of this society is bored,
> they simply go to the pleasure dome to experience the thrills.
>
> ... Despite the thrills, we can imagine that such a life would
> come to seem dreary and pointless. ... it might [also] be true
> that ennui would set in after years of this hedonistic lifestyle.

I agree with Stephen's conclusion about the envisaged land of
pleasure domes, but an immortal life would not have to be this
way. The reason many of us are not attracted to the envisaged
society is that we are not **hedonists**, and we value actively pursuing
a range of activities and projects. We value acting of our own free
will and making real connections with others and things greater
than (or at least beyond) ourselves. We care about living authen-
tically. Very little of this would be present in Stephen's society of
pleasure domes; otherwise, it is unclear why "such a life would
come to seem dreary and pointless". Our rejection of it would thus
not bear on the potential appeal of radically extended life *per se*.

As in our discussion of the curmudgeons' analogies of the
summer road trip in the family station wagon, the commuters' days

Reply to Stephen Cave   139

in the New Jersey train, and the very large but not infinite library, the extrapolation from a conclusion about the land of pleasure domes to an immortality scenario in general is unwarranted. This land is unlike certain scenarios of living forever, thus rendering any judgments about it irrelevant to an evaluation of radical life extension in general.

2.3   Four Points from Borges

2.3.1   Points (1) and (2): The Significance of Projects.

Stephen invokes the short story by Borges, "The Immortals", in seeking to argue that an immortal life would be meaningless. Stephen writes:

> If we postulate an infinite period of time, with infinite circumstances and changes, the impossible thing is not to compose the *Odyssey*, at least once. No one is anyone, one single man is all men.
>
> (Borges 1970, 145)

> The Immortals in the story have withdrawn from the world, because, as Borges writes, "in an infinite period of time, all things happen to all men."
>
> (Borges 1970, 144)

Stephen analyzes the story as follows:

> As everyone does everything, values start to become meaningless: everyone has performed 'all goodness' but also 'all perversity'. Everyone's actions balance out, leaving them characterless: there are no heroes and villains among the immortals, but each of them is both and everything in between.
>
> ... The message of Borges's story is that without the prospect of death, all this [the need to choose one path rather than another in contexts of hobbies, careers, relationships, and so forth] disappears. None of us will have a distinct identity, as we will all in time raise children—sometimes well, sometimes badly—and open a café and fight for a cause, and indeed do everything else under the sun. There will be no virtue, as we will all eventually

140 John Martin Fischer

do the right things and the wrong thing. There will be no purpose, as all things will come and go, rise and fall.

He distills these points from "The Immortal":

1. If a person lives long enough, they will eventually do an immense variety of things – even all possible things.
2. If a person does (and will do) a sufficiently immense variety of things, then individual projects will lose their significance.
3. If all people do a sufficiently immense variety of things, then they will cease to have distinct identities.
4. If all people do a sufficiently immense variety of things, then categories of virtuous and vicious, good and bad, cease to have meaning.

I find all of them dubious. (1) is a bold conjecture, but not true. Stephen concedes that this would hold of at most true immortality, in which "forever" is interpreted as "infinite time in the future". Even so, he writes that a radically extended life is long enough to generate a similar conclusion, with the result of obliterating our distinct identities. Individuals however vary greatly in what we *can* (within reason) do. I can't run a mile in under four minutes, and I know that no matter how hard and often I work out and practice, I will remain unable to do this. Same with winning the "most valuable player" award in the Super Bowl, scoring the winning goal in the World Cup, painting a beautiful painting admired by the most discerning art critics, composing a compelling piece of music, and so forth. I'm limited in my abilities, and I venture to think that very few human beings can do these sorts of things.

Further, I don't anticipate *wanting* to undertake efforts to achieve any of these (or a wide range of other) things. Simply living forever does not imply that I will want to pursue all kinds of projects over the course of my life. My character influences my interests and what projects I'll undertake. Of course, my character will change over time in a very long life (as mentioned in the discussion of personal identity in my initial essay). This does not imply that it will change in *all* ways or that during my life, even a very long one, I will choose to undertake all things. Living for all times does not imply trying all things (or wanting to or being able to).

Reply to Stephen Cave 141

I do not find (2) plausible. In a radically extended life, the individual will do many things, have many relationships, undertake many projects (individual or joint), and so forth. No denying this! Even so, I don't see why one's individual projects would lose their significance. It is important here to keep in mind that (1) and (2) posit that an individual does an immense variety of things *over the course of her life*. They do *not* envisage that the agents do these *all at once* or that large numbers of them are done at once (or during the same relatively short temporal interval).

Yes, if I were to do (or try to do) many things at once, undertaking an immense number of different sorts of projects during the same temporal interval, each would be in danger of losing its significance. It could get lost in the crowd. But if I have a manageable number of projects and activities at any given time (or interval of time), each can have significance, even if the projects were to change a great number of times as one's life goes on. As one is living one's life, even a radically extended one, the projects in the "now" or present have significance, even if they will eventually give way to others (and the individual knows this).

Stephen quotes Martha Nussbaum, stating that she captures the core of the argument that living forever (having radical life extension) would resulting in loss of meaningfulness:

> The intensity and dedication with which very many human activities are pursued cannot be explained without reference to the awareness that our opportunities are finite.
>
> (Nussbaum 1996, 229)

On this view, life is "fraught" because we do not live forever, and this gives certain choices and actions greater significance.

Human life is indeed precious, and we sometimes face crucial decisions that will have a huge impact on our lives, starting us on one path rather than another. Do these facts imply that the "finitude" or constraints must be temporal, *i.e.*, impending death? No! I discussed the worry that mortality is necessary for the precious quality of life in my initial chapter, and accordingly, I will be brief in my additional remarks here.

The shapes and "contents" of our lives matter to us—as much as anything. We care deeply about our personal and other relationships, including, most notably, our families and close friends. We are often engaged in our careers, hobbies, and so forth;

some careers are "callings". We also value natural beauty and social justice, and so many other things. That these values are expressed in life with the contours we want it to have requires difficult choices that will shape our futures, taking us in one direction rather than another.

Why, however, think that the only or primary reason why there is often an urgency to these choices and ensuing actions is the fact of our *mortality*—the looming possibility of death? Death is not the only threat; it is not the only constraint that requires us to make timely choices and pursue our goals with passion and determination. Why think that the significance of our lives—our relationships and projects—depends on the fact that we will die, rather than that we must sometimes make one choice or another, without any opportunity to go back and "erase" it or return to the sort of situation in which it was made?

Life goes on, so to speak, and the fact of radical life extension would not change this. Radical life extension obviously doesn't imply the opportunity to "rewind" the clock at will, returning to previous choice-situations or even similar ones. At a very abstract level, certain sorts of choices can be replicated in an immortal life: for example, I might ask whether I should spend more time in my career or hobbies or family. I may well be faced with such choices throughout my life, and I'll be able to answer them differently, if I so choose. But the opportunity to propose a particular business enterprise or one with a specific group of individuals or a romantic partnership with a specific person you love, will not necessarily be available again. Some opportunities are "one-off". This is an important constraint, even in a radically extended life.

Human beings must make choices to give shape to our lives, and sometimes choices rule out alternative paths—forever. It is *this* fact, rather than our mortality, that is fundamental to the significance of our choices and actions. Sometimes our mortality is precisely what forces such a choice, but even then, it is not our mortality *itself* that is fundamental in making our decisions significant. Finitude and constraint, but not necessarily death, are required for meaning: "she who hesitates is [or at least can be] lost".

2.3.2 Point (3): Identity

The third point Stephen distills from Borges is that if we do a "sufficiently immense" variety of things, then we will not have "distinct identities". The point is similar, but different, from (2), which is about particular projects or activities, rather than identities. Note first that (3)'s plausibility will hinge in part on the meaning of "sufficiently immense variety of things". How broadly are we thinking of "variety"? For example, someone who likes participating in sports might choose to play tennis, football, golf, rugby, baseball, and so forth. Within each of these categories she might try different strategies, venues, team-mates, etc. She might not however choose *all* sports (or all ways of participating in them), or all (or any) engineering careers, and similarly for various kinds of endeavors. Why suppose that immortality would imply that a given individual would choose (say) *all* sports, careers, kinds of relationships, and all ways of pursuing them? So why think that their identity could not attach at least in part to the chosen (particular) activities?

Further, at which times is it supposed to be true that the people pursuing a "sufficiently immense" variety of things will lack "distinct identities"? An individual need not be pursuing the envisaged multitude of projects *at the same time* or *during the same temporal interval*. Rather, at any given time (or interval) she is plausibly taken to be engaging in a reasonable number of activities, having a reasonable number or relationships, and so forth. It is thus not true that, at any given time (or during any given interval), the individual lacks an identity—a distinctive (particular) identity that is distinct from others' at that time. (The analysis here of distinctive *identities* is parallel to the analysis above of the significance of *projects* or *activities*.)

Consider now Borges's point (that we would lack distinct identities) from a perspective that allows for an overview of *all* times in an individual's life. The claim is not true from this perspective either. Different individuals will do different things in different ways over the course of their lives. After all, the pursuit of an immense variety of things does not entail undertaking *all things in all ways*.

Additionally, people's lives will not exhibit the *same temporal ordering of things*. Given that the shape of one's life, including the temporal sequence that structures one's activities, is part of one's distinct identity, there is no reason why we couldn't identify distinct individuals—even those who do a robustly immense variety of things—from a perspective that views the life as a whole.

144 John Martin Fischer

2.3.3 Point (4): Virtue and Vice

Consider now Stephen's fourth and last point (from Borges):

> If all people do a sufficiently immense variety of things, then categories of virtuous and vicious, good and bad, cease to have meaning.

As we've just seen, immortality (of the envisaged sort) does *not* entail eventually doing everything—performing every kind of action. More specifically, it does *not* entail that one will perform every "morally valanced" action, good *and* bad, or that one will exhibit every virtue *and* vice. Further, if I now have a good character, there is no reason to suppose that at some point my character will change so that I regularly do bad things. Why not instead suppose that virtuous persons would never fall into vice? After all, virtue is often thought to be "ampliative": acting from virtue strengthens and reinforces virtue. There is, however, no reason to think that all immortal individuals would eventually act only viciously (or, for that matter, virtuously) forever.

Considering the extreme cases, we could arguably have a concept of good, even if no one's actual behavior were an instance of it, and we could have a concept of bad, even if no one's actual behavior were an instance of it. Immortality would not necessarily obliterate our moral framework, even if all our actual actions (implausibly) were in one category.

2.4 Procrastination

There are so many reasons why we need to "get off the couch" and actively pursue what we care about in a timely way. I return to that famous immortality scholar, Dr. Seuss (Theodor Geisel), who writes:

> You're off to Great Places!
> Today is your day!
> Your mountain is waiting,
> So ... get on your way!
> (Seuss/Geisel 1990)

Other people won't necessarily wait for us to dawdle and endlessly deliberate. Opportunities for rewarding relationships—sometimes love—and professional success can be frittered away. Each of us is situated in a web of human relationships, constrained ultimately by nature. Others will need our commitments in a broad range of situations: going to a ball game, playing tennis, getting more involved in the church, becoming a romantic partner, fighting for social justice, protecting our endangered environment, and so forth. Patience wears thin, social injustice gets worse, the environment becomes increasingly fragile... ... It is not only (or even primarily) because we recognise that we will die at some point (perhaps sooner rather than later) that we cannot lollygag.

Let's pause to highlight and reflect on the idea that we are situated at a particular point in the web of human relationships. Indeed, our relationships are central to the meaningfulness of our lives. These relationships necessarily involve explicit and implicit contractual relationships or, at the very least, reciprocal expectations. I sign a mortgage with a schedule of payments, and there are deadlines I must meet, short of defaulting and losing my house. I sign a contract to make payments on my car loan; again, I must meet the specified deadlines, or I will lose the car. I get married and have children. This involves me in a complex set of duties and responsibilities, many of which require meeting deadlines: my girl needs to arrive at her ballet practice on time, my kids need to get to school in the morning, etc. Our locus in the web of human relationships determines a huge set of temporal constraints, even if we were to have radical life extension.

My explicit promises set up legitimate expectations that I will keep them. Others rely on me to do so. Similarly, implicit promises or regular behavior (in certain contexts) may establish reasonable expectations of continued similar behavior. When we don't keep our promises or do our part in conventional practices, others may rely on us to their detriment. We thus have moral, as well as prudential, duties to meet our contractual and less formal deadlines.

Stephen writes, "... death is the source of all our deadlines. If we live forever, these deadlines disappear". I do not agree. As with questions about the significance of our choices and actions, there are many challenges and obstacles to our success, and many reasons to get going. One such reason is human interdependence; we rely on others, and they on us. Others' lives don't necessarily come to a halt when I acquire radically extended life! The worry about lack of motivation in immortality has the feeling of solipsism about it, and the answers to both the worries about significance and procrastination are similar: death is not the only relevant "limit" or "constraint".

146   John Martin Fischer

In our debate, we are envisaging a scenario in which at least some others (perhaps all) with whom one interacts are also radically life extended persons. Would deadlines then disappear? I don't see why. Certainly, some would disappear as a result of mutual self-interest and prior negotiations. That is, some deadlines that are pointless or are simply in place to facilitate coordination that can wait will be renegotiated if delays are desired. It by no means follows that all, or even most, would be adjusted or eliminated. This is because there are many constraints (other than death) on our decision-making and action, especially as we aim at the goals of flourishing and leading a good, rewarding, ethically defensible life.

Nature and physics impel us to act in timely ways, especially (but not solely) when coordinated action in the face of physical constraints requires it: the avalanche is bearing down on us, the out-of-control car is coming toward us, my rock-climbing partner has slipped and is connected to me via ropes, and so forth. So does human psychology. We do not wish to be lonely or depressed for significant periods of time, and this will cause us to make arrangements with others or simply start projects that require timely action. These kinds of activities help us to lead rewarding and agreeable, rather than listless, alienated, and bored lives. We seek happiness and meaning in a world that includes physical limitations and the requirements of interpersonal interaction. At the very least, we need to get to our therapist's office on time!

2.5   Value and Scarcity

Stephen writes, "As a rule, the value of a thing is related to its scarcity. If it were infinite, time would therefore have no value". It is indeed true (in some sense) that if time is scarce, then we feel that each moment is more valuable—we must take advantage of it. Importantly, however, this does *not* imply that it would be more valuable to have a life with less time than more, and even much more. Consider, for example, having to survive for three days in a hot desert with one canteen of water. Each drop is precious—none must be wasted, and each gulp savored. Contrast this with a scenario in which you are given three large jugs of water containing much more than the canteen—more than enough to survive comfortably. Each drop of water is more precious in the first scenario, but the amount of water is preferable in the second—there is more

Reply to Stephen Cave 147

of a valuable commodity in the second scenario, and overall, it is clearly to be preferred. You would and should choose it!

Stephen offers this argument:

> ... imagine you have found the elixir and are working hard to save for a fantastic holiday to celebrate your good fortune. You are thinking of packing your bags when your employer says to you that if you work one more week she will give you a bonus of $1,000. If you were mortal, in making this decision you would have to weigh the value to you of the money with the value to you of your limited time. But as an immortal, you have all the time in the world—if you worked an extra week, you would still have an infinite amount of time ahead of you in which to take your holiday and do everything else you have ever dreamed of. So by sacrificing a week, you lose nothing. But money you still need; and the more you have, the longer you can enjoy your holiday—after all, you are only limited by the amount of cash you have; time you have in abundance.

> It is therefore rational for you to accept your employer's offer: you get much-needed extra money yet lose nothing. Next week, however, she offers you the same deal. As you still have infinite time ahead of you, it makes sense for you again to take the cash. But the week after that she offers you the deal again ... and again ... forever. Your dreams of seeing the world have turned into an eternity chained to your desk.

The problem with this argument again has to do with the nature of human lived experience. As in my initial essay, an immortal person who sprains his ankle will not say, "Oh well, I'm in terrible pain now but eventually it will go away, and, after all, I have no time pressures ...". No, he will want the pain to stop as soon as possible. We want our pain and suffering to go away quickly, and, similarly, we want our pleasures and rewarding experiences as soon as possible, other things equal. There will come a week when the marginal utility of the cash "now" (*i.e.*, at the time the choice must be made) will be less than the utility of taking the holiday. You had plans to go on a vacation, and they have had to be put on hold. During this interval of time, you have made choices that were better for you at the relevant time than going on vacation. At a certain point, however, it is better for you (your marginal utility is

148 John Martin Fischer

higher) if you refuse the offer and take the trip instead. How many weeks will go by? There's no answer to this for all people, but it is by no means inevitable that you will be trapped in an eternity of postponements of something you very much, and increasingly, want to do.

The marginal utility of the cash will diminish in accordance with the economic **Law of Diminishing Marginal Returns,** and the vacation will be more enticing as time goes by. To reiterate: at some point, the marginal utility of going on holiday is greater than the work plus cash, and you will go to Hawaii. (The "staycations" will finally become stale, no matter how much money you are raking in.) But perhaps the lure of sunshine, beautiful beaches, luaus and Mai Tais is less than compelling, and you *always*—every week—prefer the "package" of work plus $1,000 to the holiday. Well, then, you are hardly in eternal torment at your desk—you prefer this. You are no absurd Sisyphus, rolling his rock up the hill forever—with no choice about it.

Of course, you'd have to be a person who pathologically defers gratification to have a "utility function" of this sort, and very few people will. Just as it is irrational to give no weight to future well-being, it is also irrational to give *all* weight to the future. We have a dilemma: either you are within the bounds of "normalcy" as regards gratification deferral and you will not be eternally chained to your desk, or you will be one of those unhappy souls who always defers gratification, in which you will be at your desk, but not chained! Either way, no problem with radical life extension.

2.6 The Perils of Wanting True Immortality or Radical Life Extension

Stephen offers a reason why it might be psychologically bad to want to live forever. He writes:

> ... plenty of people already have difficulty living with joy, appreciation and purpose in a lifespan of 75–85 years. One of the causes of this is a failure to 'number our days'; to appreciate that our days are very limited and very precious. The pursuit of immortality does not *necessarily* entail an underappreciation of the limited days we have. But the two seem frequently to go hand-in hand. The upshot [of the literature in "terror-management theory"] is that a desire to

Reply to Stephen Cave 149

live forever and an associated faith that it is possible erode our awareness of our morality, and with that the appreciation of the preciousness of each day.

Against this, I would point out that even an extended-life individual wants her days to be both pleasant and rewarding, so far as possible. She thus has reason to treasure each day, not because the days are scarce, but because each day presents both an opportunity for immersion in what she is passionate about and the danger of wasting it and becoming depressed. She has a choice: "I can live each day to the fullest, throwing myself into relationships and projects I care about, and being mindful of the small pleasures and joys along the way. Alternatively, I can sit on the sofa and do nothing or go through the motions of life without really savoring or appreciating it". I know what she—and all of us--should choose. It is important for an extended-life individual not to let the parade of life pass her by. She will have many more days—days that could be parts of valuable and increasingly rewarding projects, or more wasted opportunities and emptiness. Activity and mindfulness would be just as important in a radically extended life as in a mortal life. It is the Zen of Immortality.

I wish to add a thought about our attitudes toward radical life extension. If you become seriously engaged with the possibility of it—either doing scientific/medical research or ruminating frequently on relevant philosophical issues—it could come as a very disappointing shock to receive a terminal diagnosis or otherwise be confronted by one's imminent death. You might feel cheated and angry.

We human beings, however, have the capacity to switch our focus as appropriate—to take different perspectives as conditions render them appropriate. I can think philosophically about radical life extension, seeking to defeat the army of curmudgeons. I can also hope fervently that medical science will soon make such a life possible for me. I must, however, remain "rooted" in reality. When I bump into the fact of my mortality, I can switch to a perspective from which I accept its inevitability with grace, not anger.

This is a special case of a general phenomenon. David Hume famously wrote that he left his skeptical reflections and conclusions "in his study", living his day-to-day life as though skepticism were false. Scientists, mathematicians, poets, and many others may be passionately immersed in their activities while in their offices or labs, or while lost in abstract thought during a walk on a lovely spring day, but they must switch to a focus on ordinary, day-to-day "reality" when it is time to leave their reflections for another day. (Of course, in one's office or lab you must be aware of smoke that may indicate a fire, and on your walk through the meadow you have to avoid stepping on jagged rocks ...).

The same capacity to shift our focus is required in the context of engagement with the possibility of radical life extension. There is a time for science and philosophical rumination, but also for accepting the reality of death—a reality that brings us (literally!) down to earth. Sometimes we must be Here, rather than There, now. Given the current impossibility of radical life extension, and the implausibility of getting there soon, we have overwhelming reason to get psychologically prepared for the shift, and to accept it with humility and grace.

3 Moral Reasons to Reject Radical Life Extension

3.1 Environmental Concerns: Overpopulation

Stephen begins with the challenge of overpopulation, distilling this argument:

A. If humans continue to be born, but no longer die, the population of humans will continue to increase indefinitely.
B. This planet (and any other reachable parts of the physical universe) can support only a limited number of humans comfortably and sustainably.
C. Therefore, if humans continue to be born, but no longer die, the population of humans will eventually exceed the number that can live comfortably and sustainably.

He goes on to point out that if the technology that enables greater and greater longevity is only accessible to a limited number of people, this will exacerbate the considerable inequity and social injustice that already exists. He boils down his concerns to a dilemma:

> ... the more people have access to life extension, the higher the risk of overpopulation; the fewer people have access to life extension, the more unjust this will be.

Stephen envisages specific ways that might be proposed by optimists to deal with overpopulation, pointing to the unacceptability of all of them. In what is perhaps the most plausible (or least unappealing) scenario, all humans (having achieved radical life extension) stop having children, thus rendering the "generation" of that moment the last one.

Stephen points to what he takes to be the injustice of favoring one generation over all future generations (in this important way), and the difficulties and horrors of enforcing a no-children policy. We already know of the terrible efforts in China to enforce a one-child policy, and it is hard to imagine how a no-child policy could be implemented in a humane and morally acceptable way. Would women be subject to involuntary abortions? Any efforts to enforce a ban on having children would inevitably involve morally unacceptable means and consequences. Further, there is the prudential concern that many human beings take having and raising children and building loving families as one of the most rewarding parts of their lives. Many simply cannot imagine life without this experience.

As I pointed out in my initial essay, having children is not *essential* to leading a good human life. After all, many couples (and individuals) cannot conceive a child, and others voluntarily decide not to for a variety of reasons. They can (and many do) still lead happy and meaningful lives. Further, couples (and individuals) have *no* obligation to have any—or additional—children. They have no duty to increase the total amount of "value" or happiness in the world, unless they adopt an overly simple version of the idea that we should always do what maximises the good of the greatest number of persons. We need not adopt any version of this doctrine, nor is it clear that a plausible version of it would imply that we need to have (more) children.

One should ask: if you were to voluntarily refrain from having a child, whom would that harm? Who is the subject of the alleged harm? You can obviously harm extant individuals, but why think you can harm a non-existent person by failing to bring them into existence? We are morally required not to harm existing persons, and not to intentionally or recklessly bring into being a person with significant impairments. We *do* have obligations to extant persons, but we have no duties regarding *merely* possible persons (those who never become actual persons), and certainly no moral requirement to bring them into existence.

152 John Martin Fischer

What if all persons were immortal and voluntarily decided not to have children? Cave suggests that this would be *unfair* to future generations. I believe that, just as you cannot harm a merely possible person, you cannot harm or treat unfairly a merely possible set of persons—a merely possible future generation. Again, who is harmed? Who is treated unfairly?

Is it immoral to allow the human species to go out of existence? I do not think so, but let's grant the point. Eventually, when enough extended-life human beings will have died, there could be a mechanism (lottery?) to encourage a subset to have enough children to achieve the continuation of the species. (Of course, this is *only* if we were to accept the controversial idea that the extinction of our species would be so bad as to generate a duty to continue it.)

The simple and basic point of my reflections just above is illustrated by the following scenario. You are a happily married couple (we are imagining now a couple, not an individual, referred to by "you") who are living a rewarding but very busy life. You are both immersed in your careers, friendships, hobbies, and love for each other. After reflection and discussion, you've decided (voluntarily and freely) not to have children. Wouldn't it be absurd if someone were to tell you that you have a *moral obligation* to have at least one child, since you need to maximise value in the world? Wouldn't it be equally ludicrous for someone to tell you that, in refraining, you are *harming* the possible person who would exist, but for your obstinate and narcissistic refusal to raise a family?

No need to state the answers explicitly: there is nothing morally wrong with your freely choosing not to have children. Unless there is something especially bad about the extinction of our species, it would not be morally objectionable for everyone to make this decision. The same would apply to truly immortal persons, except that the moral situation is even simpler: the species would continue. I have focused on voluntary and free choices by individuals, couples, and even all humans. What about a policy—applicable to all—*prohibiting* having any children? I agree with Stephen that this would be unenforceable except by means that are morally abhorrent.

Would the existence of a very small group of life-extended persons, or even clusters of such groups, *with the right to have children*, exacerbate social injustice, especially if this unequal distribution of the means of achieving such life extension is widely known? No doubt it would to some extent, although I doubt this would be a major impetus for concern about the inequitable distribution of medical care in the future. More importantly, the concern starts with the "status quo" of inequity, but this need not be held fixed in our analysis here. Going forward, we *must address the general problems of unfair and differential access to health care in general.* This needs to be part of an overall strategy for ameliorating social injustices more broadly, including radical inequalities in wealth and income. Addressing these social injustices is of utmost importance, and without making significant progress on these pressing challenges, the opportunity for only *some* to achieve medical immortality might well exacerbate social injustice to some extent.

Achieving much greater social justice, including a more equitable distribution of economic resources, will help cushion any shocks from unequal access to radical life extension. After all, social injustice and inequitable distribution of wealth and income are particularly distressing when some are not getting the resources necessary for a good life. Above this baseline, unequal access to luxuries is less worrisome. Even with a more equitable distribution of resources, however, there will be non-negligible differences in economic wherewithal (assuming some sort of "market" economy). These differences, together with the substantial price tag of radical life extension, would no doubt restrict the availability of it. The upshot is that all these facts would *significantly diminish* the effect of the right to have children on social injustice.

The analysis I've just offered treats access to racial life extension as a "luxury good", like a fancy car or a Caribbean cruise. If there is substantial social and economic justice, that some can afford these goods (while others can't) is not socially *incendiary*, significantly magnifying social injustices and threatening to produce political instability. The importance of equality in outcomes is much diminished when everyone has *enough* of the relevant goods.[1] Here: the basic goods that are required to enable people to live good and fulfilling lives are equitably distributed. This offers a model of medical immortality with the right to have children that would not appear to exacerbate social injustice or undermine political stability.

---

1. Harry Frankfurt has argued for this position in a very enlightening article: (Frankfurt 1997)

Still, one might be unsatisfied by the treatment of radical life extension as a "mere" luxury good, on a par with a Rolls Royce. For optimists, radical life extension would be "in a league of its own"—incomparably better than any other good. One might call it a "transformational" good, transforming rather than merely enhancing life. Even if there is fundamental social justice, unequal access (based on equalities of wealth and income) to *transformational* goods might be problematic.

I do not know if this is correct, but if so, there would have to be a mechanism—generally deemed "fair"—to distribute access to radical life extension. One might envisage a lottery that could be entered voluntarily, the winners of which would be given the resources enabling radical life extension. The lottery would be set up so that there would be enough people to make meaningful relationships possible, but not so many as to propel overpopulation or otherwise accelerate environmental degradation. The life-extended folks would be allowed to have children, but the eventual deaths of merely life-extended (and not truly immortal) people would balance out the additions from children. This offers another model of life-extended persons with the right to have children that does not appear to significantly exacerbate social justice or lead to political instability.[2]

3.2 Environmental Concerns: Optimistic Realism

All these points having been made to address the challenge of overpopulation, there is absolutely no doubt that pressures on our increasingly fragile environment and social injustice are two of the

---

2. In a democratic society in which some (perhaps a small minority) are immortal, they might develop significant political power, because politicians would recognise that they will get more votes from them over time (than from moral people). This recognition could lead to politicians' currying favor with the immortals and offering them "bribes" in the form of differential benefits. This sort of exacerbation of inequality is an interesting feature of any model of immortality, not just ones in which the immortal people have the right to have children. Of course, people's political views change over time (for various reasons), and no political party or candidate can reliably expect their support, even when doling out special favors and treatment. If the differential treatment becomes too much, society will enact measures to restrict or eliminate it. This and other challenges for immortality that emerge from concerns about social justice and stability bear further discussion and thought.

most, if not the most, pressing problems facing human beings today. How exactly do these issues bear on the specific question of our debate (and the bulk of the literature surrounding the desirability or worthiness of choice of immortality)? This is delicate and complex.

Should you choose radical life extension under favorable conditions? My aim here has been to address the worries of the immortality curmudgeons, as they have been developed in the literature primarily, although not exclusively, by Bernard Williams (Chair of the Bored) and his very influential followers: boredom, ennui/ hyperboredom, meaninglessness, lack of motivation/ procrastination, lack of the "stages" that make a life recognizably human, the absence of the structuring of our attitudes and values by temporal finitude (scarcity of time), the identity problem ("it wouldn't be me"), and so forth. These challenges have dominated the literature. All of them contend, in some way or another, that living forever would not be worthy of choice because of deep and central facts about human nature, such as having a specific character, set of memories, values, and attitudes, and a certain structure to our lives.

These (and other) curmudgeonly worries do not in any way flow from (or depend on) environmental deterioration due to overpopulation or any other factor; to reiterate, they putatively flow primarily—if not solely—from facts about human nature. Recall that Williams based his critique of immortality on the (alleged) fact that everything that could happen to Elina—an individual with a certain character—had already happened, thus resulting in boredom and alienation. No mention here of environmental challenges. Given the influence of Williams and the wide acceptance in philosophy (and beyond) of his arguments for his position that living forever would not be worthy of choice by any human being, I have focused on the arguments from human nature.

Recall that my interpretation of the question at issue in this debate is, "Should you choose radical life extension *under favorable conditions*"? The question is of little philosophical interest if it is about an existence in poverty or hunger or lack of shelter or inhospitable environment. Who would want to live forever in an ugly, polluted, and increasingly toxic environment? Further, why think that such an environment could sustain human longevity of the sort envisaged by radical life extension? Given that I have wished to address the primary arguments of the immortality curmudgeons, I've formulated the question with the important qualification, "under favorable conditions".

Overpopulation in the future that exacerbates already pressing challenges to a clean and hospitable environment would almost certainly issue in circumstances that are incompatible with "favorable conditions". Thus, in answering the question at the center of my reflections, I have essentially assumed that such problems have been addressed successfully, if not perfectly. This assumption posits a *hypothetical* scenario, and it allows me to home in on the problems central to the debates between the optimists and the curmudgeons. This is an important intellectual project, and I hope I have convinced you that the answer to the question, "Should you choose radical life extension under favorable conditions"? is "Yes".

Now for the bad news. I do not think it is more likely than not that we will be able to achieve the "favorable conditions" in question. Unfortunately, I believe that the challenges are great, and our ability to unite and thoughtfully address them is not as robust as necessary. The environment is rapidly reaching the "point of no return", where decent life (or life at all) for our species will not be sustainable. At the same time, the human tendencies toward immediate self-interest and denial, combined with the social and political requirements of sustained and significant cooperation to solve the problems, is a strong cocktail that distracts us and diminishes our capacity to save the planet.

I am thus an immortality optimist but also an immortality realist. (Again: "immortality" here is radical life extension.) Call me an **optimistic realist**. I'm *not* a curmudgeon—I do not believe that facts about human nature imply a negative answer to our question; in this sense, I'm an optimist. But I'm a realist in that I do not believe it is more likely than not that we will *in fact* achieve the "favorable circumstances" required to sustain greater and greater longevity. The species and our planet are going in quite the opposite direction.

Finally, despite its less-than-perky implications, realism does *not* necessarily lead to hopelessness and a kind of despair. Although I believe our achieving the required favorable conditions is unlikely, I also hold that it is *not* impossible. Given human ingenuity and the propulsive force of looming imminent demise, we have a real shot at saving the planet. Perhaps the dream of prolongevism, a motivation for human beings ever since we have existed, can provide the motivation for galvanising the ingenuity and energy required to address the obstacles. The dream of immortality (or radical life extension) is not a pipedream, but a call to action.

4 Summary

In this chapter, I have addressed Stephen's many thoughtful and challenging critiques. He divides the worries into two categories: prudential and moral. He argues that we have neither prudential nor moral reasons to choose radical life extension.

The prudential worries stem from: boredom, ennui, the significance of projects, identity, virtue and vice, procrastination, value and scarcity, and the (psychological) perils of wanting radical life extension. The moral concerns stem from overpopulation, pressure on scarce resources, and environmental degradation. I seek to address each of these challenges to radical life extension's potential worthiness of choice by human beings. In doing so I have revisited and elaborated some of my remarks in my initial essay, and I have also added some new responses.

There are many dystopian depictions of radical life extension (some of which are described in the section on apologist legends and stories in my first essay). Borges's presentation in "The Immortals", as discussed by Stephen is particularly vivid and disturbing. No one would, or should, choose radical life extension under those circumstances! This is not, however, our question. Ours is whether you should choose it under favorable conditions. It is easy to be frightened by the many dystopias of science fiction and fantasy literature, but we must keep our eyes on the ball.

Part 3

Second Round of Replies

Chapter 5

Reply to John Martin Fischer's Reply

Stephen Cave

Contents

1 Hedonism, Meaning and Moral Change	161
1.1 The Spectrum of Despond	162
1.2 Meaning and Moral Change	163
2 What We Owe Future Generations	166
2.1 Is the Idea of An Obligation to Have Children Absurd?	167
2.2 Is There an Obligation to Make Happy People?	168
2.3 Is a Future with More Generations Better?	170
3 Conclusion	173

In this short chapter—my final contribution—I will respond to a few of the many excellent arguments John makes in favour of living forever. I group them into two sections, one focussing on the prudential arguments and one on (a few aspects of) the ethical arguments. I hope, at the same time, to open up some new directions in which the debate could be taken. I will focus on:

1. The relationship between hedonism, meaningful engagement with the world, and moral change.
2. Whether we are obliged to bring future generations into existence.

Then finally, I will offer a few conclusions.

I Hedonism, Meaning and Moral Change

There is a good chance that you, dear reader, will by now have made up your mind about whether forever would be tedious. I hope you

DOI: 10.4324/9781003105442-8

162   Stephen Cave

are not growing bored of the argument: that would bode ill for an immortality of philosophical investigation. Just in case, I will not dwell too much longer on this aspect of our debate. But I do want to respond to a couple of John's points, and in doing so draw out a further dilemma for the would-be immortalist.

1.1   The Spectrum of Despond

One theme of this debate is that there are many degrees of boredom. For example, John distinguishes between boredom and hyperboredom; I have also discussed ennui and meaninglessness, and we have both alluded to various related concepts such as melancholy and depression. Though each of these is subtly different, they have something in common: a lack of interest in what is going on. This can be very temporary, as when one is standing in a long supermarket queue, impatient to get on with one's life. But it can also be more profound, as in depression, when nothing seems to matter any more.

In this way, these affects are therefore on a continuum of deepening severity (even while they might differ in other ways). Let us call this continuum **the Spectrum of Despond**. I argue that it matters that these problems are linked in this way. It matters because I believe sometimes we might be able to solve a problem at one point on the spectrum, but in doing so only increase the risk of suffering from a problem on another part of the spectrum. This was the point of my 'pleasure dome' example in Chapter 1. In that example, I asked you to imagine a society of very long-lived people. In order to stop themselves from getting bored, they have invented pleasure domes: entertainment centres that are so effective that even the most listless and cynical citizen cannot help but be swept up in the adventure. Such pleasure domes seem to me a plausible shorthand for developments that are well underway. The entertainment industry is already highly sophisticated, with blockbuster movies and compelling video games, while newer technologies such as virtual reality offer even more immersive experiences. If science and technology have one day mastered the human brain and body to the point that they can stop ageing and disease, it seems highly probable that they will also be able to keep us entertained.

However, I argued in Chapter 1 that after many years of such a life, the inhabitants of this society would start to feel ennui. Although it would be true that they would not be bored while in

Reply to John Martin Fischer's Reply   163

the pleasure domes, once out of them they would feel stale and empty. In other words, their attempt to solve boredom would just shunt them further along the Spectrum of Despond to a more profound dissatisfaction. In the last chapter, John broadly agreed with this analysis. However, he does not consider it to be an argument against immortality, but rather against hedonism—the pursuit of pleasure. John concurs that such a hedonistic life would not be worth pursuing for eternity.

However, this sits ill with his preceding section—§1.1 of Chapter 4, on boredom. In that section, John rebuffs arguments for inevitable boredom and cites a number of activities that he thinks we could pursue joyfully forever. The hitch is that all the activities he cites are hedonistic: "nice walks, a lovely glass of wine from time to time" and a colourful sunset over the mountains. These activities might not be everyone's idea of hedonism—some people might have something more orgiastic or adrenaline-pumping in mind. But John makes very clear that these are his idea of "pleasurable experiences", and argues that we should choose to continue them forever—which is pretty much a Hedonist's Manifesto.

So on the one hand, John agrees that my hedonistic pleasure domes would be unsatisfactory for eternity. But on the other hand, his own vision of living happily ever after seems to be a more sedate hedonism without the domes.

1.2 Meaning and Moral Change

Why do defenders of immortality not point to more meaningful activities than drinking wine for us to pursue *ad infinitum*? Perhaps because many activities are less obviously repeatable. The examples John offers in his chapters of this book certainly range over other varieties of experience, such as pursuing business ventures, romantic partnerships or new sports. A cynic might say that these pursuits too are merely hedonistic: there is little deeper meaning to be had from hitting balls with sticks (no matter how seriously some people take cricket and baseball) or from the cut and thrust of Wall Street. If that is so, then these activities too all belong in the allegorical pleasure dome.

However, let us grant that there are activities that go beyond mere pleasure: activities we pursue because of our values and virtues. These might include all kinds of political, social and charitable projects, from helping the homeless to fermenting the overthrow of the government. In Chapter 1, drawing on Borges's short story "The Immortal", I argued that even these kinds of activities would lose their meaning over a sufficiently long life. In particular, I argued that after a long enough time, pursuing enough of such activities, categories of virtuous and vicious, good and bad, would cease to have meaning. In §1.3.4 of the last chapter, John takes issue with this. He argues that "if I now have a good character, there is no reason to suppose that at some point my character will change so that I regularly do bad things." The good, he believes, might stay good indefinitely, and the wicked wicked.

However, I do not believe that this is realistic. Borges is exaggerating for literary effect when he writes that every immortal will perform "all goodness" but also "all perversity"—but not much. Consider the past few hundred years—a modest period for someone whose life is radically extended (let alone an immortal). John and I are both white men, he from the US, and I from the UK. We could trace our ancestry back for these past few centuries and ask for each generation: what did it mean to be a good man?

We would get a very wide range of answers, many completely at odds with each other. For example, at the end of the nineteenth century, English fathers were expected to be strict disciplinarians, ruling firmly over their households and showing little affection to their children; yet at the start of the twenty-first, they are expected to be egalitarian partners and loving parents. Today, in the circles in which John and I travel, a good man is 'colour-blind' to race at the very least, or (better) actively anti-racist. Yet two centuries ago, our ancestors were building empires justified by an ideology of white supremacy, an ideology implicated in atrocities including war, genocide, pillage, theft of lands and the destruction of countless indigenous cultures. These were not the acts of a few bad apples—these were the acts of people who thought they were doing their duty: bearing, in poet Rudyard Kipling's words, "the white man's burden" (Kipling 1899).

Such chequered pasts are not unique to the US and the UK. Think of what it meant to be a good Chinese man or woman in 1900 during the last days of the Imperial Qing dynasty, versus in 1930 under the Nationalist government, versus in 1970 during the 'Great Proletarian Cultural Revolution' instigated by communist ruler Mao Zedong, versus in the economically liberal but politically authoritarian present. Norms have changed immensely over the past centuries. Indeed, they have changed considerably in just the past decades: homosexuality was not just socially unacceptable in the UK in the mid-twentieth century, but actually illegal; today it is socially unacceptable to condemn it, and illegal to discriminate against anyone on the basis of it.

It would be foolish to think we have reached any kind of ethical apotheosis. Norms will continue to change: perhaps, one hundred years from now, it will be illegal to eat meat, or drive a car (as computers will do it much more safely), or throw away an old item instead of recycling it, or lock people for months in solitary confinement in prison. There are many reasons why our great-grandchildren might think us short-sighted and cruel.

Now recall John's argument that "if I now have a good character, there is no reason to suppose that at some point my character will change so that I regularly do bad things". My point is that the long-lived person's character does not need to change for them to do "bad things". The tumult of history will thrust it upon them. Consider someone born in the UK in 1850, who did his duty building the British Empire as a young man. By 2020, either he will have had to radically review his moral framework, such that he would view his earlier deeds as "bad" (i.e., as the exploitation and oppression of other peoples based on a spurious ideology of race), or if he kept to his nineteenth-century views, no one today would accept his claim that his racist, imperialist views were "good".

This is the reality that underlies Borges's literary flourish that the immortal would engage in "all goodness" and also "all perversity". A person who engaged deeply with their times, who strived to be the very best they could be, would over the centuries have found themselves on both sides of countless moral battles: against gay rights and for gay rights; participating in the colonisation of other lands (even pillage, slavery, and murder) and fighting racism; burning witches and campaigning for women's suffrage. Borges contends that there is only so much of this that a person can take before their will to engage with the world breaks down, and they wish only to lie in shallow pits, staring at the stars.

I started this sub-section asking why defenders of the desirability of immortality often point to simpler, hedonistic pleasures such as drinking wine, rather than more complex, meaning-laden ones such as participating in politics. The answer is that over a long enough period of time, these more complex projects seem absurd and contradictory—or worse. Engaging with such projects, and thereby experiencing repeatedly that what one once took so seriously has

166 Stephen Cave

proved to be embarrassingly wrong-headed, can hardly provide a recipe for a happy forever.

Far simpler then to stick to a nice glass of wine. Certainly, that is something people have enjoyed for millennia. (Let us leave to one side the moral back-and-forth around the temperance movement in the US, which culminated in the prohibition of alcohol from 1920 to 1933.) A retreat to the simpler pleasures is, of course, a retreat to hedonism—to the pleasure dome, albeit, as John conjures it, a dome without walls (just a well-patrolled southern border) called California, with fine wine and picturesque mountains. As lovely as this sounds, we have seen that this hedonistic vision is not lovely enough for forever—and John agrees.

So we have moved along the Spectrum of Despond, only to find ourselves slipping back to where we started. It might be possible to avoid the boredom of everyday repetition through a world of wondrous pleasures; but in the end, this is likely to leave us cold, drifting into ennui. It might be possible to avoid this ennui through more meaningful engagement with the world; but in the end, this will lead us into a tangled web of contradictory meanings that will leave us as world-weary as Borges's 'troglodytes'. But if we then seek solace in a glass of wine, we are on our way back to the shallow hedonism of the pleasure dome.

2 What We Owe Future Generations

In this section, I return to the ethical considerations relevant to whether we should choose to live forever. In Chapter 1, I argued that these considerations could be boiled down to overpopulation (if many people have access to life-extension technologies) or increased injustice (if only a few do). This is, of course, a simplification—there are many scenarios in which we could encounter both over-population and increased injustice, *and* other problems besides!

I laid out in the first chapter a range of possible policy approaches to managing the overpopulation problem in a world of very long-lived people. None were very attractive. They ranged from banning children (a policy likely to require forced sterilisation, forced abortion and infanticide) to capping lifespans at 100 (a policy likely to require the mass involuntary killing of the elderly). These are more the stuff of science fiction dystopias than modern politics. John seems mostly to agree with this assessment. However, he does take issue with one further argument I made against banning—or choosing not to have—children: that this would be unfair to (potential) future generations.

John makes two main arguments against this point. The first is that "you cannot harm a merely possible person" or "a merely possible set of persons—a merely possible future generation". The second argument is that it would "be absurd" to think we in the current generation have a *moral obligation* to have children, and so to bring future generations into existence. The two points are closely related, and I will start by addressing the second.

2.1   Is the Idea of An Obligation to Have Children Absurd?

I suggest that it is far from absurd to think we have an obligation to bring future generations into existence. In posing his rhetorical question—"wouldn't it be absurd if someone were to tell you that you have a *moral obligation* to have at least one child?"—John is assuming that you, dear reader, have the same moral intuitions as he does. Perhaps you do. But I contend that the idea that it is *absurd* to think we might have an obligation to have children is a moral intuition that is highly particular to a current time and place. It seems absurd to twentieth- and twenty-first-century North Americans (and some others in industrialised, liberal societies), because they have been inculcated with a philosophy of extreme individualism. This philosophy, which permeates American culture, emphasises the importance of individual desires and goals over the interests of any larger social group. Of course, for an individualist, it is absurd that someone would suggest they should have children if they don't want to.

But the majority of people throughout history have *not* been individualists in this sense. Indeed, the term (*individualisme*) was coined in France in the eighteenth century as a pejorative to describe (and denigrate) an emerging group who were seen to place their own interests above those of the collective (Lukes 2020). Most ancient peoples and most non-Western peoples conceive of themselves as parts of greater wholes: of communities that extend not just across space, but also backwards and forwards in time.

Consider this epitaph from the tombstone of a member of the ancient Roman Scipio family: "By my conduct I added to the virtues of my family; I begat offspring and sought to equal the deeds of my father. I maintained the glory of my ancestors, so that they rejoice that I was their offspring; my honours have ennobled my stock" (Clarke 1956, p. 3). This member of the Scipio family is proud to have fulfilled his duty to his ancestors, a crucial part of which was ensuring there would be descendants. A combination of Greek philosophy and Hebrew (Judaeo-Christian) religion slowly undermined this worldview in Europe over the subsequent centuries, giving rise to the philosophy of individualism. Nonetheless, the idea that people have a duty to produce the next generation persisted well into the twentieth century: for example, in the 1930s and '40 s the German state awarded the *Mutterkreuz*—the Cross of Honour of the German Mother—in gold, silver or bronze to women who had sufficient children (my own children's maternal great-grandmother was awarded silver for her seven offspring).

This worldview would be instantly recognisable to people from China, Japan, Korea, India and many parts of Africa today. For example, Hinduism has a notion of the 'three debts' that each individual owes and must repay: to the gods, to the sages and to one's ancestors. The debt to one's ancestors is repaid by—you guessed it—having children (Vyas 1992, p. 76). So, whether you personally believe in it or not, it is not *absurd* to think we might have a moral obligation to have children—indeed this looks to have been the mainstream view throughout the history of humanity.

2.2 Is There an Obligation to Make Happy People?

However, I have not argued for a moral obligation for *each individual* to have children. I am assuming that in the ordinary course of things, enough people will want to have children to ensure that there will be future generations. In my view, we can therefore happily leave to people's individual preference whether to have children. The question I posed is whether it would be morally wrong to *ban* a population from having children, if that population were in return permitted to live indefinitely. There are various reasons to think such a ban would be wrong with regard to the population to whom it applies—for example, if we consider their right to have children to be fundamental. But what I also suggested is that this would be wrong with regard to the potential future generations that would have existed were it not for the ban. This is what John disputes.

John's position is shared by many philosophers. But it is far from the only position, even within the narrow confines of contemporary Anglo-American philosophical debate. The question of what responsibilities we have to future generations is in fact an exciting and lively area of current research. It is also a hugely important one, given that decisions we make today about (e.g.) our use of natural resources will have impacts far into the future (for millions of years in the case of nuclear waste, or forever in the case of loss of species).

John makes two main arguments to support his view that we are not obliged to bring future generations into being. He argues that we *are* morally required "not to intentionally or recklessly bring into being a person with significant impairments" but that we *are not* morally required to bring unimpaired people into existence. He further argues that as these future generations do not currently exist, there are no identifiable people who will actually suffer harm through our action (or inaction). He writes: "You can obviously harm extant individuals, but why think you can harm a non-existent person (by failing to bring them into existence)?"

These two arguments are in tension with each other. If we have no obligations regarding "merely possible persons", as John puts it, then it is not clear how we can be obliged not to intentionally bring into being someone whose life would be one of suffering. After all, this is also a "merely possible person". John's position reflects an *asymmetry* that is well known in population ethics. The asymmetry is between how some thinkers regard the question of bringing into existence people whose lives would be bad (they think we shouldn't) and how they regard bringing into existence people whose lives would be good (they are neutral, rather than thinking we should). Numerous philosophers have attempted to defend this asymmetry, but without a great deal of success.

First, some philosophers, such as John in the preceding chapter, write as if this asymmetry were obvious; as if we all share the moral intuition that we have an obligation to *not* bring into being suffering people, but have no obligation to bring into being happy people. But the only study to systematically test this intuition on a large group of people does not support this. In a recent survey of 157 people, a Harvard psychologist and his colleagues found that participants "considered a world containing an additional happy person better and a world containing an additional unhappy person worse", with "no significant differences in the strength of these two preferences" (Caviola et al. 2022).

Second, the asymmetry position produces some uncomfortable results. Let us assume John's position that a world with an additional

170   Stephen Cave

happy person is no better or worse than a world without that person. Let us call the world without an additional person World 0, or W0. Now imagine a couple face a choice. They can choose to conceive a child now, knowing that this child will have a life that is worth living but interspersed with periods of severe illness (let us call this World 1, or W1). Or they can wait three months before conceiving, at which time they can access a new treatment that is given at birth, and which will ensure their child will not have this severe illness (W2). If we follow the asymmetry view, according to which there is no reason to morally favour a world with an additional happy person over a world without that person, then both W1 and W2 are no better or worse than W0. But if both W1 and W2 are no better or worse than W0, then W1 and W2 are no better or worse than each other.

I think most people would disagree with this. I (and—from what we can infer from the survey mentioned above—others too) think that W2 is better than W1, and that the couple should wait. In which case, we *do* think that the degree of happiness of 'merely possibly people' is morally relevant. The simplest way out of the conundrum posed by this example is to admit that W2 is better than W1 because it is a world with greater happiness than W1, and that both W2 and W1 are better than W0, because they both are worlds with greater happiness than W0 (I take this argument from MacAskill 2022, pp. 176–177). If one possible future is better than the other, then we have a prima facie moral reason to bring it about, if it is in our power to do so. To relate this back to our debate: if the possible future in which there are new generations is a happier one than the possible future without such generations, and it is within our power to bring into existence these new generations, then, other things being equal, we have a moral reason to bring them into existence.

2.3   Is a Future with More Generations Better?

Would a possible future with new generations be better than one in which a single generation lives forever? In this subsection, we shall explore this question. But first, a note on the approach I am taking. The example above of worlds W0 to W2, and my discussion below will take a utilitarian approach. Simply put, **utilitarianism** is the view that ethics boils down to maximising happiness and minimising suffering. Utilitarianism isn't the only contemporary ethical tradition to have brought future generations into the sphere of moral consideration. For example, those who subscribe to a rights-based approach have argued that future people might have rights that we ought to respect (Gosseries 2012), and followers of contractarian approaches have included future people in the (imagined) social group who must agree a contract of norms that is binding on us today (Rawls 1971). But in recent years, utilitarianism has been the most influential ethical tradition for considering our obligations to future generations, so it is the one I will draw on here.

The utilitarian approach begins with accepting that our moral obligations extend across time as well as space. So, for example, if I break a bottle in a children's playground, it doesn't matter whether a toddler cuts herself on the shards tomorrow or five years from now—the harm done is the same. Therefore if I break the bottle today and know the playground won't be used for five years, my moral obligation to clean up the glass is undiminished by the fact that it is only toddlers who have not yet been born who will be harmed. There are many different versions of utilitarianism, but broadly speaking, this approach to ethics obliges us to work towards a world with the greatest happiness and least suffering over time. For some—a growing movement of 'longtermists' (see box)—this means taking seriously the well-being of generations far into the future (MacAskill 2022).

Longtermism and Effective Altruism

Longtermism is an ethical stance that gives weight to future generations and the long term future of humanity. It is an important concept in **Effective Altruism**, a movement that aims to use evidence and reason to determine the best way of doing good. Both longermists and effective altruists frequently draw on utilitarian ethics, inspired by the philosopher Peter Singer. Influential effective altruists such as William MasAskill have argued for focussing on (among other things) risks that technology could pose to the future of civilisation, such as from a powerful rogue AI. This has made both longtermism and effective altruism controversial, as critics argue that they de-prioritise real, present-day suffering in favour of mitigating highly speculative possible future harms.

172   Stephen Cave

We cannot do full justice to the question here, but we can briefly ask how a utilitarian might see the question of whether it would be ethical for a particular generation to become immortal (or very, very long-lived) and abstain from having children. From a utilitarian point of view, the question is which scenario is more likely to generate the greatest happiness: one in which a single generation (us, for example) lives indefinitely, or one in which each generation dies and new generations are born. In asking this question, we are of course deeply into the realm of speculation. But this speculation relates very directly to all the prudential arguments for and against living forever that we have been examining in this book so far.

In the first scenario, we would have a generation free from ageing and disease, free to pursue countless hobbies, professions, relationships and so on. No doubt this could be a happy prospect for many years. Though as we noted in Chapter 3, if these people were radically life-extended, they would not be immune to death, and therefore not free from mortal dread. Indeed, as we discussed, their fear of death might be exacerbated by knowing they have much more to lose. We have also discussed at length the many other woes that might beset them, such as boredom, meaninglessness and becoming stuck in all kinds of ruts.

In the second scenario, by contrast, countless new generations will take their turns facing the joys and tribulations of life. We can imagine many different variations on this theme. But if we are genuinely facing a choice of whether to radically extend the lives of one generation or not, it is safe to assume that the technology will exist to substantially reduce physical suffering. Would a scenario in which 100 generations of people live to the age of 100 produce more overall happiness than a scenario in which a single generation lives to the age of 10,000? My view is that it would: that those successive generations would be more full of creativity, inspiration, optimism and joy than a single generation of Methuselahs would be. In which case, a utilitarian approach to ethics would oblige us to bring these other generations into being.

But this is hard to prove, and others might see it differently. I also do not think that utilitarianism is the only useful approach to ethics, though it can be illuminating. My original argument in Chapter 1 did not appeal to any particular theory of ethics, but something vaguer—an intuition of wrongness. Recall that I have divided arguments for and against living forever into the prudential, which concern self-interest, and the ethical, which concern our

Reply to John Martin Fischer's Reply 173

obligations to others. From a prudential point of view, it might be rational to live as long as one wants, with no regard to future generations (though I have of course argued that this might not be in one's interest.) But from an ethical point of view, it is not clear that it is right for one generation to declare themselves the last, and to hog this planet forever, instead of handing the baton on to countless further generations that could follow. At the very least, it seems selfish—an attribute we generally consider a vice, and the opposite of virtues such as benevolence, generosity and concern for others.

I won't pursue this argument further: John agrees that prohibiting having children "would be unenforceable except by means that are morally abhorrent", and it seems likely that some people will want to continue having children. Therefore, while he argues against a moral obligation to create future generations, he offers a scenario in which there nevertheless would be future generations. How then will overpopulation be avoided? By the market: because radical life extension treatment is likely to be affordable only by a few. But that, of course, leads to the other horn of the dilemma— the problem of social injustice.

3 Conclusion

In this brief chapter, I first explored further some of the prudential worries about living forever. I argued that the various forms of boredom, ennui and meaninglessness to which the immortal could be prone, can be seen as all lying on a **Spectrum of Despond**. Solving a problem at one point on the spectrum could just push one towards a problem at another point. For example, the immortalist might avoid boredom with hedonistic pleasures, such as a glass of wine while watching a lovely sunset, or perhaps something more adrenaline-pumping. But such pleasures, no matter how fine or how exciting, would likely pale after enough repetition, leading to ennui. Such ennui could perhaps be avoided by a deeper engagement with the great issues of one's day. But we saw that over a long enough period of time, these engagements would seem absurd and contradictory, leading to meaninglessness. And so on.

Second, I have attempted to defend the idea that we might be morally obliged to pass on the baton to future generations. I pointed out some difficulties with the *asymmetry* position that John assumes, according to which we *are* obliged to *not* bring into being future people who would suffer, but we are *not* obliged to bring into being future people who would be happy. While noting that other ethical theories also include obligations to future people, I sketched a *utilitarian* argument for why it would be morally better for generations to succeed one another much as they do now, rather than for one generation to inherit the Earth.

I will now briefly sum up what I have argued in my contributions to this book—and also what I have not argued. The latter matters, because my position can easily be misread. If one argues against the *possibility* of immortality (as I have elsewhere[1]) and against the *desirability* of immortality (as I have in this volume), then one can find oneself portrayed as an 'apologist' for death, as someone who thinks our allotted three score years and ten are always sufficient (Gruman 1966). Certainly, there are such thinkers, but I am not one of them. I hope that when I am 70 or 80, I will be as happy and healthy as I am now, and I am sure that if I am so lucky, then I will want to continue living. If in 2050 I am offered an elixir that would grant me a few more decades, I am fairly sure I would accept that offer. Contrary to John's assessment, I do not think I am a curmudgeon now, and I hope I won't become one any time soon.

But for how long would I want to keep taking such an elixir? To help answer this, we can summarise how the arguments we have considered in the preceding chapters relate to our four modes of 'living forever'.

The literal interpretation of 'living forever' is what we have called **true immortality**—a condition in which one cannot die. John has agreed with me that this condition is not one we should choose, for various reasons. For example, it could result in us being condemned to eternal suffering with no way out. Even if we were not so condemned—even under what John calls 'favourable conditions'—I have argued that the problems of boredom, meaninglessness, and so on, would become inevitable for a finite human being given infinite time. It is notable that John and I concur that true immortality would not be worthy of choice, not only considering it is the literal interpretation of the question we are debating, but also considering that billions of people around the world believe that they *are* truly immortal.

---

1. (Cave 2012)

We have also considered **contingent immortality**: a condition in which a person could live (literally) forever, but could also choose to end it. As with the true immortal, I believe that the problems of boredom, meaninglessness, etc., would catch up with the contingently immortal person eventually. Such a person would, however, have a get-out clause: unlike the true immortal, they could choose to end it all if the millennia began to drag. However, I argued in Chapter 3 that it is very hard to see how the contingent immortal could ever rationally use such an exit clause, in which case it offers less reassurance than at first sight.

Our next category is **radical life extension**, a condition in which we are immune to ageing and disease. This is John's favoured interpretation of 'living forever', and he has aimed to defend its desirability 'under favourable conditions'. Would it be rational to swig an elixir that promised this condition? Of the various problems with immortality that I have sketched in the preceding chapters, which of them would apply to someone who has swigged such an elixir would depend greatly on their particular circumstances. For example, certain personalities are more prone to boredom and ennui than others, or to procrastination; certain material conditions are more attractive, and others more likely to induce ennui. John has argued that it is imaginable that at least some people in at least some material circumstances could be happy for millennia, and that therefore for them, under those conditions, radical life extension could be worthy of choice. I have argued that these conditions have never pertained for significant lengths of time in this world, and that it would therefore not be prudentially rational to choose radical life extension. Whether you think it might be anyway worth giving it a go—to try it and see, as it were—could depend on how you see the question of the 'exit clause' mentioned above.

In addition to these considerations, I have argued that the question of whether we should choose radical life extension also has ethical elements. I suggested that the two main ethical considerations form a dilemma: if many people have access to radical life extension there will be a problem of overpopulation; but if only a few do, then this will exacerbate social injustice.

Finally, we have also considered **moderate life extension**. This is not a very plausible interpretation of 'living forever', but it is interesting because it is conceivably within the grasp of our civilisation in the foreseeable future. In my view, the prudential problems

176 Stephen Cave

of immortality, such as boredom, meaninglessness and procrastination are *not* inevitable for someone with a life expectancy of 160. For a society that had made the breakthroughs necessary for moderate life extension, I suggest that the ethical problems of overpopulation and social injustice would be much more pressing. But that is not to say they would be insurmountable, and any resulting downsides would have to be weighed against the potential increase in wisdom and happiness that could come from longer lives.

On the one hand, the question of whether we should live forever is an ancient philosophical topic, which can help us to understand what matters most to us, and how we should think of life in the face of death. But on the other hand, with scientific, technological and medical advances only accelerating, the question of how much longer it is prudential and ethical to want to live is one that is topical, even urgent. While my and John's duty in this debate book has been to sharpen our points of difference, it has been illuminating to see the many points of convergence, and the emerging consensus on what the issues are. In the next chapter, John will have the last word. But let me end my contribution to this book by agreeing with him that the dream of living longer can be a call to action: let us work to ensure that everyone can enjoy long and happy lives on a planet that can sustain us and other species far into the future. That should keep us busy for many generations to come.

Chapter 6

Reply to Stephen Cave's Reply

John Martin Fischer

Contents

1 Introduction 177
2 What Am I Arguing For? 180
3 Rationality and Procrastination 182
4 The Zen of Immortality 183
5 Life-Stages, Values, and Recognizability 187
6 Societal Adjustments 187
7 Summary 189

I Introduction

Stephen's second essay, like his first, is elegant and insightful, and offers challenges to my views that invite (and require!) me to clarify them. In particular, he homes in on important questions about what exactly I'm arguing for, in contending that you *should* choose radical life extension under favorable circumstances. If I don't believe the various conditions involved in "favorable circumstances" will be satisfied, what does it mean for me to contend that you should choose such radical life extension? Further, what is the role of an "exit strategy" in my thinking about the choice worthiness of radical life extension?

Stephen returns to the problems of procrastination and rational planning for the future in a radically extended life. I have pointed out that the nature of lived human experience places importance on the "now"; we want our pains (and negative experiences) to end as soon as possible, other things equal, and we want our pleasures (and positive experiences) to start as soon as possible, other things equal.

DOI: 10.4324/9781003105442-9

But how does this priority of the present relate to the importance of giving appropriate weight to yourself in the future (your "future selves")? Doesn't rational planning sometimes require sacrifice now for better outcomes later? After all, no pain, no gain.

I have suggested that at least some (if not most) of the seductive appeal of immortality curmudgeonliness (based on the boredom worry) stems from taking an extractive, rather than immersive, view of the activities of human life. Stephen points out that even an immersive orientation cannot insulate us from boredom and alienation, given enough time. Further, he describes an "irony" in my invocation of mindful meditation, which comes originally from a Buddhist tradition that aims for the achievement of "nirvana" or a "blowing out" of the self, as in the extinguishing of a flame. This doesn't seem much like living forever/radical life extension!

Stephen presses on Samuel Scheffler's point that our mortal lives have a distinctive set of stages, which would not exist in a radically extended life, thus rendering such a life unrecognizable as a human life worthy of choice. He concedes that the last century has brought roughly a doubling of average human lifespan but points out that this is largely due to the significant reduction of childhood mortality. He thus argues we don't have evidence of our capacity to adapt to and recognise, human lives with radically different stages (or structures of stages). He raises additional concerns about the recognizability of human life with a very different set of stages, especially regarding the currently understood purposes and possible accomplishments at each stage.

Finally, he raises challenges immortality would pose for our social structures and expectations. One might reasonably wonder what would happen to education, marriage, careers, mortgages and other "contracts," public benefits, health insurance, and so forth. Even though we might be able to imagine radical changes to our institutions and practices, he reminds us that the social changes needed to implement them would be considerable. Mere imaginability does not entail feasibility.

There is much to address here, and I am grateful for the opportunity. This debate has opened my eyes to issues I hadn't fully appreciated and heightened my view that offering a satisfying—and convincing—answer to the question of our book is not easy or straightforward. Like with all great perennial philosophical questions, there is much to be said on each side.

Reply to Stephen Cave's Reply 179

Before I jump into a discussion of each of Stephen's points just sketched, I wish to defend Sunday afternoons! He points out that Susan Ernz noted that some who desire immortality can't even figure out what to do on Sunday afternoons, and Douglas Adams describes "that terrible listlessness which starts to set in at about 2:55 [Sunday afternoons], when you know that you've had all the baths you can usefully have that day, ... and you will enter the long dark tea-time of the soul."

The way I feel about it is different! For many, Sunday afternoons provide us a space to take a break from work (or perhaps study) and explore activities of our own choosing. To start with what might seem a trivial example, Sunday afternoons in the USA feature the National Football League, and many fans look forward to the season with great anticipation, in some cases deeply identifying with their teams and "living and dying" with their fortunes. Perhaps Ms. Ernz is not an NFL fan, but athletics in general, participating or observing, can be rewarding and engaging on a Sunday afternoon. Playing, or watching, the "beautiful game" of football (or what Americans call "soccer") can also be a pleasant way to spend a Sunday afternoon.

Perhaps, though, Ernz is not a huge soccer fan either. How about a walk in a lovely garden, park, or bustling urban neighborhood, a game of chess with a good friend, cooking and enjoying a delicious supper with family, going to an art gallery or concert? And don't forget about a leisurely Sunday brunch, extending into the afternoon, lingering over one too many mimosas! Ok, a cup of pedestrian tea accompanied by stale cookies might lead to a dark tea-time of the soul, but what about High Tea at the Ritz Carleton in London, shared with old and cherished friends? The cup of tea might be half-full, not half-empty (although one's wallet might be)!

Yes, we can take a dreary perspective on life. This is characteristic of depression, and it can manifest itself chronically even in persons who are not clinically depressed. There are people who cannot squeeze much joy out of life, and there are days when tea-time is dark for all of us, even in California! This bleakness is obviously not *unique* to immortality, and, I suggest, not *necessary* in it either. Why do so many people say, "Thank God it's Friday"? Because it leads to Saturday and even Sunday afternoon!

2 What Am I Arguing For?

I have emphasised that I would not choose radical life extension under *unfavorable* circumstances—terrible, unrelenting physical and/or mental pain, extreme poverty, inadequate food, shelter, water, medical care, a filthy, overcrowded environment, and so forth. The question of whether to choose such a life is just not interesting, nor is it the one that philosophers have addressed. In the contemporary literature, almost all discussions of the potential worthiness of choice of radical life extension have started with Bernard Williams's discussion of Elina Makropulos. Williams quite explicitly contends that Elina is an example of the inevitability of boredom and alienation in such a life, *even under favorable circumstances*. As I emphasised in my second essay in this debate, the problems with radical life extension on which Williams focuses come from *human nature*, not pollution, overpopulation, poverty, and so forth. Most, although certainly not all, contemporary discussions of immortality, both pro and con, have focused on the question of whether radical life extension would be necessarily boring and/or alienating for a human being "with a certain character" (in Williams's phrase).

This then is the primary (although not sole) question I seek to explore here: is there something about human nature that would inevitably lead to a dark night, or even tea-time, of the soul, including hyperboredom and detachment from life, in a radically extended life? Boredom is not the fundamental worry for Stephen, and we have discussed a range of other issues, including problems of motivation and procrastination, the stages of life and recognizability, meaningfulness, value, and so forth. By focusing on radical life extension under favorable conditions, we can figure out whether these worries are significant (and even decisive). That is, we want to know whether a significantly longer life, simply in virtue of being so and not because of a deterioration of circumstances, would issue in the indicated problems. In order properly to evaluate the various objections, we need to figure out whether the circumstances of radically extended life themselves would lead to the indicated problems.

The curmudgeons present objections, which contend that specific problems would emerge from a radically extended life, simply by being so. We can then evaluate these claims, assuming favorable circumstances, unlikely as they may be. Is this strategy like that of

Reply to Stephen Cave's Reply   181

the benighted Professor Merman, who proclaims that we should build a city under the sea?

My claim, in contrast to his, is *qualified*. I seek to convince you that you should choose radical life extension, *under favorable circumstances*. Now the good Professor Merman might retreat to the claim that the citizens of the city should build a metropolis under the sea, *assuming* its feasibility (which he deems highly unlikely). I would have no objection to this, but, of course, there would be no point in his going "from conference to symposium to City Hall" asserting this sort of highly qualified and conditional claim. The claim might be correct, but its assertion is pointless.

Stephen writes:

> John argues that we should choose to live forever if (and only if) we can be sure that a long list of conditions will be met.
>
> We cannot be sure that this long list of conditions will be met. Indeed, the lesson of history is that it is highly unlikely that these conditions will be met.
>
> We therefore should not choose to live forever.

He adds, "The debate therefore seems to be won."

But we must proceed with caution here, being careful not to violate the philosophical speed limits. Despite the question in the title of the book, and perhaps some dramatic flourishes, I have not been addressing the question of whether you should choose radical life extension, without qualification. To reiterate: my project has been to argue that you should choose radical life extension, assuming favorable circumstances.

Even though it seems absurd for Merman to implore the city council to build a city under the sea, when he believes it nearly impossible to do so, it does *not* follow that it would be absurd for me to assert that you should choose radical life extension under favorable circumstances, even though I recognise that it will be difficult to bring about such circumstances. I believe it is still very much an open question whether we will solve the challenges to our continued flourishing; I do not think it is nearly impossible (or worse). I'm an immortality realist, but the concerns about favorable conditions are a call to action, not necessarily a path to despair.

In true immortality you would have no exit strategy, and thus choosing it would be extremely risky. In contrast, in radical life

182 John Martin Fischer

extension there would indeed be the possibility of ending one's life. Stephen points out that suicide, even physician-assisted suicide under prescribed conditions, is not universally accepted as morally acceptable, nor is it possible to implement it in an unobjectionable way. I believe however that, in our current mortal lives, we should be granted the right to physician-assisted suicide, even when not suffering from a terminal disease. Death with dignity should be recognised as a basic human right, even more so in a radically extended life.

This would admittedly require a change in our institutions and laws, and perhaps even in our moral understanding of these issues, but, in my view, so be it. I believe forcing someone to live, or withholding the reasonable opportunity for assistance in suicide, when he or she is in intolerable pain or otherwise does not want to continue to live, is morally unacceptable. Of course, we will need to fashion laws to ensure that the choice to die is genuinely voluntary and not the result of curable depression.

So: what am I arguing for? I contend that you should choose radical life extension, under favorable circumstances. Radical life extension, by definition, opens the possibility of an exit strategy, if things get bad enough. Would it never be rational to take this opportunity? After all, as Stephen points out, given enough time, one might be able to escape one's misery and even live a happy life. For some, this bare possibility would be enough, but I'd be more comfortable with the "fallback" option of being able to have assistance in ending my life, if I were to believe that it will most likely involve great suffering and misery (physical or mental). I would want this option, even if I were to know that it would be *possible* that this belief is incorrect. Although most depressed people do in fact recover, many do not and suffer chronic, severe, and "intractable" depression.

Rationality does not require certainty. I am even feisty enough to wish to put aside the question of rationality and express a preference for the availability of an exit option freely chosen, rational or not. As normally understood, *autonomy* does not require rationality, and it is autonomy that we must respect here.

3 Rationality and Procrastination

I have argued that the nature of human experience constrains our practical reasoning in certain ways regarding pleasures and pains. We have a **temporal bias** toward the immediate present: we want

Reply to Stephen Cave's Reply | 183

our pains over, and our pleasures present, as soon as possible. Stephen correctly points out, however, that the generalization of a very strong form of this sort of temporal bias would lead to problems. Mick fritters away his life, chasing the pleasures of the moment. Prudence requires a global, not just local, maximation of good. Further, Stephen finds it puzzling how a rational agent could reasonably aim for global maximation in a radically extended life.

I agree that we should not always privilege the present to the significant detriment of our future selves. With respect to severe pain, the present takes almost absolute precedence, but in most contexts, we will need to make decisions about our present and future interests, where these may conflict. In seeking a *local* maximum, we will adopt our preferred policies here, some **discounting the future** heavily, others treating the future just like the present, and most choosing something in-between. Presumably, severe pain and intense pleasure would be weighted significantly in determining a plausible local maximum.

How would one conceive of a *global* maximum in a radically extended life? This is a good question, and it points to another instance of the ways in which such a life would be different from a mortal life. I think we would simply have to select a "time horizon" relative to which we aim at maximization, realising that this structure would be flexible and may change as we go on in life. It is not too different from how we think of things in our mortal lives, as we sometimes establish time horizons for maximation that do not extend all the way to the (envisaged) end of our lives, and we need to stay flexible. We might think of our practical reasoning within these time-horizons as in-between seeking only a local maximum and a "totalizing" global maximum.

4 The Zen of Immortality

I have commended an immersive, rather than an extractive, model of the value of experience and activity. I suggested that much of the resistance to radical life extension might stem from an explicit or implicit acceptance of an extractive model. We shouldn't ask what we can "get out of" an activity, but how best to "get into it". Mindfulness meditation and aiming for "flow-states", as discussed in Chapter 2, can enhance our ability to immerse ourselves in life. We are thereby at home in the world, rather than tourists.

Stephen's friend was a world-class opera singer, who fully immersed herself in the music and performances over two decades.

184 John Martin Fischer

(In the play and opera, Elina Makropulos was also an opera singer!) This however was not enough to keep up her interest, even in a finite life, and she got "burnt out" due to the "downsides," including "the physical demands [and] relentless competition for the top roles, and so on." Stephen concludes, correctly in my view, that immersion does not *guarantee* immunity to boredom.

Note however that specific problematic features of Stephen's example would not need to be present in a radically extended human life (just as they are not in all mortal lives). As in our discussion above of the importance of "rotating one's pleasures," it is important that one can fully immerse oneself in a deeply rewarding activity without having to pursue it relentlessly—without pause to rest and live a balanced life containing other similarly rewarding activities. One needs to distribute one's activities in a sensible way, and it is optimal to have a variety of activities, immersion in which can be deeply meaningful or even just pleasurable. Additionally, of course, I am assuming, as part of our thought experiment in this debate, a level of physical health and strength that would sustain an active schedule over time and would not diminish (in contrast to our finite lives). Even in our ordinary lives, some opera singers, musicians in general, artists, academics, and so forth *never* tire of pursuing their passions. They have probably learned how to do so within the context of at least some balance.

Stephen observes that my appeal to meditative practices of the sort associated with Buddhism is "ironic". He contends that Buddhism is a "pessimistic" doctrine that aims at the extinction of the self. The package of views he attributes to Buddhism does not seem to commend itself to a defense of the potential desirability of certain forms of radical life extension as embodied human beings.

It is perhaps unfair to dwell on this observation of Stephen's, so far as he presents it as merely "ironic", but it might be instructive to explore it a bit. First, "mindfulness", although associated with Buddhism, is not unique to it. The main *initial* goal is to "still the chatter" in the mind (to tame the "wild tiger" of mental wandering), but this is not an end in itself. The *ultimate* goal is to prepare us to see reality as it is. All spiritual paths have practices that are similar to this. What distinguishes Buddhism is the particular account of ultimate reality, where this is "emptiness", including the view that the "self" never existed. These doctrines, however, should not lead us to despair; rather, they allow us to resist interpretations of reality that result in frustration and deep sadness.

Reply to Stephen Cave's Reply   185

Buddhism is not a "pessimistic" doctrine. Its account of *dukka* (suffering) is stated in the Four Noble Truths. They are generally taken as offering a medical model: describing a disease, its causes, the cure, and a course of treatment. Here's a brief version:

1. There is suffering—dissatisfaction, "dis-ease".
2. There is the origination of suffering: suffering arises from causes.
3. This is the cessation of suffering: suffering can be prevented.
4. There is a path to the cessation of suffering: *The Noble Eightfold Path.*

The key to avoiding unnecessary (self-inflicted) suffering lies in our desires. Stephen is right about this, but the Buddha knew (from experience) that asceticism doesn't work. Desire can't be eliminated or fully overcome—some desires, such as hunger and thirst are "hard-wired." He also knew that all action, including trying to relieve suffering, requires desire. Rather than eliminating all desires, we must eliminate those rooted in a false conception of who we are. The Buddha distinguishes a *specific set* of desires that are problematic and the root of suffering. These are "**cravings**". The key is to give up the cravings, not desire *per se*.

Stephen incorrectly equates **Nirvana** with non-existence, "the end of the person as an individual." We need to distinguish the **person** from the **self**. For our purposes, the self can be understood as the **simple self,** as in our discussion, "Would it be me?" in Chapter 2. **Buddhism** does indeed deny that the "self" exists, conceived of as a simple self—a "particular" that has mental states and persists through time. We are not "selves," so understood, at the basic metaphysical (or analytical) level. But the rejection of the existence of simple selves does *not* entail a denial that we exist as persons, as we ordinarily take ourselves to be. (Mark Siderits develops this sort of interpretation of the "**no-self view**" in Siderits 2021, and I rely on it, as well as his presentation, here.)

The no-self view is *not* that we don't exist, only that we don't exist *understood in a certain way*. It might be called, "the no-simple-self" view. We can acquire this view and thus achieve **enlightenment** through meditation. Nirvana then is not the extinction of the person (or a "place"). Rather, it is *living* in recognition of the fact that we are not, and never have been, simple selves. Given this enlightened re-orientation, we can be released from craving, and thus we can escape *dukkha*, sometimes defined as "pain", but perhaps better understood as unfulfilled desire (or, perhaps, the suffering that comes from unfulfilled desires).

One of the major interpretations of Buddhism emphasises the *psychological insights* provided by its main tenets. There are even "Buddhist psychotherapists". So understood, Buddhism offers important ways of enhancing the quality of our lives. It could offer helpful techniques for living a psychologically healthy radically extended life. Radical life extension would also give us all the more time to help to relieve suffering, an ideal of certain forms of Buddhism.

Buddhism is completely compatible with living a (desirable) radically extended life as an embodied person—a person in the "ordinary" sense. Further, enlightenment is precisely the path to a happy, rewarding life—an escape from the cycle of transitory pleasures and suffering that characterises our unenlightened life. Given that Nirvana is not annihilation, but the end of unnecessary suffering, a Buddhist can embrace the possibility of radical life extension. The doctrine of reincarnation is also fully compatible with radical life extension.

Buddhism

Is Buddhism a religion? In some ways it is. Religions are concerned with the afterlife and the possibility of "salvation" or the achievement of something better after death. A distinctive feature of religious views is belief in an afterlife, of some sort or another. Although the question is complex, it is fair to attribute this sort of view to Buddhism in the form of reincarnation. (Buddhism comes in many varieties, and not all have the same views of the afterlife and the notion of survival, but they share *some* view to the effect that we survive the death of our current bodies.)

In another way, Buddhism is not a religion, because it lacks a "creation story" and a supreme or "perfect" being—a God, who created the universe. The answer to our question, then, is "yes and no." Buddhism is a religion in some ways, and not in others. It is undoubtedly a philosophy and offers significant psychological insights.

5 Life-Stages, Values, and Recognizability

I have invoked the fact that our average lifespan has roughly doubled in the last century (or so) in support of my contention that we have already got used to significant changes in the lengths (and thus ratios) of our life-stages. Stephen correctly points out that much of the doubling is due to a significant decrease in infant mortality, although he also concedes that "extra years are being added to the elderly". Indeed, more and more people are living into older age--their seventies, eighties, and even nineties.

I agree that this increase in life-expectancy does not show that we have adjusted to *radical* changes in the stages. A more careful formulation is that we have in fact adjusted seamlessly to considerable changes, especially in the length of "adulthood" (roughly speaking). As I pointed out, this resulted in Erik Erikson's wife adding a new stage to their iconic presentation of the (previously) eight stages of human life. I do not see why we couldn't recognise human lives with certain differences in the stages (to accommodate even longer life-expectancy). This could involve conceiving of stages as longer or adding stages (or both).

The contention that we could not recognise human lives with different stages implies an undue conservativism. Stephen agrees that it would have been disastrous if we had accepted a version of Scheffler's argument in 1900, and I do not see how the circumstances are relevantly different now. It would have been arbitrary to have accepted 40 as the maximum number of years consistent with recognizability of life-stages. Why wouldn't it be any less arbitrary to adopt 80 now?

Values may well attach to stages, as Scheffler contends, but why not suppose that the values change or are repurposed, given a different sequence of stages (or stage-lengths). If we need to recognise stage-dependent values to grasp a distinctively human life, this is fully compatible with the stages and values changing. The problem would come if recognizability of a distinctively human life would require recognition of the *specific* stage-dependent values we *currently* have, but I do not see why this would be so (and Scheffler hasn't offered an argument for this stronger claim).

6 Societal Adjustments

Stephen is correct to point to the many changes in our "widely shared norms and social expectations, public institutions, laws, the structure of the economy, and so on" that would be required if some (perhaps sizable) group of human beings were to attain radical life-extension. This would be on top of other significant changes we have discussed, including conceptualizations of our lives as narratives, the lengths and ratios of life-stages, rational planning, motivation, certain values, and so many more.

I have emphasised that we should not expect radically extended lives to be just like our mortal lives. They could be *sufficiently similar* to the mortal lives we currently lead to be recognizable as human lives worthy of choice. Given all the required changes noted above, however, a reasonable question emerges as to whether the envisaged lives are indeed enough like our mortal lives to be recognizable as (potentially desirable) human lives. Recall that we might conclude that radically life extended persons would not have children. This in itself would be a major change.

I believe we could come up with—and I have suggested--ways of addressing *each* necessitated change—each difference in ways of seeing ourselves and others, and in structuring social norms, expectations, and laws. Even so, the changes would *add up* to a totality that might represent such a huge departure from our ordinary, mortal lives that the lives under consideration would indeed be unrecognizable as human lives (capable of being happy and meaningful). I do not think we must draw this conclusion, but I also do not think we can easily dismiss the concern.

Whereas it might seem relatively easy and straightforward to imagine an immortal existence, this is very far from the truth. There are importantly different ways of defining or specifying the kind of immortality in question, and many significant adjustments in our conceptions of ourselves and others, and our social institutions, that would be required.

Stephen and I have clarified different notions of immortality and have focused especially, but not exclusively, on radically extended life (under favorable circumstances). I have taken the view that the individual adjustments, considered one by one, do not force changes that are too big, but I fully agree that, taken together, the emerging picture of living forever (even "merely" radical life extension) is going to be very different from our current, mortal lives. Immortality—even radical life extension--is hard to wrap our minds around. Given this, I cannot be confident that I'm fully grasping what such a life would be like, and thus I must temper my enthusiastic recommendation that you choose radical life extension (assuming favorable circumstances). I still urge a positive answer to the question of this book, but with a due respect for its complexity. This should not be surprising, given that debates about these issues have raged for millennia. To grapple with the issues, especially with a thoughtful partner like Stephen, is both deeply rewarding and humbling.

7 Summary

The central point I have made in this final contribution is a clarification of exactly what I've been arguing for. I've argued that you should choose radical life extension, assuming favorable circumstances. In making this assumption, I concede that it is not likely that these will obtain, but I also insist that they may. (We should certainly make heroic efforts to ensure that they do.) I do not fall into immortality despair. I have thus been concerned with the primary issues in the philosophical debates about radical life extension's worthiness of choice: boredom, alienation, procrastination, recognizability, value, meaning, and so forth. I have argued that *these* would not necessarily characterise radical life extension.

Throughout my essays in this debate, I have emphasised certain themes. One should not expect radical life extension to be *just like* living a mortal life. One should not apply a double standard, and also it is enough that the envisaged lives be *sufficiently similar* to ordinary mortal human lives. We shouldn't conceive of a radically extended life as full of merely extractive activities, pursued in a single-minded, relentless way, or extrapolate from the manifest suffering and deterioration of many elderly people in our current circumstances to conclusions about very different ones.

Just as with mortal lives, we need to conceive of radically extended lives as containing a sensible distribution of activities within social contexts that allow for flourishing. This will certainly involve rethinking our social structures along with our personal lives—aspirations, expectations, schedules and plans, expenditures of energy, relationships, and families. Some of these could, arguably, benefit from serious and thoughtful reconsideration in any case, especially as we evolve in our moral and political views, and pressures on our planet become increasingly worrisome.

The idea of moving toward a more immersive life, present in the "now" and deeply connected to the wondrous beauty of human beings and nature, is an attractive goal, living forever or not. Mindfulness meditation is one (although not the only) way of aligning with these values. We do not have to accept any particular religious framework in adopting practices to induce flow-states and reject extractive models of human flourishing. Being "grounded" and undistracted is a good platform upon which to pursue our projects, which would not lose their importance in a radically extended life, as well as to seek happiness. We can venture out from a safe harbor to fight the battles against social injustice and environmental degradation. To the extent that reflection on radical life extension brings all this to the fore, it is valuable, no matter how one comes down on the specific question we have debated.

Further Readings

We list here some important or useful articles and books about topics treated in this debate. Some of them have been referred to in these essays, but are included here to emphasize their significance *as a whole* (not just the specific elements to which we refer in the text). John has treated many of the elements of this debate, along with related issues, in his *Death, Immortality, and Meaning in Life* (Oxford University Press 2020). Stephen has previously covered a number of the philosophical and historical aspects of the quest to live forever in his book *Immortality* (Crown 2012).

Two thoughtful and accessible introductions to the philosophical issues posed by death and immortality are Todd May's *Death* (Acumen 2009) and Geoffrey Scarre's *Death* (Acumen 2007). The classic analysis of fictional and historical efforts to achieve immortality is Gerald G. Gruman, *A History of Ideas about the Prolongation of Life: The Evolution of Prolongevity Hypotheses to 1800* (American Philosophical Society 1966; reissued by Springer, 2003). Historian David Boyd Haycock's *Mortal Coil: A Short History of Living Longer* (Yale University Press 2008) covers some of the same ground, but brings the story up to the twenty-first century. For a contemporary discussion with an emphasis on the colorful figure Aubrey de Gray, see Jonathan Weiner, *Long for this World: The Strange Science of Immortality* (HarperCollins 2010).

Immortality requires persistence (forever) of the person—the *very same* person. Otherwise, the story is not one of one person's radically extended life, which is the subject of our book. There are helpful discussions of the philosophical concept of a person, and the identity of particular persons over time, in John Perry, ed., *Personal Identity* (University of California Press 1975), especially

192 Stephen Cave

the introductory essay; and John Perry, *A Dialogue on Personal Identity and Immortality* (Hackett Publishing Co. 1978). A more recent overview of theories of personal identity is found in Eric Olson's *What Are We? A Study in Personal Ontology* (Oxford University Press 2007).

Boredom is fascinating! Martin Heidegger discussed boredom in *The Fundamental Concepts of Metaphysics* (Indiana University Press 1995 [originally 1938]). Cheshire Calhoun's *Doing Valuable Time: The Present, the Future, and Meaningful Living* is especially insightful and helpful, and John relies on it in the text. An early and influential work (in contemporary research) is Otto Fenichel, "On the Psychology of Boredom," in *The Collected Papers of Otto Fenichel* (W.W. Norton 1953). See also Lars Svendsen, *A Philosophy of Boredom*; Sean Desmond Healy, *Boredom, Self, and Culture*; Patricia Meyer Stacks, *Boredom: The Literary History of a State of Mind*; and Andreas Elpidou, *Propelled: How Boredom, Frustration, and Anticipation Lead us to the Good Life* (Oxford University Press 2020), and Andreas Elipdou, ed., *The Moral Psychology of Boredom* (Rowman and Littlefield 2021). Elpidou's work and collection contain references to interesting empirical work on boredom, as well as philosophical reflections.

There is a large literature surrounding Bernard Williams's classic article on the Capek play's main character, "EM"/Elina Makropulos, discussed in the text. An interpretation and alternative formulation of Williams's argument is presented in Samuel Scheffler, *Death and the Afterlife* (Niko Kolodny, ed., Oxford University Press 2015). For critical discussions, see John Martin Fischer, "Why Immortality Is Not So Bad," *International Journal of Philosophical Studies* 2 (1994); and John Martin Fischer and Benjamin Mitchell-Yellin, "Immortality and Boredom," *Journal of Ethics* 18 (2014): 353–72. There is an excellent and in-depth study of Williams's article and the issues it raises in Connie S. Rosati, "The Makropulos Case: Reflections on Immortality and Agency," in Ben Bradley, Jens Johansson, and Fred Feldman, eds., *The Oxford Handbook on the Philosophy of Death* (Oxford University Press 2013). Jeremy Wiznewsky connects the contemporary discussions of Williams's curmudgeonly attitude toward immortality with Heidegger's views in "Is the Immortal Life Worth Living?" *International Journal for Philosophy of Religion* 58 (2005).

An influential recent discussion of obligations to future generations is found in William MacAskill's book *What We Owe The*

Future (Oneworld Publications 2022). This book is also a good introduction to the broader "longtermist" movement. MacAskill is an influential advocate of "effective altruism" (e.g., see his *Doing Good Better: Effective Altruism and How You Can Make a Difference*, Random House 2015), alongside Peter Singer—e.g., *The Most Good You Can Do: How Effective Altruism Is Changing Ideas About Living Ethically* (Yale University Press 2015). Somewhat more detailed, highly influential discussions of our obligations to future generations can also be found in Derek Parfit, *Reasons and Persons* (Oxford University Press 1984), and Jonathan Glover, *What Sort of People Should There Be?* (Penguin 1984).

Two fine explorations of the ethics and impacts of life extension are: John Davis, *New Methuselahs: The Ethics of Life Extension* (MIT Press 2018) and Christine Overall, *Aging, Death, and Human Longevity: A Philosophical Inquiry* (California University Press 2003). Two influential advocates of life extension from the transhumanist camp are the philosopher Nick Bostrom (e.g., "The Transhumanist FAQ: A General Introduction: Version 2.1", 2003, and "A History of Transhumanist Thought", 2005—both available online) and the futurist and inventor Ray Kurzweil (e.g., in *The Singularity is Near: When Humans Transcend Biology*, Viking, 2005, and *Fantastic Voyage: Live Long Enough to Live Forever*, with Terry Grossman, Rodale Books 2004).

For particularly helpful and clear explanations of philosophical ideas in Buddhism, see: Mark Siderits, *Buddhism as Philosophy*, 2nd Edition (Hackett 2020); and Amber Carpenter, *Indian Buddhist Philosophy* (Ancient Philosophers) (Routledge 2014). There is an excellent presentation of psychological insights of Buddhism in Robert Wright, *Why Buddhism Is True: The Science and Philosophy of Meditation* (Simon and Schuster 2017). For a "how-to" manual for "insight" or "mindfulness" meditation, see Joseph Goldstein and Jack Kornfeld, *Seeking the Heart of Wisdom: The Path of Insight Meditation* Reprint Edition. (Shambala Publishers 2001 (originally 1987)).

Kieran Setiya's groundbreaking books are insightful and wise explorations of the limitations of "project-based" conceptions of meaningfulness in life (among other topics). He emphasizes the importance of "atelic" activities (those that do not aim at an independent goal or purpose) in a rewarding life, and mindfulness meditation as a way of finding meaning in the "now", so to speak. See his *Midlife: A Philosophical Guide*, (Princeton University Press 2018) and *Life Is Hard: How Philosophy Can Help Us Find Our Way* (Riverhead Books 2022). A classic and still relevant exploration of the meaning and length of life is *On the Shortness of Life* by the Roman Stoic philosopher Seneca (in many translations, e.g. by C.D.N. Costa, Penguin 2012).

There are many fascinating (and equally many terrible) explorations of life extension in fiction. In this book, we have explored the 1922 play *The Makropulos Secret* by Karel Čapek, and the 1947 short story "The Immortal" by Jorge Luis Borges. In addition, technologically-enabled life extension is a staple theme of science fiction. Some classics of this genre include Rudy Rucker's *Ware Tetralogy*, which starts with *Software* (Ace Books 1982) and Robert Heinlein's tales of Lazarus Long, such as *Methuselah's Children* (Gnome Press 1958) and *Time Enough for Love* (G.P. Putnam's Sons 1973). More recent additions include Robert J. Sawyer's exploration of mind-uploading *Mindscan* (Tor 2005), and Cory Doctorow's utopian novel *Walkaway* (Tor 2017). Some of these are analyzed in John's essay (with Ruth Curl) "Philosophical Models of Immortality in Science Fiction", in *Immortal Engines*, Eric S. Rabkin, George Slusser, Gary Westfahl, eds., (University of Georgia Press 1996), and Stephen's essay "AI: Artificial Immortality and Narratives of Mind-Uploading", in *AI Narratives: A History of Imaginative Thinking about Intelligent Machines*, Cave, Dihal and Dillon, eds., (Oxford University Press 2020).

Glossary

Antediluvian Theme (Antediluvian) The view that in previous times (long ago) some people lived **Radically Extended Lives**. **Primitivism** adds to the contention that some such lives were attractive.

Apologist Gruman's term for proponents of the belief that immortality would not be worthy of choice. Fischer employs the term **Immortality Curmudgeon** or **Curmudgeon**.

Boredom A feeling characterised by a lack of interest in one's current activity, or a more general state of disengagement and indifference.

Carrying Capacity The maximum population size of a species that can be sustained by a specific environment. The "carrying capacity of the Earth" often refers to the maximum population of humans sustainable on this planet.

Contingent Immortality The state of being able to live forever (e.g., immune to ageing and disease, accident or violent death, etc.,) but also being able to die (e.g., by ceasing to take some **Elixir of Life**). Contrast with **True Immortality**, a state in which one cannot die.

Cravings Unhealthy desires, according to Buddhism. They cannot be satisfied, and this leads to **Dukkha** and the suffering that comes from unsatisfied desires.

Discounting the Future Giving less weight to one's own welfare in the future than in the present. A form of **Temporal Bias**. It is rational to discount the future to some extent, although people will differ on how much.

Dukkha In Indian religions such as Buddhism, the suffering that comes from, or is simply constituted by unsatisfied desires.

196 Glossary

Elixir of Life A potion (or similar substance) that grants the drinker immortality or **Radically Extended Life**, e.g., through immunity to ageing and disease.

Ennui Cave's term for **Hyperboredom**—deep and profound **Boredom** that presents itself as impossible to escape.

Ethical Reasons In contrast to **Prudential Reasons**, considerations that count in favor of actions, from a viewpoint that takes into account others' interests, as well as one's own.

Flow (Flow States) A process wherein one is fully immersed in what one is doing, not being aware of oneself, but, rather, the external world. Time seems to slow down or stop. The term "flow" was introduced for this concept by the psychologist Mihaly Csikszentmihalyi.

Fountain Theme The idea that there are somewhere magical waters (e.g., a river or spring) that grant the drinker immortality or **Radically Extended Life**, e.g., through immunity to ageing and disease. See also **Elixir of Life**.

Hyperboredom A deep and profound **Boredom** that presents itself as impossible to escape. Cave's term is **Ennui**. (To be distinguished from the very different concept **Hyperboreanism**.)

Hyperborean Theme (Hyperboreanism) The view that in some faraway places people live attractive immortal (or very long) lives. (To be distinguished from the very different concept **Hyperboredom**.)

Identity Criterion The requirement that a scenario purporting to describe immortality (or **Radically Extended Life**) genuinely describes the same person persisting through time. This will depend on the **Personal Identity Theory** one adopts.

Immortality Curmudgeon (Curmudgeon) Fischer's term for the view to which Gruman's term "**Apologist**" refers, according to which immortality would necessarily be unworthy of choice.

Immortality Optimist (Optimist) Another name for the view to which Gruman's term, **Prolongevist**, refers, according to which immortality could be worthy of choice (under certain circumstances).

Life Expectancy The amount of time (usually expressed in years) that a person of a given age in a given population is expected to live based on statistical averages (e.g., "life expectancy at birth for those born in 1950 in the USA"). Contrast with **Lifespan**.

Life Extension interventions to extend the **Lifespan** of particular humans, and/or the maximum human **Lifespan**.

Lifespan The actual number of years that a person lives (in contrast to **Life Expectancy**). "Maximum lifespan" refers to the longest that a member of a given species could live under ideal conditions, and is often set at the lifespan of the longest-lived member of that species reliably recorded—e.g., the maximum human lifespan is (currently) 122.

Longevity Having long life (e.g., living longer than the **Life Expectancy** for the relevant population).

Longtermism An ethical stance that gives substantial weight to future generations and the long term future of humanity. It is an important concept in "effective altruism", a movement that aims to use evidence and reason to determine the best way of doing good.

Meaninglessness A condition in which nothing seems to have significance.

Medical Immortality Another term for **Radically Extended Life**. Cave introduced this term in previous work, and Fischer has also employed it.

Mindfulness Meditation A form of meditation associated with various different traditions, including Buddhism, according to which one focuses the mind on an item or process (such as breathing) in an effort to be more "present" and avoid distraction.

Moderate Life Extension Interventions that result in an increase in **Life Expectancy** for a given population to c.120–160 years, so equalling or moderately exceeding the current maximum human **Lifespan**.

Nagel's Thought-Experiment You are asked to choose, each week, whether to continue to live (under favorable circumstances) one more week.

Nirvana Term from Indian religions (such as Buddhism, Hinduism, and Sikhism) referring to a state of liberation from suffering and the cycle of birth, death and rebirth.

Narratives Stories of a special sort. Typically they are thought to have meaning holism, emotional engagement, and endings.

No-Self View Buddhist view, similar to John Locke's memory theory of personal identity over time, according to which we are not **Simple Selves**. We are, nevertheless, **Persons** as we normally think of ourselves.

Optimistic Realism The view, propounded by Fischer in this debate, that it is possible, although not likely, that we will live

198 Glossary

attractive **Radically Extended Lives** in the future. It is "optimistic" in the sense that nothing about human nature rules out **Radical Life Extension,** but "realistic" in acknowledging pressing challenges from global climate change.

Overpopulation when the population of a given species (e.g., humans) exceeds the **Carrying Capacity** for a given environment (e.g., the planet).

Person The term we use for ourselves, understood as an individual with a **Narrative** and a set of memories, values, and so forth. Not all such properties are necessary for the persistence of a person, but some are (depending on one's **Personal Identity Theory**). In the text we distinguish **Persons** and **Simple Selves** as regards the Buddhist **No-Self View.**

Personal Identity Theory In philosophy, a theory of what kind of thing human people are (e.g., a **Soul** or an animal or a set of data), which also determines the conditions for their persistence over time (e.g., the survival of the **Soul,** or the continued biological function of the animal, or the continuity of certain psychological data). See also **Identity Criterion.**

Primitivism Combined with **Hyperboreanism,** the view that some lived attractive **Radically Extended Lives** in the remote past.

Procrastination Delaying or postponing an activity.

Prolongevists Gruman's term for the view to which "**Optimists**" refers, according to which immortality can be worthy of choice (under favorable circumstances).

Prudential Reasons In contrast to **Ethical Reasons,** considerations that count in favor of actions, from a self-interested point of view.

Radical Life Extension (Radically Extended Life, Radically Life-Extended Person) Another term for **Medical Immortality,** in which one does not die from aging, diseases, or "spontaneous" biological catastrophes, such as cardiac arrests and strokes. Where **Radical Life Extension** is possible, **Life Expectancy** will depend on the accident rates for the given population (so could vary from decades in war-torn countries to millennia in safe, peaceful ones).

Simple Selves A self that is not constructed out of memories or understood in terms of personality or social position. It is "basic". If our mental states (including memories and intentions) can be considered analogous to a stream of consciousness,

Glossary   199

it is the riverbed that persists even when the stream changes. Sometimes associated with a view that humans have or are a Soul.

Social Justice   A fair distribution of wealth and opportunities in a society.

Soul   In philosophy and theology, an immaterial (i.e., non-physical) part of a person, often considered to be immortal (or at least able to survive the death of the person's physical body).

Suicide   When a person voluntarily and intentionally ends their own life. Physician-assisted suicide (PAS) is where a medical professional assists in this process. PAS is similar to voluntary euthanasia, in which the medical professional ends a person's life at that person's request.

Temporal Bias   Giving greater weight to one's welfare, depending on its "time"—present, past, or future. Discounting the Future is a certain kind of temporal bias—toward the present over the future. (It is considered rational under certain circumstances and to some extent.) Caring more about future welfare than past is also a form of temporal bias.

Terror-Management Theory   Developed by social psychologists inspired by the work of Ernest Becker, the view that much of what human beings do is to manage the fear of death. This would include adopting religious beliefs, funeral practices, art, architecture, and so forth.

Transhumanism   A movement that advocates for the use of advanced technology to significantly improve the human condition, including through Radical Life Extension.

True Immortality   In contrast to Contingent Immortality and Radical Life Extension, the view that a being will live forever in the sense of never dying or being able to die by any means.

Utilitarianism   An approach to ethics that equates the rightness or wrongness of an action with its consequences for the sum total of happiness for a specified population (such as "all humans", or "all sentient beings on the planet").

References

Adams, D. (2009). *The Restaurant at the End of the Universe*. Basingstoke: Pan Macmillan.

Agar, N. (2010). "Humanity's End: Why We Should Reject Radical Enhancement." 10.7551/mitpress/9780262014625.001.0001

Ahmed, Nabil, Anna Marriott, Nafkote Dabi, Megan Lowthers, Max Lawson, and Leah Mugehera. (2022). *Inequality Kills: The Unparalleled Action Needed to Combat Unprecedented Inequality in the Wake of COVID-19*. Oxfam International. 10.21201/2022.8465.

Anonymous. (1800) BCE/1960). *The Epic of Gilgamesh*, N.K. Sanders Trans. London: Penguin Classics.

À bout de souffle. (1960). Les Films Impéria, Les Productions Georges de Beauregard, Société Nouvelle de Cinématographie (SNC).

Aquinas, S.T. (1266). *Summa Theologiae*.

Bacon, Francis. (1638/2005). *The History of Life and Death, or The Prolongation of Life*. Whitefish, MT: Kessinger Publishing.

Becker, E., (1997). *The Denial of Death*. 1st Free Press paperbacks edition. New York: Simon & Schuster.

Beckett, Samuel. (1993). *Dream of Fair to Middling Women*, Eoin O'Brien and Edith Fourmier eds. Dublin: Arcade.

Beglin, David. (2017). "Should I Choose Never to Die: Williams, Boredom, and the Unthinkability Condition." *Philosophical Studies* 174(8): 2009–2028.

Bishop, S.R., M. Lau, S. Shapiro, L. Carlson, N.D. Anderson, J. Carmody, Z.V. Segal, S. Abbey, M. Speca, D. Velting, and G. Devins. (2004). "Mindfulness: A proposed operational definition." *Clinical Psychology: Science and Practice* 11, 230–241. 10.1093/clipsy.bph077

Borges, Jorge Luis. (1970). "The Immortal," in *Labyrinths: Selected Stories and Other Writings*. London: Penguin.

Bricker, Phillip (2020). *Modal Matters: Essays in Metaphysics*. Oxford: Oxford University Press.

References 201

Byron, Lord George Gordon. (1819/1966). "Don Juan." In E.H. Coleridge, ed., *The Works of Lord Byron*. New York: Octagon Books.

Calhoun, Cheshire. (2018). *Doing Valuable Time: The Present, the Future, and Meaningful Living*. New York: Oxford University Press.

Campbell, Denis. (2021). "Life Expectancy Gap in England 'a Growing Chasm' Exacerbated by Covid." *The Guardian*, 10 October 2021, sec. Society. https://www.theguardian.com/society/2021/oct/10/life-expecta ncy-gap-england-growing-covid.

Čapek, Karel. (1990). "The Makropulos Secret." Translated by Yveta Synek Graff and Robert T. Jones, in Peter Kuiss, ed., *Toward the Radical Center: A Karel Čapek Reader*, 110–177. North Haven, CT: Catbird Press.

Cave, Stephen. (2012). *Immortality: The Quest to Live Forever and How It Drives Civilization*. New York: Crown.

Caviola, L., D. Althaus, A.L. Mogensen, and G.P. Goodwin. (2022). "Population ethical intuitions." *Cognition* 218, 104941. 10.1016/j.cognition.2021.104941

Clarke, M.L. (1956). *The Roman Mind: Studies in the History of Thought from Cicero to Marcus Aurelius*. Cambridge, MA: Harvard University Press.

Csikszentmihalyi, Mihalyi. (1965). *Beyond Boredom and Anxiety: The Experience of Play in Work and Games*. San Francisco, CA.: Jossey-Bass.

Davis, John K. (2018). *New Methuselahs: The Ethics of Life Extension*. Basic Bioethics. Cambridge, MA: The MIT Press, 2018.

De Grey, Aubrey with Michael Rae. (2005). *Ending Aging: The Rejuvenation Breakthroughs that Could Reverse Human Aging in Our Lifetimes*. New York: St. Martin's.

Durkheim, Emile (1951). *Suicide: A Study in Sociology*. (1951; originally 1897) Translated by John A. Spaulding and George Simpson, George Simpson, ed. New York: Macmillan, The Free Press.

Erikson, Erik H. (1982). *The Life Cycle Completed*. New York: W.W. Norton and Company.

Erikson, Erik H., and Joan M. Erikson. (1997). *The Life Cycle Completed* (Extended Edition). New York: W.W. Norton and Company.

Ertz, Susan. (1943). *Anger in the Sky*. New York: Harper & Brothers.

Feldman, Fred. (1992). *Confrontations with the Reaper: A Philosophical Study of the Nature and Value of Death*. New York: Oxford University Press.

Fischer, John Martin. (2020). *Death, Immortality, and Meaning in Life*. New York: Oxford University Press.

Fischer, John Martin, and Benjamin Mitchell-Yellin. (2014). "Immortality and Boredom." *The Journal of Ethics* 18: 353–372.

Frankfurt, Harry G. (1999). "Equality and Respect." In H.G. Frankfurt, ed., *Necessity, Volition, and Love*, 146–154. Cambridge: Cambridge University Press.

Freidan, Betty. (1964). *The Feminine Mystique*. New York: Dell.

202 References

Fukuyama, Francis. (2002). *Our Posthuman Future: Consequences of the Biotechnology Revolution.* London: Profile Books.

Gawande, Atul, MD. (2014). *Medicine and What Matters in the End.* New York: Metropolitan Books.

Gorman, August. (forthcoming). "Holism, Particularity, and the Vividness of Death." *The Journal of Ethics.* Online 2/16/2022.

Gosseries, A., (2012). "On Future Generations' Future Rights*." In *Environmental Rights.* New York: Routledge.

Grey, Aubrey de. (2004). "We Will Be Able to Live to 1,000." *BBC News,* 3 December 2004. http://news.bbc.co.uk/1/hi/uk/4003063.stm.

Grey, Aubrey de, and Michael Rae. (2008). *Ending Aging: The Rejuvenation Breakthroughs That Could Reverse Human Aging in Our Lifetime.* Reprint edition. New York: St. Martin's Griffin.

Gruman, Gerald G. (1996/2003). *A History of Ideas about the Prolongation of Life.* Philadelphia: American Philosophical Society, 1996; reissued by Springer, 2003.

Harris, John. (2000). "Intimations of Immortality." *Science* 288 (5463): 59–59. 10.1126/science.288.5463.59.

Healy, Sean Desmond. (1984). *Boredom, Self, and Culture.* Cranbury, NJ: Associated University Presses.

Hilton, James. (1933). *Lost Horizon.* New York: William Morrow and Company.

Hoffman, Bjorn. (2018). "Young Blood Rejuvenates Old Bodies: A Call for Reflection when Moving from Mice to Men." *Journal of Medicine and Hemotherapy* 45(1): 67–71.

Holy Bible: King James Version. (1997). Oxford World's Classics. Oxford: Oxford University Press.

Janecek, Leos. (1925). *The Makropulos Case* [opera].

Johnson, Samuel. (1578–60/1963). "The Idler and the Adventurer." In John W. Bullit, W.J. Bait, and L.F. Powell, eds., *The Yale Edition of the Works of Samuel Johnson,* Vol. 2. New Haven, CT: Yale University Press.

Kagan, Shelly. (2012). *Death.* New Haven, CT.: Yale University Press.

Kass, L. (ed.). (2003). *Beyond Therapy: Biotechnology and the Pursuit of Happiness.* HarperCollins.

Keown, D. (2000). *Buddhism: A Very Short Introduction, (Very Short Introductions).* Oxford: Oxford University Press.

Kierkegaard, Soren. (1843/1994). *Either/Or.* Translated by David F. Swenson, Lillian Marvin Swenson, and Walter Lowrie. Princeton, NJ: Princeton University Press.

Kipling, R., (1899). *The White Man's Burden. The Times.*

Lamont, Corliss. (1965). "Mistaken Attitudes toward Death." *The Journal of Philosophy* 62(2): 29–36.

References 203

Lipsenthal, Lee. (2012). *Enjoy Every Sandwich: Living Each Day As If It Were Your Last*. London: Bantam Press.

Lukes, S.M. (2020). "Individualism: Definition, History, Philosophy, Examples, & Facts." *Encyclopædia Britannica*. URL https://www.britannica.com/topic/individualism (accessed 9.3.22).

Luper, S. (2009). *The Philosophy of Death*. Cambridge: Cambridge University Press.

MacAskill, W. (2022). *What We Owe the Future*. New York: Basic Books.

McDannell, Colleen, and Bernhard Lang. (1988). *Heaven: A History*. 2nd ed. New Haven, CT: Yale University Press.

Moore, Natasha. (2021). "We Asked Australians If They Believe in God or the Supernatural. Here's What They Said." *ABC News*, 3 April 2021. https://www.abc.net.au/news/2021-04-04/spiritual-supernatural-realities-australians-weig-in-this-easter/100046122.

Nagel, Thomas. (1986). *The View from Nowhere*. New York: Oxford University Press.

Nagel, Thomas. (2014, Jan. 9). "After You've Gone Away." *The New York Review of Books*.

Nuland, Sherwin. (1994). *How We Die: Reflections on Life's Final Chapter*. New York: Alfred A. Knopf.

Nussbaum, Martha. (1996). *The Therapy of Desire: Theory and Practice in Hellenistic Ethics*. Princeton, NJ: Princeton University Press.

OED. (2021). "Forever, Adv., n., and Adj." In *OED Online*. Oxford University Press. http://www.oed.com/view/Entry/73245.

Overall, Christine. (2003). *Aging, Death, and Human Longevity: A Philosophical Inquiry*. Berkeley, CA: University of California Press.

Plato. (2015). *Symposium*. Translated by Benjamin Jowett.

Pengra, Bruce. (2012). *One Planet, How Many People? A Review of Earth's Carrying Capacity*. UNEP Global Environmental Alert Service.

Percy, Walker. (1975). *The Message in the Bottle*. New York: Farrar, Strauss, and Giroux.

Perry, John, ed. (1975). *Personal Identity*. Berkeley, CA: University of California Press.

Perry, John. (1978). *A Dialogue on Personal Identity and Immortality*. Indianapolis, IN: Hackett Publishing Co.

Pessoa, Fernando. (2002). *The Book of Disquiet*. Richard Zenith, trans. and ed. London: Penguin Classics.

Pew Research Center. (2018). "Being Christian in Western Europe." https://www.pewforum.org/2018/05/29/being-christian-in-western-europe/.

Rada, A.G., (2021). "Spain Will Become the Sixth Country Worldwide to Allow Euthanasia and Assisted Suicide." *BMJ* 372, n147. 10.1136/bmj.n147

Ratzinger, Joseph. (2007). *Eschatology: Death and the Eternal Life* (second edition). Washington DC: The Catholic University of America Press.

Rawls, J., (1971). *A Theory of Justice*. Oxford: Oxford University Press.

204 References

Regalado, Antonio. (2021). "Meet Altos Labs, Silicon Valley's Latest Wild Bet on Living Forever." MIT Technology Review. 4 September 2021. https://www.technologyreview.com/2021/09/04/1034364/altos-labs-silicon-valleys-jeff-bezos-milner-bet-living-forever/.

Rosati, Connie. (2013). "The Makropulos Case: Reflections on Immortality and Agency." In Ben Bradley, Fred Feldman, and Jens Johansson, eds., *The Oxford Handbook on the Philosophy of Death*. New York: Oxford University Press.

Roser, M., (2019). "Mortality in the past – around half died as children." Our World in Data. URL https://ourworldindata.org/child-mortality-in-the-past (accessed 8.21.22).

Rustomji, Nerina. (2009). *The Garden and the Fire: Heaven and Hell in Islamic Culture*. New York: Columbia University Press.

Santhanam, Laura. (2021). "COVID Helped Cause the Biggest Drop in U.S. Life Expectancy since WWII." PBS. 22 December 2021. https://www.pbs.org/newshour/health/covid-helped-cause-the-biggest-drop-in-u-s-life-expectancy-since-wwii.

Sartre, Jean-Paul. (1944/1989). *No Exit*. In *No Exit and Three Other Plays*. Stuart Gilbert, trans. New York: Vintage: Reissue Edition.

Scheffler, Samuel. (2013). "Fear, Death, and Confidence." In Niko Kolodny, ed., *Death and the Afterlife*. New York: Oxford University Press.

Setiya, Kieran. (2017). *Midlife: A Philosophical Analysis*. Princeton, NJ, and Oxford: Princeton University Press.

Setiya, Kieran. (2022). *Life Is Hard: How Philosophy Can Help Us Find Our Way*. New York: Riverhead Books.

Seuss, Dr. (Theodor Geisel). (1990) *Oh, The Places You'll Go*. New York: Random House.

Shakespeare, W. (1599/2006). *As You Like It*, 3rd edition. ed. London: The Arden Shakespeare.

Siderits, Mark. (2021) *Buddhism as Philosophy*, second edition. Indianapolis, IN: Hackett.

Silver, Laura, Patrick Van Kessel, Christine Huang, Laura Clancy, and Sneha Gubbala. (2021). "What Makes Life Meaningful? Views From 17 Advanced Economies." Pew Research Center. https://www.pewresearch.org/global/2021/11/18/what-makes-life-meaningful-views-from-17-advanced-economies/.

Solomon, S., J. Greenberg, and T. Pyszczynski. (2015). *The Worm at the Core: On the Role of Death in Life*. New York: Random House.

Spacks, Patricia. (1995). *A Literary History of a State of Mind*. Chicago: University of Chicago Press.

Svendsen, Lars. (2005). *A Philosophy of Boredom*. London: Reaktion Books.

Swift, Jonathan. (1726/1997). *Gulliver's Travels*. London: Wordsworth Editions, Ltd.

The Global Health Observatory. (2022). "Life Expectancy at Birth (Years)." World Health Organization. 2022. https://www.who.int/data/gho/data/indicators/indicator-details/GHO/life-expectancy-at-birth-(years).

The World Bank. (2021). "Fertility Rate, Total (Births per Woman) | Data." The World Bank. 2021. https://data.worldbank.org/indicator/SP.DYN.TFRT.IN.

Tibbetts, Carl, dir. (2014). 'White Christmas'. *Black Mirror*.

Vyas, R., (1992). *Nature of Indian Culture*. Delhi: Concept Publishing Company.

Weiner, Jonathan. (2010). *Long for the World: The Strange Science of Immortality*. New York: HarperCollins.

Index

Adams, Douglas 110, 119, 179
Allen, Woody 9
antediluvian 56–57
anti-ageing medicine 56, 59
anti-ageing research 15, 36
apologist 69–71, 88, 106, 174
As You Like It (Shakespeare) 127
Avatar (Cameron) 87

Bacon, Francis 58–59
Becker, Ernest 55, 110–111
Beckett, Samuel 95
Benedict XVI, Pope 24
Bezos, Jeff 15, 44
Bible; *see* Gospels
Black Mirror, TV show 7
blood, preventing ageing 59
boredom 19–25, 38, 89–90, 180;
    Bernard Williams's 92–93;
    circumstances of 91; contingent
    immortality 23–24; endless
    journeying 99–103; ennui
    138–139; extractive *versus*
    immersive views of life 122–125;
    and hyperboredom 90, 93, 94,
    119, 138, 155, 162, 180;
    immortality and 89–90; math
    activities 99; mindfulness
    meditation 102; pleasure dome
    and 26; pleasures and enjoyable
    experiences 95–98; projects
    102–103; radical life extension
    23; religions on 31–32; repetition
    and 94–95; seriousness of 23;

true immortality 24–25;
unthinkability requirement 94;
valuable activities in 98–99
Borges, Jorge Luis 18, 26–29
Bostrom, Nick 16
brain scanning 7–8
breathing exercises 8;
    see also mindfulness meditation
Buddhism 124–125, 184–186

Calhoun, Cheshire 94
Camus, Albert 103–104
Capek, Karel 59, 71, 91
carrying capacity 43–44
child mortality 127; *see also* infant
    mortality
Christianity/Christians 24, 31–32,
    111, 125
companionship 67–68
contingent immortality 6, 8, 17,
    23–24, 36–37, 39;
    meaninglessness 31;
    overpopulation problem 41;
    procrastination 34–35
Conway, Hugh 57
COVID-19 pandemic 15, 50, 86
cravings 185
cryogenic preservation 56
Csikszentmihalyi, Mihalyi 101

Davis, John K. 5, 41–42, 48
Davoudpour, Shahin 41–42
Day of Judgement 10, 111
deadlines 32, 120, 145–146

death: exit strategy 117–120; fear of 110–113; suicide/voluntary euthanasia 118–120, 182; terror management theory 111–113
discounting the future 183
Doctor Faustus (Christopher) 70
dukkha 186
Durkheim, Emile 100–101

effective altruism 171
elixir of life 117
enlightenment 16, 124–125, 185
ennui (listlessness) 25–26, 38, 138–139
The Epic of Gilgamesh 56, 69–70
Erikson, Erik 86–87
Erikson, Joan 86
Ertz, Susan 22
eternal life 7
ethical and political philosophies 48–49
ethical reasoning 13–14, 17, 166–167
exit clause 23–24, 117–120
extractive approach to life 122–125

Faust story 70
fear of death 110–113
The Feminine Mystique (Freidan) 91
fertility rate 40–42
Fischer, John 74–75; memories and values 76
flow(flow states) 101
fountain theme 58, 61
friendships 67–68
Fukuyama, Francis 49–50
future generations 166–167; effective altruism 171; longtermism 171; obligation to 167–168; utilitarianism 170–171

Geisel, Theodor (a.k.a. "Dr Seuss") 144–145
goals/preferences 12, 17, 35–36
God, being with 24

Gospels 15, 31, 33
Gruman, Gerald 56, 69
Gulliver's Travels (Swift) 68, 70–71

Harry Potter books 84
health inequalities 49
hedonism/hedonists 162–163; Spectrum of Despond 162–166
Hinduism and life stages 128, 129
human value framework 81–83
hyperborean theme (hyperboreanism) 57
hyperboredom 90, 93, 94, 119, 138, 155, 162, 180

identity 142–143; identity criterion 7–9, 8; numerical identity 9–10: personal identity theory 10–11, 17; qualitative identity 9–10
immersive approach to life 122–125
'The Immortal' (Borges) 18, 26–29, 139–142; distinct identities 142–143; projects, significance of 139–142; virtue and vice 144
immortality 6, 28; *see also* living forever; boredom 89–90; desirability of 62; interpretations of 56–57; life and living 62–63; and meaningless 28; medical 5n1; preference of 61–62; and society 120; true immortality *vs.* radical life extension 7, 63–66; wars and rejection of 69
immortality curmudgeon 71, 94–95, 105, 155, 178
immortality optimist 18, 21, 22, 26, 29, 71, 114, 116, 117, 146, 156
immortality realism 71n8
individual's longevity 74; personal identity 75
individual's longevity: basic self 77–78; self constructed from memories 75–77; subject of consciousness 77

208 Index

infant mortality 15, 40, 127
invulnerable to death 61, 63
Islam 24

Janacek, Leos 59
Jesus 15, 31
Johnson, Samuel 101
journeying 99–103

Kafka, Franz 91
Kagan, Shelly 99–100, 122–123
Kierkegaard, Soren 89, 95–96, 100
Kurzweil, Ray 16

Lamont, Corliss 97–98
Lang, Bernhard 24
legends and stories 55–60, 103
Leon, Ponce de 58
The Life Cycle Completed
    (Erickson) 86
life expectancy 5–6, 8, 15–16,
    48–49, 126–128, 131, 133, 187
life extension 36, 42–51, 42–52;
    see also radical life extension
lifespan 5, 6, 15, 31; attitude 16;
    for minority 49–50; moderate life
    extension 36; radical life
    extension 33; for welathy 48, 50
life stages 126, 187; adaptation to
    127; Hinduism 128, 129;
    recognizability 187; social and
    economic consequences 128; and
    society 131–132; timescales 130;
    values 187
longtermism 171
loss and harmness 82–83
Lost Horizon (Hilton) 57

The Makropulos Secret (Čapek)
    18, 19
Marlowe, Christopher 70
marriages 67–69
MasAskill, William 171
McDannell, Colleen 24
meaninglessness 26–32, 38
Measure for Measure
    (Shakespeare) 55
medical immortality 5n1, 64, 80

memories 75–77
The Metamorphosis (Kafka) 87
mindfulness meditation 102,
    124–125, 183–186
moderate life extension 5, 8, 16,
    30, 36
mortal life 28–29, 61, 84, 99,
    161, 189
motivation and values 78; body
    functioning 82; human value
    framework 81–83; loss and
    harmness 82–83; loving
    relationship 79–80; pains and
    pleasures 121; and timely action
    78–79
Musk, Elon 44

Nagel's thought-experiment
    60–61, 73
Nagel, Thomas 60–61, 104–105
narratives 83–84; and stages of
    durations 85–89
New Testament 15, 31
nirvana 124–125, 185
no-self view 185
numerical identity 9–10
Nussbaum, Martha 29, 141

Occupy Movement 49
Odyssey (Homer) 27
optimistic realism 154–156
Overall, Christine 22
overpopulation 39–47, 50,
    150–154

Page, Larry 15
Percy, Walker 90
personal identity 10–11, 72, 75
Pessoa, Fernando 90
pleasure domes 25–26, 124,
    138–139, 162–163
practical reasoning 12
preferences/goals 12, 17, 35–36
primitivism 57
procrastination 32–35, 38,
    144–146; pains and pleasures
    121; problem and relevant
    feelings 120–122; radical life

extension 79–80; rationality and 182–183
projects 98–103, 139–142
prolongevists 69, 71, 106
prudential reasoning 12–14, 17, 35–37, 135
Psalms 33
Putin, Vladimir 48

qualitative identity 9–10

radical life extension 5, 8, 17, 23, 30, 36–37; boredom 135–138; companionship 67; distinct identities 142–143; ennui 138–139; favorable circumstances 182; good human life 66–69; marriages 67–69; optimistic realism 154–156; overpopulation 150–154; physician-assisted suicide 182; procrastination 79; projects, significance of 139–142; prudential reasons 135; rejecting reasons of 150; risky behavior 67; stages of lives 85–89; true immortality *vs.* 63–66, 148–150; unfavorable circumstances 180–182; in United States 66; valuable activities in 98–99; value and scarcity 146–148; virtue and vice 144
rationality and procrastination 182–183
reason for action 135
reincarnation 6–8, 14, 87, 125, 186
rejuvenating substances 58–59
resurrection 10, 14, 62, 64, 111
risky behavior 67
Rufus, Marcus Flaminius 26–28

Scheffler, Samuel 81–82, 85–87, 128, 178

scientific and technological progress 15
self constructed from memories 75–77
selfinterested reasoning 12
Shangri La 57–58, 78
simple selves 185
social justice 48–51
societal adjustments 187–189
society 39, 51, 120; life stages and 131–132
Socrates 9
souls 130; beliefs 6–7
Spacks, Patricia 91
Spectrum of Despond 162–166
Steinach, Eugen 111
suicide/voluntary euthanasia 118–120, 182
supercentenarians 18

techno-optimism 16
temporal bias 182–183
terror management theory 55, 59, 111–113
The Denial of Death (Becker) 110–111
theocentric accounts 24
transhumanism 16
true immortality 7, 8, 14, 17, 24–25, 63; radical life extension *vs.* 63–66

unequal society 48–49
unthinkability requirement 94
utilitarianism 170–171

valuable activities 98–99
voluntary euthanasia 118–120, 182

Williams, Bernard 87, 92–95, 104

Printed in the United States
by Baker & Taylor Publisher Services